Praise for *Nonprofit AI*

We are deeply grateful for the generous endorsements and thoughtful reviews from some of the nonprofit and technology industries' most esteemed thought leaders. Their insights and support underscore the urgency and importance of Nonprofit AI as a guide for mission-driven organizations navigating this transformative era. This book is dedicated to helping nonprofits harness artificial intelligence responsibly, ensuring greater impact while upholding the values of trust, transparency, and community. We extend our sincere thanks to each leader who took the time to share their perspective and reinforce the vital role of AI in shaping the future of philanthropy.

"This powerful guide looks at how AI can revolutionize the work of the non-profit sector, for both the people involved in fundraising and the communities their non-profits serve. The authors provide practical and easy-to-understand advice for those just starting on the AI journey and those who are already on their way."

-**Alice Ayres,**
President and CEO,
Association for Healthcare Philanthropy

"Working with thousands of nonprofits at AWS over the last 10 years has shown me that successful AI adoption isn't about size or budget - it's about intentional implementation. This book finally gives organizations of all sizes the roadmap they need to transform their operations and increase their impact."

- **Rick Buettner,**
Director of Nonprofits at Amazon Web Services (AWS)

"Wealth is great, but connection is better when it comes to finding and engaging donors. That's where they prove AI (and all of the other vowels) come in."

– **Paul Clolery,**
vice president & editorial director,
The NonProfit Times.

"Nonprofit AI is more than just a guide to technology—it's a blueprint for the future of philanthropy. By weaving together real-world examples, ethical frameworks, and actionable strategies, this book empowers nonprofits to embrace AI confidently and responsibly. It's an indispensable resource for any organization ready to innovate while staying mission-focused."

- Gabe Cooper,
CEO, Virtuous

"I have read many books on AI meant to be a guide, but this one isn't just one of those guides; this book is a call to action for our nonprofits to step up and lead with courage. Through every chapter and example, authors make AI feel approachable and doable while reminding us of our tremendous responsibility in shaping its use for social good. This book is a must-read for anyone who cares about impact – in other words, our entire social sector."

- Meena Das,
CEO, Namaste Data

"Nonprofit AI offers nonprofit leaders an accessible and practical guide to using AI to enhance their impact without adding to their burnout. Chappell and Rosenkrans cut through the noise to show how AI can support, not replace, the human side of fundraising."

- Mallory Erickson,
Author of What the Fundraising: Embracing and Enabling the People Behind the Purpose

"I highly recommend Nonprofit AI: A Comprehensive Guide to Implementing Artificial Intelligence for Social Good and I commend Nathan and Scott for putting it together. This book is packed with practical advice and real examples that show nonprofit leaders how to use AI in ways that actually make sense for their mission. It cuts through the noise and fluff and makes AI feel less intimidating, which is exactly what so many organizations need right now. If you're looking to make smarter decisions and get back to the work that really matters, this book is for you."

- Shereese Floyd,
AI Consultants for Nonprofits

"Nonprofit AI is a must-read for nonprofit leaders looking to leverage artificial intelligence to amplify their mission while navigating the complexities of responsible adoption. With a pragmatic approach, this book demystifies AI and provides real-world strategies for integrating technology in a way that enhances efficiency, engagement, and long-term impact. In a rapidly evolving digital landscape, this is the guide that every mission-driven organization needs to stay ahead while staying true to its values."

- Lori Freeman,
Global GM & VP, Salesforce for Nonprofits

"Whether you're new to AI or looking to refine your strategy, this book offers the tools and knowledge necessary to explore its promise and potential while tackling the critical work needed to promote and achieve ethical AI—ensuring that the future of the nonprofit sector advances social good."

- Alesia Frerichs,
President & CEO, Lutheran Services in America

"AI is becoming a fundamental part of the nonprofit sector. Nonprofit AI explores how organizations can adapt and innovate with AI. Their insights provide a practical perspective on leveraging AI responsibly to maximize impact."

- Randall Hallett,
CEO and Founder, Hallett Philanthropy

"As a nonprofit CEO implementing AI daily, I can affirm this isn't just another tech manual - it's the definitive playbook our sector desperately needs, transforming AI from buzzword to practical tool for amplifying our missions. Just as our predecessors couldn't imagine running a charity without electricity, this book shows us why we won't remember how we served communities without AI."

- Dan Kershaw,
Executive Director at Furniture Bank

"This book is for the innovators who see AI as a mission multiplier. It's for nonprofit leaders ready to scale their impact without scaling their workload. It's for the change-makers who know that in a world of algorithms, authentic human connection matters more than ever. And it's for those who believe that compassion plus innovation is how we'll solve humanity's greatest challenges. For those who hope the future looks like the past, or that AI is a passing fad, this book will change your mind."

- **Tim Lockie,**
Founder and CEO, The Human Stack

"This book perfectly frames how the balance of human touch, advanced technology and mission impact can amplify philanthropy. Nonprofit AI is the ideal bridge to connect fundraising progress with practical application, today."

- **Justin McCord,**
Chief of Staff, RKD Group

"Nathan and Scott provide the expertise and ethical clarity nonprofits need to navigate the rapidly evolving world of AI. This book turns complex concepts into actionable strategies, ensuring organizations can harness AI for real, mission-driven change."

- **Ben Miller,**
SVP of Data Science and Analytics, Bonterra

"Over 30 years in technology and the past decade implementing AI in organizations, I have seen nonprofits struggle to keep pace with private enterprises and governments. Nathan and Scott deliver a commonsense roadmap designed specifically for nonprofit leaders navigating the AI revolution. Their guide bridges technological innovation with practical implementation, offering insights and real-world case studies to empower responsible fundraising and boost operational efficiency."

- **Shawn Olds,**
Co-Founder, boodleAI

"Nonprofit leaders should race to read this essential nonprofit AI playbook and empower their teams to rapidly adopt AI technology responsibly and ethically across every nonprofit job to be done. The organizations who put Chappell and Roseknrans's data-driven AI best practices to work in responsible and ethical ways are the ones who are going to secure the most funding, deliver the greatest mission impact, and establish their program relevance for decades to come."

- **Erin McHugh Saif,**
Chief Product Officer, Microsoft Tech for Social Impact

"Having witnessed the evolution of AI for nonprofits from its earliest stages, it's clear that Nonprofit AI stands out as an essential resource for organizations navigating this new frontier. This must-read book bridges cutting-edge technology with the unique needs of the sector, offering actionable strategies that prioritize both innovation and ethical stewardship."

- **Salvatore Salpietro,**
Chief Community Officer, Fundraise Up

"This groundbreaking work by Chappell and Rosenkrans delivers exactly what today's nonprofits need: a practical blueprint for using AI to connect with your community, move them to action, and simplify your operations. It's both visionary and actionable - a must-read for any organization ready to transform how they deliver social impact."

- **Tim Sarrantonio,**
Director of Corporate Brand, Neon One

"As social and economic inequities deepen, nonprofits must leverage AI to drive impact—but for many, its potential remains out of reach. Nonprofit AI cuts through the hype, offering a clear and practical guide to using AI responsibly to address the very inequities it risks exacerbating."

- **Michael Sheldrick,**
Co-Founder, Global Citizen & Policy Entrepreneur; Author, From Ideas to Impact: A Playbook for Influencing and Implementing Change in a Divided World

"Chappell and Rosenkrans reveal why embracing AI is not just an opportunity but a mission-critical imperative for nonprofits, offering an inspiring vision of AI as a tool for service, not just profit."

- **Eric Siegel,**
CEO of Gooder AI and author of "The AI Playbook"

"Nonprofit AI is the ultimate guidebook for social impact leaders looking to harness AI ethically and effectively to drive real change in the world."

- **Amber Melanie Smith,**
Social Impact Expert

"From fundraising and donor engagement to program delivery and impact measurement, Nonprofit AI provides practical guidance for mission-driven organizations. Whether you're new to AI or an experienced data scientist, this book makes the field accessible and actionable. Thank you, Scott and Nathan, for your passionate leadership!"

- **Angie Stapleton,**
Executive Director, Research & Prospect Development, Vanderbilt University

"This guide is a game-changer for the nonprofit sector. It doesn't just talk about AI—it shows how to use it. With clear examples and practical advice, it equips nonprofits to make data-driven decisions, engage stakeholders, and scale their impact like never before."

- **Bill TeDesco,**
CEO and Founder, DonorSearch

"In Nonprofit AI, Nathan and Scott provide the definitive guide for nonprofits to bridge the gap between visionary ideas and actionable AI/ML strategies, empowering organizations of any size to predict donor behavior, personalize engagement, and optimize resources for maximum impact. Drawing on over a decade of experience as AI pioneers in the nonprofit sector, they share real-world case studies, actionable insights, and lessons on change management to help leaders navigate the complexities of innovation responsibly and effectively."

- **Jon Thompson,**
AVP of Philanthropic Strategy & Technology at the Children's Hospital of Philadelphia

"For anyone who believes in the power of technology to amplify human compassion and drive meaningful change, this book is an essential companion. It's not just a guide—it's a call to action for a brighter, more impactful future."

- **Tammy Zonker,**
Award-winning Major Gifts Expert,
Keynote Speaker, and Founder of Fundraising Transformed

Nonprofit AI

Nonprofit AI

A COMPREHENSIVE GUIDE TO IMPLEMENTING
ARTIFICIAL INTELLIGENCE FOR SOCIAL GOOD

Nathan Chappell
Scott Rosenkrans

WILEY

Copyright © 2025 by John Wiley & Sons. All rights reserved, including rights for text and data mining and training of artificial intelligence technologies or similar technologies.

Published by John Wiley & Sons, Inc., Hoboken, New Jersey.
Published simultaneously in Canada.

No part of this publication may be reproduced, stored in a retrieval system, or transmitted in any form or by any means, electronic, mechanical, photocopying, recording, scanning, or otherwise, except as permitted under Section 107 or 108 of the 1976 United States Copyright Act, without either the prior written permission of the Publisher, or authorization through payment of the appropriate per-copy fee to the Copyright Clearance Center, Inc., 222 Rosewood Drive, Danvers, MA 01923, (978) 750-8400, fax (978) 750-4470, or on the web at www.copyright.com. Requests to the Publisher for permission should be addressed to the Permissions Department, John Wiley & Sons, Inc., 111 River Street, Hoboken, NJ 07030, (201) 748-6011, fax (201) 748-6008, or online at http://www.wiley.com/go/permission.

Trademarks: Wiley and the Wiley logo are trademarks or registered trademarks of John Wiley & Sons, Inc. and/or its affiliates in the United States and other countries and may not be used without written permission. All other trademarks are the property of their respective owners. John Wiley & Sons, Inc. is not associated with any product or vendor mentioned in this book.

Limit of Liability/Disclaimer of Warranty: While the publisher and author have used their best efforts in preparing this book, they make no representations or warranties with respect to the accuracy or completeness of the contents of this book and specifically disclaim any implied warranties of merchantability or fitness for a particular purpose. No warranty may be created or extended by sales representatives or written sales materials. The advice and strategies contained herein may not be suitable for your situation. You should consult with a professional where appropriate. Further, readers should be aware that websites listed in this work may have changed or disappeared between when this work was written and when it is read. Neither the publisher nor authors shall be liable for any loss of profit or any other commercial damages, including but not limited to special, incidental, consequential, or other damages.

For general information on our other products and services or for technical support, please contact our Customer Care Department within the United States at (800) 762-2974, outside the United States at (317) 572-3993 or fax (317) 572-4002.

Wiley also publishes its books in a variety of electronic formats. Some content that appears in print may not be available in electronic formats. For more information about Wiley products, visit our web site at www.wiley.com.

Library of Congress Cataloging-in-Publication Data is Available:

ISBN 9781394316649 (Cloth)
ISBN 9781394316656 (ePub)
ISBN 9781394316663 (ePDF)

Cover Design and Image: Wiley

SKY10100181_031825

To the amazing humans who wake up each day with a desire to make the world a better place, armed with the courage and curiosity to amplify their mission with AI.

Contents

Our Commitment to Responsible and
Beneficial AI in Writing Nonprofit AI xvii

Introduction xix

Chapter 1: The Need for Innovation in the Nonprofit Sector Has Never Been Greater 1

Chapter 2: AI Deconstructed: Separating Myth, Hype, and Reality 13

Chapter 3: AI Fluency and the Future Nonprofit Workforce 33

Chapter 4: The AI-First Nonprofit 47

Chapter 5: AI for Program Development and Impact Measurement 57

Chapter 6: AI for Fundraising, Resource Development, and Donor Experience 67

Chapter 7: AI for Volunteer Engagement and Management 79

Chapter 8:	AI for Nonprofit Marketing and Communications	89
Chapter 9:	AI for Administration and Human Resources	99
Chapter 10:	AI Transformation Is a Journey, Not a Destination	111
Chapter 11:	Beyond AI Ethics: The Nonprofit Sector's Imperative for Responsible and Beneficial AI	125
Chapter 12:	Evaluating AI for Nonprofits	145
Chapter 13:	Humanity or Utility? New Questions for a New World	159
Chapter 14:	Overcoming Challenges in AI Adoption	167
Chapter 15:	Building an AI Strategy for Your Nonprofit	179
Chapter 16:	Training and Capacity Building	189
Chapter 17:	The Future of AI for Nonprofits	197
Chapter 18:	Parting Thoughts	209

Appendix: Resources for AI Governance Templates and Frameworks	*215*
Glossary	*219*
References	*229*
About the Authors	*235*
Index	*237*

Our Commitment to Responsible and Beneficial AI in Writing Nonprofit AI

In writing Nonprofit AI: A Comprehensive Guide to Implementing Artificial Intelligence for Social Good, we sought to blend our collective 30+ years of experience in the nonprofit sector with the very tools we advocate for in this book. Generative AI played a supporting role in this process—not as a replacement for our insights, but as an amplifier of our expertise. By leveraging AI, we were able to organize complex ideas, explore diverse perspectives, and refine our messaging to resonate with the needs of nonprofit professionals.

We approached this collaboration with care, ensuring every AI-assisted contribution was rigorously reviewed, edited, and supplemented by our deep knowledge of philanthropy, technology, and ethical leadership. Our goal was to demonstrate, through the creation of this book, how responsibly using AI can enhance—not diminish—human creativity, experience, and judgment.

This transparency reflects the ethos of responsible and beneficial AI adoption we advocate for throughout these pages, and we hope it serves as an example of how technology can support, rather than replace, the humanity at the heart of nonprofit work.

Introduction

"The landscape of American generosity is marked as much by decline as it is by increase. In recent years, surveyors of that landscape have begun to give as much attention to decline as to growth" (Soskis, 2024). The persistence of these undercurrents signals that **doing things the same way will not meet today's challenges**.

Now, More than Ever

The nonprofit sector is an indispensable pillar of the global economy, contributing significantly to societal well-being and economic stability. Collectively, nonprofits and NGOs manage trillions of dollars in economic activity and employ tens of millions of hard-working professionals worldwide. These individuals and the mission-centered organizations they serve fill critical gaps that neither governments nor corporations can address alone, often acting as the thread of decency, love, and hope that together bind the fabric of society. Their contributions range from providing essential human services to protecting the planet, reducing inequalities, and educating future generations to fostering community resilience and beyond, making them essential agents of change in an increasingly complex and interconnected world.

Amidst a backdrop of fractured societies, declines in civic engagement, government stand-offs, and an escalation of humanitarian crises of seemingly every variety, the need for nonprofit services has never been greater. Yet, the sector stands at a pivotal moment marking the urgency for rapid innovation more pronounced than at any time in history.

Exacerbating an ever-increasing demand in nonprofit services is a sobering reality that in many developed nations, the number of people donating to or volunteering with nonprofits has seen systemic declines, making the delivery of mission-critical initiatives increasingly challenging.

In a period of dramatic societal and technological change, doing things the same way will not enable the nonprofit community to support the humanitarian demands of this or future generations.

Yet, despite the confluence of headwinds facing the modern nonprofit ecosystem, there is great reason to maintain a hopeful and even optimistic stance about the sector's ability to solve many of humanity's greatest challenges with greater speed, precision, and efficiency than ever imagined.

While the advent of artificial intelligence (AI) is anything but new, the recent explosion of accessible and affordable AI heralds a pivotal shift, opportunity, and responsibility to rethink every facet of nonprofit work. The significance of this moment cannot be oversold. It's our firm belief that the future of the nonprofit sector will depend largely on how swiftly and responsibly the organizations themselves accept or reject this technological milestone. How much and how well the nonprofit sector embraces AI will determine the speed and degree by which the digital divide becomes a digital chasm. There is little doubt that the winners of the digital divide will be represented by organizations that adopt new technologies to support their mission, while the losers will be those that do not. Ultimately, the success, consolidation, or dissolution of underperforming nonprofit organizations will lead to a more streamlined yet less diverse philanthropic landscape, making an immeasurable impact on humanity at large.

AI Adoption Is Not Enough

While AI adoption is inevitable, responsible and beneficial use of AI is not.

As the landscape of charitable giving undergoes significant shifts, understanding and leveraging AI technologies to amplify nonprofit missions becomes crucial for sustaining and enhancing organizational efforts. AI's increasingly broad role in supporting nonprofit success will pave the way for more strategic and precise philanthropic endeavors. To successfully navigate this tectonic shift in nonprofit business, mission-oriented organizations must not trivialize the vastness of AI's potential, but also be mindful to leverage this breakthrough technology in ways that are responsible and beneficial. As guardians of public trust, nonprofit organizations must prioritize the beneficial utilization of AI while maximizing immediate impact and safeguarding the long-term sustainability of the sector. In this dynamic environment, this book serves as an essential guide for any nonprofit professional, leader, volunteer, donor, or advocate seeking to execute and amplify their nonprofit mission in an algorithmic world.

The nonprofit sector, often constrained by limited resources and funding, stands to benefit immensely from the efficiencies and capabilities that AI can provide. However, the transition to becoming an AI-first nonprofit is not without its challenges. This book addresses these challenges head-on, offering practical tools, case studies, and templates designed to facilitate a smooth and effective AI transformation.

Drawing on our collective 30 years of nonprofit experience and global leadership on the responsible and beneficial use of AI within a nonprofit orientation, this book is crafted to serve you and your organization well. *Nonprofit AI: A Comprehensive Guide to Implementing Artificial Intelligence for Social Good* is not just a theoretical exploration of AI technologies. It is also a practical handbook to equip nonprofit stakeholders with the knowledge and tools to successfully navigate the AI transformation. The book provides actionable tools that can be readily applied to various aspects of nonprofit operations. From fundraising and donor management to program delivery, operations, and impact measurement, readers will find resources that can help them integrate AI into their daily activities.

Learning from the experiences of others is invaluable. This book includes numerous case studies from diverse nonprofit organizations that have successfully implemented AI solutions to best support their mission. It also takes forensic audit to the myriad reasons why others have failed. Learning from these real-world examples offers insights into best practices, common pitfalls, and innovative approaches that can inspire and guide other organizations on their AI journey. To further support those embarking on their AI transformation, this book offers a variety of tips and resources that can be customized to meet the specific needs of different organizations, covering strategic planning, project management, data governance, and more, providing a solid foundation for AI initiatives.

Imagine a future where nonprofits can predict donor behavior with remarkable accuracy, personalize engagement strategies to resonate deeply with supporters, and optimize resource allocation to achieve maximum impact. This is not a distant dream but a near-term reality achievable through AI. As you immerse yourself in the chapters ahead, you will discover how AI can be harnessed to amplify your mission, drive efficiency, and foster innovation.

The accelerated adoption of AI in the nonprofit sector is not merely an option; it is an imperative. As we look toward a future influenced by algorithms, it is clear that those who embrace these technological advancements will lead the way in creating more effective, efficient, and impactful organizations.

In an era where the need for innovation is paramount, this book stands as a beacon, lighting the path toward a future where technology and social good work hand in hand to create a better world for all. Your investment of time in reading through these pages promises significant returns, empowering you to scale your mission and amplify your impact through the thoughtful, responsible, and beneficial integration of AI technologies.

AI Transformation Is a Journey, Not a Destination

As you embark on this journey, remember that innovation is not just about adopting new technologies; it is also about embracing a mindset of continuous improvement, curiosity, collaboration, and courage. The future of the nonprofit sector is being written today, and with AI as your ally, there are no limits to what we can achieve together in support of a more equitable world for this and future generations.

1

The Need for Innovation in the Nonprofit Sector Has Never Been Greater

What Got Us Here Won't Get Us There: The Nonprofit Sector at a Crossroads

As we stand on the precipice of a new era shaped by unprecedented technological advancements and global challenges, the imperative for innovation in the nonprofit world has never been more critical, nor more laden with potential for transformative impact.

Nonprofits and artificial intelligence (AI) are a match made in heaven. There's no industry that works harder, with constrained resources, delivering tremendous impact, than the nonprofit sector. The return on investment (ROI) of AI has been proven time and again through numerous studies, often involving A/B tests with diverse groups. Whether it's college students or white-collar professionals, those who incorporate AI into their work consistently perform better, faster, and with higher satisfaction, not only helping to combat burnout—a challenge endemic in the nonprofit sector— but also enhancing overall efficiency, improving decision-making, and enabling a deeper focus on creative, mission-critical tasks (Microsoft, 2024). By taking on repetitive and administrative duties, AI frees up nonprofit professionals to concentrate on strategic initiatives, innovation, and cultivating meaningful donor relationships, ultimately amplifying their ability to create impact.

The nonprofit sector, a cornerstone of civil society, finds itself at a pivotal crossroads. On one hand, the need for its services has never been greater, with global crises multiplying, inequalities increasing, and societal factions deepening. On the other, the sector faces a combination of factors that threaten its traditional modes of operation and funding. This chapter explores the multifaceted landscape in which nonprofits now operate, the modern challenges they face, and the urgent need for innovation—particularly through the lens of artificial intelligence—to not just survive, but thrive in this new reality.

The Nonprofit Sector: A Pillar of Global Economy and Social Well-being

Before exploring the myriad challenges and opportunities that lie ahead, it's crucial to understand the vital role the nonprofit sector plays in our global society and economy. Far from being peripheral, nonprofits and NGOs collectively manage trillions of dollars in economic activity and employ tens of millions of dedicated professionals worldwide.

> "Nonprofits are the hands that catch people when they fall through the gaps."
>
> —Randima Fernando, Center for Humane Technology (Fundraising.AI, 2025, 21:45)

These mission-first organizations fill critical gaps that neither governments nor corporations can address alone. From providing essential human services to protecting the environment, from educating future generations to fostering community resilience, nonprofits often act as the thread of decency, compassion, and hope that binds the fabric of society together.

Consider, for instance, the role of nonprofits in disaster relief. When Hurricane Katrina devastated New Orleans in 2005, nonprofits like the

Red Cross and Habitat for Humanity were on the front lines, providing immediate aid and long-term rebuilding assistance. Similarly, during the COVID-19 pandemic, food banks across the nation scaled up operations dramatically to meet surging need, with Feeding America reporting a 60% increase in food bank users (Feeding America, 2022). Innovative nonprofit organizations like The Farmlink Project swiftly emerged to close the gap between the farmers with surplus food who lacked transportation and food banks with mile-long lines of hungry families.

The economic impact of the sector is equally significant. In the United States alone, nonprofits contribute approximately $1 trillion to the economy annually, comprising 5.6% of GDP (International Monetary Fund, 2023). Globally, the nonprofit sector is the third-largest employer, behind only retail and manufacturing. These statistics underscore the immense responsibility and potential impact that rests on the shoulders of nonprofit organizations.

The Confluence of Circumstances: A Perfect Storm for Nonprofit Innovation

Despite their crucial role, nonprofits find themselves navigating increasingly turbulent waters. An alignment of conditions has created a perfect storm that demands rapid and thoughtful innovation. Let's examine these factors in detail.

Global Pandemic: A Catalyst for Change

In many ways, the COVID-19 pandemic acted as an unprecedented catalyst for change across all sectors, but its impact on nonprofits has been particularly profound.

The pandemic's sudden onset exposed both the vulnerabilities and the potential of nonprofits in the information age. Organizations on the path to digital transformation found themselves better equipped to handle the crisis, ready to mobilize human and capital resources to areas of the greatest need, while those relying on traditional methods struggled to adapt.

While many nonprofits traditionally relied on in-person gatherings to raise funds for their causes, the pandemic forced a dramatic shift in strategy. Organizations across the sector quickly pivoted to virtual events and digital fundraising, embracing technology to maintain engagement and sustain their missions. Despite the challenges posed by restrictions on group gatherings, this swift adoption of digital formats enabled many nonprofits to continue generating significant support and making a meaningful impact during an unprecedented time.

However, the pandemic also exacerbated existing inequalities within the sector. Many smaller, community-based organizations lacked the resources to make rapid digital transitions, highlighting the need for sector-wide support and innovation to ensure that all nonprofits can thrive in the digital age.

Financial Uncertainty: A Convergence of Macro Economic Factors

The economic fallout from the pandemic, coupled with ongoing geopolitical tensions, created a climate of financial uncertainty for nonprofits. According to the 2021 Nonprofit Finance Fund State of the Nonprofit Sector Survey, 88% of nonprofits reported that financial uncertainty was a significant challenge (Nonprofit Finance Fund, 2021).

This instability is compounded by changing patterns in philanthropy. The continued rise of donor-advised funds, impact investing, and newer forms of giving, like cryptocurrency donations, are reshaping traditional funding models. Highlighting the gravity of this significant shift, The Giving Block, a crypto donation platform, reported a 1,558% increase in crypto donations from 2020 to 2021 (The Giving Block, 2022).

While these new funding streams offer exciting opportunities, they also require nonprofits to adapt quickly and develop new skills. Organizations must now be fluent not just in traditional fundraising methods, but also in emerging data-fueled technologies and strategies.

Moreover, the economic uncertainty over the past decade has led to increased scrutiny of nonprofit financials. Donors, both individual and institutional, are demanding greater transparency and efficiency in how their contributions are used. This pressure, while challenging, also presents an opportunity for nonprofits to innovate in their financial reporting and impact measurement practices.

Technological Advancements: The Double-Edged Sword

The rapid pace of technological advancement offers immense potential for nonprofits to increase their impact. Artificial intelligence, big data analytics, blockchain, and other emerging technologies promise to revolutionize how nonprofits operate, from fundraising to program delivery.

Consider the success of charity: water in leveraging technology. Their use of remote sensors to monitor water projects in real time improves their operational efficiency and provides donors with unprecedented transparency. This level of real-time impact reporting is setting new standards in the sector.

However, as Gabe Cooper and Mckenna Bailey (The Nonprofiteers, 2020) argue in *Responsive Fundraising*, these advancements also raise the bar for donor expectations, creating a digital divide between technologically savvy organizations and those still relying on transactional engagement efforts. The risk is that this divide could lead to a concentration of resources in a smaller number of tech-enabled nonprofits, potentially reducing the diversity of the sector, thus decreasing the intrinsic democratic nature of the nonprofit sector overall.

The ethical implications of these new technologies cannot be ignored. While AI promises tremendous opportunities to amplify nonprofit mission, it also brings concerns about data privacy, algorithmic bias, and the potential for dehumanizing relationships between nonprofits and their constituents. Nonprofits must grapple with these ethical considerations as they adopt new technologies.

Changing Donor Expectations: The Demand for Personalization and Impact

Today's donors, particularly millennials and Gen Z, expect a level of personalization and impact transparency that was unheard of a decade ago. Mallory Erickson (2022), in her work on nonprofit leadership, emphasizes the shift toward donor-centric fundraising, where supporters expect to be treated as partners rather than mere checkbooks.

This shift is evident in the rise of peer-to-peer fundraising platforms and the success of *giving days* like GivingTuesday, which helped nonprofit organizations generate $2.7 billion in the United States alone in 2021 (GivingTuesday, 2021). These trends underscore the need for nonprofits to innovate in how they engage with supporters, moving beyond transactional relationships to create meaningful, personalized connections.

Nonprofits must not only do good work, but also demonstrate their impact in concrete, data-driven ways. The demand for impact transparency is equally pressing. Donors increasingly demand to see measurable results from their contributions.

Increasing Competition for Connection: Breaking Through the Noise

In an era of information overload, nonprofits face intense competition for attention, not just from other causes, but from the entirety of the digital landscape. This challenge is particularly acute on social media platforms, where algorithm changes can dramatically impact a nonprofit's reach. Organizations like the American Civil Liberties Union (ACLU) have responded by adopting a multi-channel, content-rich approach, using everything from Instagram stories to podcasts to engage different segments of their audience (American Civil Liberties Union, n.d.).

The competition for attention also extends to the fundraising realm. With so many worthy causes vying for support, nonprofits must find innovative ways to tell their stories, secure volunteers, and demonstrate their unique value proposition to those who could benefit from their services. This requires not just compelling narratives, but also sophisticated use of data and technology to reach the right audiences with the right messages at the right time.

If the ROI of AI weren't impressive enough, consider these numbers. A recent study showed 74% of nonprofit employees are looking for or considering a new job within the year, with 65% unsure if they would continue to work in this sector (The Nonprofiteers, 2024). The primary reason: too much responsibility and not enough support. Nonprofit employees are continually on the brink of burnout. However, this trend can be reversed by leveraging AI to do more creative work quicker and feel better about it, keeping nonprofit employees satisfied and continuing to do good.

The Generosity Crisis: A Sobering Reality

Exacerbating the challenges outlined in the preceding section is a sobering trend: in many developed nations, the number of people donating or volunteering with nonprofits has seen systemic declines. This "generosity crisis" is making the delivery of mission-critical initiatives increasingly challenging.

In *The Generosity Crisis*, authors Chappell, Crimmins, and Ashley (2022) explored how the percentage of U.S. households giving to nonprofits fell from 66% in 2000 to less than 50% by 2018, making givers a minority in the United States for the first time in American history. This phenomenon, often manifested as "dollars up, donors down," highlights a paradox where total donations are sustained, but the donor base is shrinking. This concentration of giving, volunteering, and advocating among a smaller number of individuals creates a fragile system that is vulnerable to economic volatility.

The volunteerism crisis is equally concerning. According to AmeriCorps (2023), formal volunteerism in the United States dropped from 30% in 2019 to just 23% in 2021, marking the steepest decline in decades. This shortage is further straining nonprofits, especially small, community-based organizations that depend heavily on volunteer labor.

Several factors contribute to this generosity crisis:

- Changing societal norms and decreased community engagement and civic engagement
- Economic pressures, including rising costs of living and stagnant wages
- Shifting generational attitudes toward philanthropy
- Information overload by the increased number of nonprofit organizations leveraging multiple channels, subsequently leading to compassion fatigue
- Decreased trust in institutions, including nonprofits
- Changes in tax incentives and government involvement
- Declines in religious participation, which traditionally serves as a place where new generations learn the roles, responsibilities, and virtues of giving back

- The dramatically increased role that algorithms play in capturing and steering attention toward their specific purpose
- Competition with for-profit entities, with robust research and development budgets to leverage big data and AI

This is not a comprehensive list; the generosity crisis is exacerbated by myriad factors. This crisis underscores the urgent need for nonprofits to innovate in how they engage supporters, build trust, and demonstrate impact. Traditional methods of fundraising and volunteer recruitment are no longer sufficient in this changing landscape.

The Imperative for Innovation

As management guru Peter Drucker (1985) wisely noted, "The greatest danger in times of turbulence is not the turbulence itself, but to act with yesterday's logic."

In light of these challenges, it's clear that doing things the same way will not enable the nonprofit community to support the humanitarian demands of this or future generations. Yet, with the confluence of headwinds facing the modern nonprofit ecosystem, there is great reason to maintain a hopeful and even optimistic stance about the sector's ability to solve many of humanity's greatest challenges with greater speed, precision, and efficiency than ever imagined.

For nonprofits, clinging to outdated methods and mindsets is no longer an option. The sector must embrace innovation not as a one-time effort, but as an ongoing process of adaptation and creativity.

The AI Revolution: A Pivotal Shift

While the advent of AI is anything but new, the recent explosion of accessible and affordable AI heralds a pivotal shift, opportunity, and responsibility to rethink every facet of nonprofit work. The significance of this moment cannot be oversold. In fact, it's our firm belief that the future of the nonprofit sector will depend largely on how swiftly and responsibly organizations accept or reject this technological milestone.

The AI landscape offers nonprofits a powerful toolkit to tackle complex challenges and maximize their mission impact. By strategically integrating AI, nonprofits can revolutionize their operations and amplify their capabilities. Below, we explore some key opportunities that AI provides to nonprofits today:

- **Create Tremendous Efficiency:** AI-driven tools allow nonprofits to streamline their operations significantly by automating repetitive tasks, managing schedules, and optimizing workflows. For instance, AI-powered CRM systems can automate donor follow-ups, handle event scheduling, and even assist in basic financial management. By doing this, nonprofits can save substantial amounts of time and financial resources, enabling them to allocate these savings toward activities that directly serve their mission. With AI, a nonprofit's human capital becomes more focused on strategic, creative, and mission-critical tasks, which increases overall productivity and impact.
- **Personalize Stakeholder Engagement at Scale:** Stakeholder engagement becomes much more effective when personalized, and AI can do this at a scale unimaginable for traditional teams. AI models can analyze data to understand donor preferences, predict the right time for outreach, and tailor messages that resonate individually with each stakeholder. For example, generative AI can help craft highly personalized emails, and machine learning algorithms can predict a stakeholder's giving patterns based on their past behavior. This leads to more meaningful interactions that cultivate deeper relationships and ultimately foster greater loyalty.
- **Analyze and Optimize Resource Allocation and Program Delivery:** AI's ability to analyze data and predict outcomes provides nonprofits with insights that help in optimizing resource allocation. Predictive models can help determine which programs are likely to succeed in certain communities, how resources can be distributed more efficiently, and where potential gaps may lie. This level of analysis ensures that the nonprofit's efforts are focused where they will yield the most impact, allowing for a more strategic approach to program delivery and ensuring resources are put to the best possible use.
- **Predict Trends and Needs in the Communities They Serve:** AI can help identify and predict emerging trends and pressing needs

within communities, allowing nonprofits to be more proactive in their approaches. Machine learning algorithms analyze vast sets of data from both internal and external sources to identify shifts in the social, economic, and environmental landscape. For example, analyzing social media posts or government data can highlight areas of increased hardship, helping nonprofits respond to developing crises before they become overwhelming. This means that nonprofits can anticipate community needs rather than just react to them, ultimately providing more timely and effective support.
- **Automate Routine Tasks, Freeing Up Staff for More Strategic Work:** By automating routine tasks such as scheduling, data entry, or even initial responses to donor inquiries, AI frees up nonprofit staff to focus on higher-value activities such as strategic planning, building relationships, and advocacy. Virtual assistants powered by AI can handle much of the administrative burden, such as sorting emails or booking meetings, thus allowing human talent to be used in areas where creative problem-solving, empathy, and interpersonal skills are crucial.
- **Enhance Impact Measurement and Reporting:** AI tools can collect and analyze data much faster and more accurately than traditional methods. This allows nonprofits to measure the impact of their initiatives in real time. For example, AI-driven dashboards can visualize metrics on project outcomes, donor engagement, and community impact, giving a clear and accessible overview to both the organization and its stakeholders. With AI, reporting becomes less burdensome and more insightful, providing the kind of granular detail that helps to refine and improve programming, secure funding, and communicate value to stakeholders.
- **Improve Decision-Making through Data-Driven Insights:** One of AI's most powerful benefits is its capacity for predictive analytics. For nonprofits, this means that data-driven insights can guide strategic decision-making, from determining the focus of future initiatives to deciding which donor segments to target for specific campaigns. AI can spot patterns that are often too subtle for human analysts, providing actionable insights that

lead to smarter decisions. Whether it's predicting future donor behavior, identifying the most impactful program activities, or understanding what messages resonate with the community, AI enables nonprofits to be more informed, strategic, and effective in their decision-making.

However, the adoption of AI also comes with significant responsibilities. Nonprofits must ensure that their deployment and use of AI is ethical, transparent, and aligned with their mission. They must guard against algorithmic bias and protect the privacy of their constituents. Most importantly, they must use AI to enhance, not replace, the human connections that are at the heart of their work.

The digital divide within the nonprofit sector is at risk of becoming a chasm. The speed and degree to which organizations adopt and effectively use AI will increasingly distinguish those that thrive from those that struggle. This could lead to a more streamlined but less diverse philanthropic landscape, with far-reaching implications for the communities served by nonprofits.

A More Charitable Future: The Promise of AI for Nonprofits

The accelerated adoption of AI in the nonprofit sector is not merely an option; it is an imperative. As we look toward the future influenced by algorithms, it is clear that those who embrace these technological advancements will lead the way in creating more effective, efficient, and impactful organizations.

AI transformation is a journey, not a destination. As you embark on this journey, remember that innovation is not just about adopting new technologies; it is about embracing a mindset of continuous improvement, collaboration, and courage. The future of the nonprofit sector is being written today, and with AI as your ally, there are no limits to what we can achieve together in support of a more equitable world for this and future generations.

As we conclude this chapter, it's clear that the nonprofit sector stands at a critical juncture. The challenges are significant, but so too are the opportunities. By embracing innovation, particularly through the responsible and strategic use of AI, nonprofits can not only weather the current storm but emerge stronger, more efficient, and better equipped to fulfill their missions.

In the chapters that follow, we will explore in depth how artificial intelligence can be leveraged across various aspects of nonprofit operations, from fundraising and donor engagement to program delivery and impact measurement. We'll examine case studies of organizations that are leading the way in AI adoption, discuss the ethical considerations that must guide this process, and provide practical strategies for implementing AI in your own organization.

The future of the nonprofit sector will be shaped by those who are willing to innovate, adapt, and harness the power of new technologies. As we embark on this exploration of AI in the nonprofit world, remember that the ultimate goal is not technological advancement for its own sake, but the amplification of your organization's ability to create positive change in the world.

The need for innovation in the nonprofit sector has never been greater. The time to act is now. Let's begin this journey together, toward a future where technology and human compassion work hand in hand to build a better world for all.

2

AI Deconstructed: Separating Myth, Hype, and Reality

The AI Revolution in Context

Before we dive into separating the reality of artificial intelligence (AI) from the hype and myths that surround it, it's important to recognize something profound—AI is not just another technological advancement; it represents a transformational shift in the way humanity operates, akin to the discovery of electricity. When Dr. Andrew Ng claimed that "*AI is the new electricity*," in 2017 during a talk at Stanford University, he was making a statement that might have seemed outlandish at the time, but it captures the magnitude of AI's potential to reshape our world (Ng, 2017). Just as electricity revolutionized every aspect of life—powering cities, transforming industries, and changing how we lived and interacted—AI is poised to do the same, permeating every facet of modern society.

Electricity, when first discovered, fundamentally altered the trajectory of human history, bringing light to darkness, powering machinery, and enabling previously unimaginable advancements. Today, AI holds the same promise of profound change. It is not merely a tool, but the foundation upon which the next era of human progress will be built. From healthcare to education, from nonprofits to global businesses, AI is becoming the driving force behind new innovations and efficiencies that will touch every person, every community, and every organization.

To understand AI's gravity, think of a world before electricity—dark, labor-intensive, and disconnected. The advent of electricity was a beacon that sparked an industrial and social revolution, improving quality of life and connecting humanity in unprecedented ways. Similarly, AI is ushering us into a new age where tasks that once required significant human labor are automated, where decisions can be data-driven and predictive, and where personalization and efficiency redefine how we interact with technology, each other, and the world. The idea of AI as the new electricity is not just a metaphor; it is a call to recognize the breadth of change unfolding in front of us and to actively participate in shaping that transformation.

Before we dive into separating the reality of AI from the hype and myths that surround it, it's also essential to recognize that AI itself owes much of its origin to philanthropy. In fact, the term *artificial intelligence* was coined at an event funded by one of the most influential philanthropic institutions in history, the Rockefeller Foundation.

In 1956, John McCarthy, Marvin Minsky, Nathaniel Rochester, and Claude Shannon organized a historic conference at Dartmouth College, aiming to explore the possibilities of machines that could simulate human intelligence. It was during this gathering that the term *artificial intelligence* was born, thanks to the Rockefeller Foundation's grant. Their funding laid the groundwork for this pioneering summer research project, which ultimately launched AI as a recognized field of study. McCarthy and his team (1955) proposed that "every aspect of learning or any other feature of intelligence can in principle be so precisely described that a machine can be made to simulate it."

Philanthropy's foundational role in the birth of AI is not only an intriguing historical fact, but also deeply symbolic. Nonprofits and foundations like the Rockefeller Foundation have long been committed to advancing human progress through scientific and technological innovation. Today, nonprofits continue to stand at the crossroads of innovation and social impact—working to ensure that new technologies, like AI, serve the common good.

As AI begins to permeate every facet of modern life, nonprofits have a responsibility not only to adopt these technologies but also to steer them in directions that protect equity, enhance trust, and amplify the missions of organizations dedicated to improving humanity. Just as philanthropy helped foster the development of AI in the mid-20th century, the nonprofit sector can—and must—help guide its ethical and responsible use in the 21st century.

Deconstructing AI: The Reality Behind the Myths

AI is no longer just the stuff of science fiction or futuristic speculation—it is here, already woven into the fabric of our daily lives. From smart devices to data-driven decision-making tools, AI is transforming industries and institutions at an unprecedented rate. But with AI's rise comes a host of misconceptions, fears, and uncertainties. Nonprofits, in particular, may find themselves at a crossroads, unsure of how to approach this technology in a way that serves both their operational needs and their ethical commitments.

In this chapter, we will explore AI in its truest form—breaking down what it is, what it can do, and what it can't do. By cutting through the noise, nonprofits will gain the clarity they need to make informed decisions about adopting AI and using it in a way that aligns with their mission.

The Evolution of AI: From Checkers to Charitable Giving

To appreciate where we are with AI today, it's helpful to understand significant milestones within a rich historical context. In fact, the concept of artificial intelligence dates back to ancient myths and legends, but the field as we know it today began to take shape in the mid-20th century.

- **1950s–1960s: The Birth of AI**

    The term *artificial intelligence* was coined in 1956 at a conference at Dartmouth College. Early AI research focused on problem-solving, symbolic methods, and learning the strategies of simple rule-based games like checkers. This period was characterized by optimism and big promises, not unlike some of the AI hype we see today.

- **1970s–1980s: The First AI Winter**
  Limitations in computing power led to reduced funding and interest in AI research. This "winter" serves as a cautionary tale about the dangers of overpromising and underdelivering in the field of AI.
- **1990s–2000s: The Rise of Machine Learning**
  Increased computing power and the availability of large datasets led to significant advances in machine learning (ML) algorithms. This period saw AI begin to tackle real-world problems, including some applications in the nonprofit sector, such as early attempts at donor database analysis.
- **2010s–Present: The Deep Learning Revolution**
  Breakthroughs in neural networks and deep learning, coupled with vast amounts of data and powerful graphics processing units (GPUs), have led to dramatic improvements in AI capabilities. This is the era that has brought us technologies like **large language models (LLMs)** and generative pre-trained transformer (GPT) capabilities, which power many of the AI writing, creative, and analysis tools that nonprofits are beginning to explore.

For nonprofits, this evolution means that AI is no longer the realm of science fiction or the exclusive domain of tech giants. Accessible and affordable AI tools are now within reach, offering unprecedented opportunities to enhance operations, engage donors, and amplify impact.

The Current State of AI: A Perfect Technological Opportunity

The rapid advancement of AI isn't the result of any single breakthrough but rather a perfect convergence of several key elements that, when taken together, have accelerated the capabilities and accessibility of AI technologies. This shift is particularly important for nonprofits, who are beginning to realize AI's transformative potential to help them achieve their mission-driven work.

At the center of this transformation is the remarkable rise of big data. In the digital age, data flows from virtually every interaction—whether it's donor records, social media engagement, program outcomes, or broader societal data that directly impacts nonprofit missions. The sheer volume of this data provides a treasure trove for AI systems to "learn" from, identifying patterns and generating insights that were previously unimaginable. Nonprofits, which may once have struggled to make sense of their fragmented datasets, can now tap into this ocean of information, applying AI to uncover donor behavior trends, optimize program efficiency, and even predict future community needs.

Equally critical is the rise of increased computing power. In the past, processing the massive amounts of data required for AI was a prohibitive task, but innovations in hardware—especially in the form of GPUs—and the advent of cloud computing have made it possible to process data at unprecedented speeds. This means that even smaller nonprofits can now access the kind of computing power previously reserved for tech giants, leveling the playing field in powerful new ways.

No longer is AI development solely within the domain of highly technical organizations with massive budgets. Thanks to cloud platforms, nonprofits can now integrate sophisticated AI tools into their workflows without needing to build these systems from scratch. The democratization of these technologies opens doors for organizations of all sizes, allowing them to benefit from AI without the need for specialized infrastructure.

The open-source community has also been an invaluable driver of AI innovation. Researchers and developers around the world share their work freely, fueling faster innovation and allowing smaller organizations—including nonprofits—to take advantage of cutting-edge tools and approaches that would have otherwise been beyond their reach. This collaborative spirit aligns with the ethos of many nonprofits, fostering a culture of shared knowledge that benefits society as a whole.

Add to this the intense investment and competition within the AI space. As major tech companies race to outdo each other with new innovations, nonprofits become indirect beneficiaries of these advancements. The AI tools and platforms being developed for commercial use can often be repurposed for social good, giving nonprofits access to technology that might have once been out of their grasp.

Lastly, the increasing focus on ethical and regulatory frameworks has emerged as an essential counterpart to AI's rapid growth. As AI technology advances, so do the efforts to create guidelines that ensure responsible and beneficial AI use. For nonprofits, this is particularly important; their mission-driven work requires a level of trust with the public that cannot be compromised. The growing ethical focus on fairness, transparency, and accountability in AI provides nonprofits with a pathway to deploy these tools in ways that align with their values while safeguarding public trust.

As these factors coalesce, nonprofits are presented with an unprecedented opportunity to harness the power of AI. However, with this potential comes the responsibility to approach AI thoughtfully, ensuring that it amplifies the organization's mission rather than complicates it. The truth is, the worst AI you will ever use is today's. Tomorrow's iterations will only grow more powerful, capable, and far-reaching. For nonprofits, this means the time to act is now. By embracing AI today, nonprofits can position themselves ahead of the curve, optimizing their operations, engaging with communities more deeply, and driving their missions forward with greater impact.

Defining the Science: More Than Robots and Sci-Fi

AI offers nonprofits a unique opportunity to extend their reach, increase their impact, and solve complex societal challenges in ways that were previously unimaginable. From optimizing mission delivery to advancing conservation efforts, health initiatives, and donor engagement, AI's broad range of applications has transformative potential. As nonprofits continue to innovate and grow, AI can enhance their ability to gather data, make informed decisions, and scale their efforts in real time.

Nonprofits working in conservation, for example, can harness AI to analyze satellite imagery and detect deforestation trends or wildlife movement, allowing organizations to take early preventive action. Similarly, in public health, AI can analyze data to predict disease outbreaks and ensure that healthcare resources are directed to the right areas. In the humanitarian sector, AI can identify people in crisis or need—whether through image analysis in disaster zones or predictive models based on population movements—helping nonprofits respond more effectively to emergencies.

Donor, volunteer, and advocate engagement also benefits greatly from AI. Machine learning can predict giving patterns and help nonprofits tailor their outreach and engagement strategies, while generative AI tools can be used to personalize and automate donor communications and create personalized messaging at scale. Overall, AI offers a powerful way for nonprofits to optimize resource use, enhance mission delivery, and drive greater impact across a variety of sectors.

Let's break down the key technical areas of AI and how they can be applied:

- **Machine Learning (ML):** ML is a foundational subset of AI that focuses on enabling machines to learn from data and improve over time without being explicitly programmed. ML algorithms are ideal for analyzing vast datasets and identifying patterns that can help nonprofits with predictive analytics, donor segmentation, and understanding behavior trends. For example, ML can predict donor engagement, helping organizations know when and how to engage donors for maximum impact.
- **Deep Learning:** Deep learning is an advanced form of machine learning that uses neural networks to mimic human brain function. It is particularly effective at analyzing unstructured data such as images, video, and audio. Deep learning can help nonprofits in environmental conservation, where it can process satellite imagery to monitor ecosystem health or identify deforestation. Similarly, deep learning could be used in health-related initiatives, such as processing medical data to diagnose conditions in remote or underserved areas.
- **Generative AI (GenAI):** GenAI refers to a class of artificial intelligence models that can create content—such as text, images, video, or even music—based on input data. This technology uses advanced algorithms like LLMs, which are designed to understand, generate, and interact with human language at scale. Generative AI doesn't just analyze and interpret data; it actively creates new material from it, making it highly valuable for nonprofits that need to scale communication and engagement efforts. Nonprofits can

leverage generative AI to create personalized outreach content, automate communications, develop educational materials, or even generate marketing assets.

- **Natural Language Processing (NLP):** Natural Language Processing enables computers to understand, interpret, and generate human language. Nonprofits can use NLP for donor engagement, automating communication, and even content creation. Chatbots powered by NLP can respond to donor inquiries, freeing up staff time while maintaining personalized interactions. NLP also makes it possible for organizations to conduct sentiment analysis on public feedback, allowing nonprofits to gauge donor satisfaction or public opinion.
- **Computer Vision:** Computer Vision allows machines to "see" and interpret visual information, such as images or video. This technology is particularly valuable for nonprofits involved in disaster response, conservation, or monitoring social projects. Computer vision can be used to assess damage after a natural disaster or track endangered species. It can even monitor human activity in conflict zones to ensure that humanitarian aid reaches the right people. As this technology improves, it will become an essential tool for nonprofits working in fields that require large-scale visual data analysis.
- **Reinforcement Learning:** Reinforcement Learning involves teaching AI systems to learn from trial and error, rewarding successful decisions and penalizing poor ones. In the nonprofit sector, reinforcement learning can help organizations optimize resource allocation, such as determining the most efficient ways to distribute aid during crises or optimizing supply chains for disaster relief efforts. It can also be used to find the best strategies for volunteer management and scheduling, ensuring maximum impact with limited resources.
- **Robotics:** Robotics combines physical machines with AI to perform complex tasks autonomously or semi-autonomously. In the nonprofit space, AI-powered robots can assist in areas like logistics, where drones or autonomous vehicles can deliver aid to remote or dangerous regions. Robotics can also play a role in environmental cleanup efforts, such as deploying robots to clear debris or monitor pollution levels in oceans or forests.

- **Internet of Things (IoT):** The Internet of Things refers to a network of connected devices that collect and exchange data in real time. When paired with AI, IoT can give nonprofits access to valuable insights that can be used to optimize programs or monitor field conditions. For instance, environmental nonprofits can use IoT sensors to track wildlife migration patterns, monitor pollution levels, or collect climate data. Health-related nonprofits could use IoT devices to monitor patients' vitals and share that information with medical teams in real time, leading to faster interventions and better outcomes.

By understanding and applying these core areas of AI, nonprofits can enhance their ability to tackle global challenges and improve mission delivery. The future of AI in the nonprofit sector is bright, with endless possibilities for solving pressing problems—from climate change and poverty to health and education—with greater efficiency and precision.

The Future of AI: Trends and Possibilities

As AI continues to advance, the next 3–5 years promise to bring transformative changes that will shape how nonprofits leverage this powerful technology to support their missions. The trends emerging today will not only improve operational efficiency but also open new pathways for personalized outreach, deeper constituent and stakeholder engagement, and real-time decision-making. Let's explore the most relevant trends and how they can impact the nonprofit sector.

- **Explainable AI (XAI):** AI models will increasingly become more transparent, enabling organizations to understand and explain how decisions are made. This is particularly important for nonprofits, where transparency and trust are essential for maintaining strong relationships with donors, beneficiaries, and the public. XAI will allow nonprofits to ensure accountability and gain greater buy-in from stakeholders who might otherwise be skeptical of AI-driven decision-making.
- **Generative AI and Multimedia Creation:** Generative AI is quickly evolving to handle more complex tasks, including creating

images, videos, voice, and text with remarkable sophistication. Nonprofits can leverage this technology to produce high-quality multimedia content, engaging donors through personalized messages, immersive virtual experiences, or AI-generated social media campaigns. These innovations will reduce costs while creating richer, more compelling and personalized narratives.
- **Federated Learning:** Privacy remains a concern for many nonprofits, especially those dealing with sensitive donor or beneficiary data. Federated learning allows organizations to collaborate on AI model training without sharing raw data, helping preserve privacy while expanding data-driven capabilities. This could be especially useful for collective fundraising efforts or cross-organizational collaborations on social issues like disaster relief.
- **AI-Powered Personalization:** AI will continue to evolve in its ability to deliver highly personalized experiences for donors. With advances in machine learning and NLP, nonprofits can tailor their outreach to the individual level, automating personalized thank-you videos, customized email content, and targeted campaigns based on donor behavior and preferences. The impact on donor retention and engagement is expected to be significant.
- **Edge AI for Resource-Constrained Environments:** Nonprofits working in regions with limited internet connectivity could benefit from Edge AI, which processes data locally on devices without requiring cloud-based infrastructure. For example, humanitarian organizations could deploy AI tools in remote areas to manage logistics, deliver services, or monitor environmental changes, all without relying on high-speed internet.
- **AI for Social Good Initiatives:** A growing movement is applying AI to solve global challenges such as climate change, poverty, and public health crises. From AI models that predict food insecurity to machine learning tools that track environmental degradation, nonprofits have an opportunity to leverage AI for significant social impact. This aligns closely with the missions of many organizations that focus on long-term, systemic change.

- **Agentive AI and Autonomous Systems:** While still in its early stages, agentive AI (AI systems that act on behalf of users) has already shown the potential to revolutionize nonprofit operations. These AI agents can autonomously manage tasks such as monitoring grant deadlines, responding to routine emails, or even making real-time decisions on resource allocation based on predefined rules. This could free up nonprofit staff to focus on higher-level strategic initiatives.

In addition to these specific technologies, the next few years are expected to bring increased investment in sustainability practices for AI, as organizations work to mitigate the environmental impacts of AI-driven systems. Nonprofits can play a role by advocating for ethical and environmentally responsible AI deployment, ensuring that their use of AI not only advances their missions but also aligns with global sustainability goals.

These emerging trends offer exciting possibilities for the nonprofit sector, but they also underscore the need for ongoing learning and adaptation. As AI continues to evolve, so must the strategies and frameworks nonprofits use to harness its power responsibly.

Why Understanding These Technologies Matters for Nonprofits

Understanding the wide range of AI-related technologies allows nonprofits to make informed decisions about how to best apply these tools for their specific needs. Each of these technologies has unique strengths, and nonprofits must determine which combination will deliver the most value based on their goals and available resources. We will go into detail throughout this book to highlight ways in which nonprofits can amplify their mission by leveraging AI to create tremendous efficiencies, personalize outreach efforts, and analyze opportunities to scale impact.

By tapping into the full spectrum of AI technologies, nonprofits can improve operations, increase donor engagement, and scale their impact in ways that were previously unimaginable.

AI Myths versus Reality

As with any revolutionary technology, the rapid rise of artificial intelligence has led to a whirlwind of misconceptions, confusion, and even fear. For the nonprofit sector, these myths can create hesitation, preventing organizations from leveraging a tool that could significantly amplify their impact. To fully harness the benefits of AI, nonprofit leaders must cut through the noise and separate the myths from reality. Doing so will allow them to implement AI solutions that truly serve their mission and the communities they support.

- **Myth 1—AI Will Replace Human Workers:** One of the most persistent fears is that AI will displace human workers, replacing staff and volunteers in droves. This misconception stems from AI's ability to automate repetitive tasks, leading to the assumption that it could render many human roles obsolete. However, the reality is that AI is most effective when it augments, rather than replaces, human effort. In the nonprofit sector, AI can handle time-consuming administrative work, such as data entry or donor segmentation, freeing up staff to focus on relationship-building, strategic planning, and empathy-driven interactions that AI cannot replicate. As a result, AI acts as a partner, not a replacement, enabling staff to dedicate more time and energy to mission-critical work.
- **Myth 2—AI Is Only for Large Corporations:** There's a misconception that AI is only accessible to well-funded, large organizations with sophisticated tech infrastructures. But today, with the democratization of AI technologies through cloud services, open-source platforms, and no-code AI tools, even smaller nonprofits can leverage AI's power. Tools for tasks like automating social media, predicting donor behavior, or generating reports are no longer out of reach. Starting with small-scale projects, like using AI to enhance donor engagement or optimize volunteer management, can set the stage for deeper AI integration over time. AI isn't just for tech giants—it's for anyone looking to work smarter and more strategically.
- **Myth 3—AI Is Infallible:** Another misconception is that AI systems are flawless and should be trusted to make decisions

without oversight. However, AI is only as reliable as the data and algorithms used to train it. If the data is biased or incomplete, the AI's outputs can reinforce existing inequalities or make incorrect predictions. A cautionary tale comes from a hiring tool that inadvertently discriminated against female applicants because it was trained on biased historical data. Nonprofits, which often deal with sensitive data and vulnerable populations, must implement robust oversight to ensure that AI models are aligned with their values of equity and inclusion. Ongoing human oversight and continuous monitoring are essential to prevent unintentional harm.

- **Myth 4—AI Is Too Complicated for Nonprofits to Implement:** The perception that AI is too complex or technical for nonprofits without dedicated data science teams can discourage organizations from exploring AI's benefits. But AI doesn't always require advanced technical expertise. Many AI tools are designed for ease of use, with intuitive interfaces and step-by-step guides. Furthermore, cloud-based AI services offer a range of functionalities—from sentiment analysis to predictive analytics—without needing in-house AI expertise. The key is for nonprofits to start with manageable, well-defined projects, learn from these implementations, and scale up as their confidence and capacity grow.
- **Myth 5—AI Requires Perfect Data to Work:** While data quality is certainly a factor in AI performance, perfect data is not a prerequisite for effective AI deployment. Many AI models can handle messy or incomplete data, and some are designed to identify and correct data inconsistencies. For nonprofits, this means that AI can be a catalyst for improving data hygiene over time. AI can help highlight gaps in datasets, uncover hidden patterns, and guide organizations on where to focus their data improvement efforts, rather than being paralyzed by the idea that they need flawless data before getting started.
- **Myth 6—AI Is a One-Size-Fits-All Solution:** It's easy to get caught up in the hype and view AI as a magic wand that can solve all of an organization's problems. However, AI is only effective when applied to specific, well-defined challenges. For instance, AI can help automate donor communications, but it

won't automatically improve donor loyalty if it's not combined with a strong engagement strategy. Similarly, AI can analyze data to predict trends, but those predictions are only valuable if acted upon thoughtfully. Nonprofits must remain strategic, defining clear objectives and success metrics before diving into AI implementations.

- **Myth 7—AI Will Make Decisions Without Human Oversight:** Another fear is that AI will begin to make autonomous decisions that could negatively impact the people nonprofits serve. In reality, AI is a tool for decision support, not a replacement for human judgment. In areas like donor outreach, program planning, or resource allocation, AI can offer data-driven insights, but it is up to human leaders to apply these insights in ways that are ethically sound and mission-aligned. Human oversight ensures that AI recommendations are contextualized within the organization's unique values and goals, maintaining the essential balance between efficiency and compassion.
- **Myth 8—AI Can't Be Ethical:** Many believe that AI is inherently unethical or that ethical AI is impossible to achieve. However, the ethics of AI are determined by the individuals and organizations developing and implementing these systems. Ethical AI frameworks are being developed by researchers, practitioners, and organizations to ensure that AI is transparent, accountable, and aligned with human values. Nonprofits, with their commitment to public good and social equity, are uniquely positioned to lead by example in ethical AI deployment, ensuring that the technology is used to uplift, not undermine, the communities they serve.
- **Myth 9—AI Will Stagnate Human Creativity:** There is a concern that as AI becomes more capable—particularly with advancements in Generative AI and LLMs—it will limit human creativity and originality. Just as calculators didn't replace the need for mathematical comprehension but rather enhanced our ability to tackle complex problems, AI can be a source of inspiration and a tool for even greater creative exploration. It can generate ideas, assist with brainstorming, and even create initial drafts of content, allowing humans to focus on refining and

enhancing these outputs. Rather than replacing creativity, AI can serve as a co-creator, sparking new ways of thinking and expanding what is possible.
- **Myth 10—AI Is Just a Passing Trend:** Some view AI as a buzzword or a fleeting trend that will fade away. But AI is here to stay, and its influence will only continue to grow. In the next 3–5 years, AI will become even more embedded in the fabric of everyday life, and organizations that ignore it will risk falling behind. As we've shared, the "worst" AI we'll ever use is what we have today, and as AI capabilities rapidly advance, nonprofits must be proactive in adopting and shaping these tools to ensure they are used ethically and effectively.

By dispelling these myths, nonprofits can approach AI with realistic expectations, a clearer understanding, and a strong foundation for leveraging its potential. The goal is to embrace AI in a way that strengthens the human aspects of nonprofit work—compassion, empathy, and ethical decision-making—while using technology to achieve more substantial, scalable impact.

Artificial Intelligence versus Augmented Intelligence: Synergy, Not Competition

In the nonprofit sector, it's particularly useful to think in terms of "augmented" rather than "artificial" intelligence. The goal is not to create machines that think like humans, but to create tools that enhance human decision-making and capabilities.

This nuance is crucial because nonprofits operate in a realm where human connection, empathy, and values are paramount. AI should be seen as a tool to augment these human qualities, not replace them. For example, an AI system might analyze donor data to identify potential major givers, but it's the human fundraiser who will build the relationship and make the ask.

A common misconception surrounding AI is the belief that it competes with human intelligence, often stirring fears of replacement and redundancy. However, the true power of AI lies not in rivalry but in complementing and augmenting human capabilities. This synergy between artificial intelligence and human intelligence is what allows for innovative breakthroughs, especially within sectors like nonprofits, where empathy, human connection, and mission alignment are central to the work.

AI and human intelligence each excel in distinct areas, and understanding these strengths is critical for nonprofits looking to leverage AI effectively.

AI is unparalleled in its ability to:

- **Process vast amounts of data:** AI systems can analyze and interpret massive datasets at speeds and volumes that far surpass human capability, making it ideal for tasks like donor data analysis or trend prediction.
- **Identify patterns:** AI can recognize patterns and trends at far deeper levels that would remain invisible to human analysis, enabling nonprofits to detect emerging needs or opportunities more quickly.
- **Perform repetitive tasks:** Whether it's automating administrative work, categorizing donations, or handling routine communications, AI can manage tasks without fatigue, ensuring consistency and freeing up human staff for more complex responsibilities.
- **Predict outcomes:** Drawing from historical data, AI can forecast behaviors such as donor likelihood or community needs, allowing nonprofits to better anticipate and respond to challenges.

However, human intelligence excels in areas that AI simply cannot replicate, such as:

- **Emotional intelligence and empathy:** Nonprofit work is deeply human, often involving vulnerable populations, and requires empathy-driven interactions. AI can analyze data, but it cannot replace the human touch when building meaningful relationships with donors, volunteers, or beneficiaries.
- **Creative problem-solving:** Humans excel at thinking outside the box and adapting to unforeseen challenges. In contexts where flexibility and innovation are crucial, AI can provide tools, but human insight drives the solution.

- **Contextual understanding:** AI can process information, but only humans can interpret nuances and the broader context of situations, which is critical for making informed, ethical decisions in a nonprofit setting.
- **Ethical decision-making:** Human values, ethics, and moral considerations play a central role in nonprofits. While AI can provide data-driven insights, it is ultimately up to humans to make decisions that align with their organization's mission and ethical standards.

For nonprofits, the real power lies in harnessing this complementary relationship. AI should be seen not as a replacement for human workers but as a powerful tool that enhances their ability to make more informed, strategic, and compassionate decisions. As Gabe Cooper and Mckenna Bailey (2020) note in *Responsive Fundraising*, the most effective strategies combine AI's data-driven insights with the personal touch only humans can provide. This dynamic is especially relevant in fundraising, where AI can identify potential major donors based on historical giving data, but it's the human fundraiser who can interpret the nuances of a donor's motivations, values, and personal connections.

The future of AI in nonprofits is not about choosing between human or machine; it's about creating a partnership where AI enhances human intelligence, helping organizations reach new heights in service of their mission while at the same time humans utilize AI in ways that thoughtfully and strategically prioritize humanity over utility.

The AI Hype Cycle: Navigating the Wave of Expectations

Like many transformative technologies, Artificial Intelligence often becomes the subject of overblown enthusiasm, driven by inflated promises of revolutionary changes and instant results. This phenomenon is captured in what is known as the "hype cycle," a model developed by Gartner (2021) to illustrate the stages of adoption for emerging technologies. The AI hype cycle unfolds in predictable phases:

1. **Technology Trigger:** The initial breakthrough or innovation generates significant buzz and media coverage, drawing attention

from both enthusiasts and skeptics. In the case of AI, this stage includes the rise of machine learning, generative models, and NLP systems that captivated industries across the globe.
2. **Peak of Inflated Expectations:** At this stage, excitement builds, and there's widespread belief that AI will solve a vast range of problems, often with little understanding of its practical limitations. Wild projections about its potential lead to inflated promises, causing many to jump on the bandwagon without fully grasping the complexities involved.
3. **Trough of Disillusionment:** As with any new technology, reality eventually sets in. The lofty expectations created earlier aren't met, and AI starts to lose its appeal among those expecting immediate, all-encompassing results. Missteps or overly ambitious projects often contribute to disappointment.
4. **Slope of Enlightenment:** After the disillusionment phase, organizations and industries begin to adopt a more pragmatic view of AI, recognizing both its strengths and limitations. Case studies of successful, practical AI implementations begin to emerge, and organizations gain a clearer understanding of where AI can add value.
5. **Plateau of Productivity:** This final stage reflects widespread, mature adoption of AI technologies, where the benefits are well understood, and the technology's impact becomes both measurable and sustainable. By this point, AI is no longer seen as novel but as a powerful tool integrated into daily operations.

Currently, many aspects of AI are hovering at or near the "peak of inflated expectations," with promises of radical transformation dominating much of the discourse. However, the nonprofit sector, in particular, must approach AI adoption with caution, avoiding the trap of thinking AI is a one-size-fits-all solution. Instead, nonprofits should take deliberate steps to ensure AI is used effectively, in ways that truly align with their mission.

AI: An Imperative, Not an Option

As AI continues to grow more ubiquitous, the nonprofit sector has an opportunity—and an obligation—to lead the way in leveraging this technology for social good. It is not enough to merely keep pace with technological change; nonprofits must actively shape how AI is used to ensure that it reflects the values of equity, justice, and transparency. This requires a proactive approach, one that includes ongoing investments in technology, training, and ethical governance.

Nonprofits that fail to adopt AI risk falling behind, losing relevance in a world that is increasingly driven by data and automation. But those that embrace AI—using it to deepen relationships with donors, streamline operations, and enhance service delivery—will be well-positioned to create lasting, transformative change.

As we explore AI's potential, we must remember that philanthropy once played a key role in giving birth to this transformative technology. Now, nonprofits stand at a similar crossroads, with the chance to guide AI's evolution in ways that align with their missions and values. By embracing AI not as a luxury but as a necessity, nonprofits can lead the charge in creating a future where technology serves humanity, not the other way around. Through thoughtful integration, continuous learning, and a steadfast commitment to ethical principles, the nonprofit sector can ensure that AI becomes a tool for amplifying compassion, justice, and equity, just as it was always intended to be.

Embracing AI with Eyes Wide Open

As we've explored in this chapter, AI is a powerful tool with enormous potential for the nonprofit sector. However, it's a tool that must be wielded with care, understanding, and a clear-eyed view of its capabilities and limitations.

By separating myth from reality, hype from substance, and fear from opportunity, nonprofits can position themselves to leverage AI effectively. This means not just adopting new technologies, but also fostering a culture of innovation, data-driven decision-making, and continuous learning.

As we move forward in this book, we'll peel back the proverbial onion into specific applications of AI in nonprofit operations, fundraising, and program delivery. We'll explore case studies of organizations that are leading the way in AI adoption, and provide practical guidance for implementing AI in your own organization.

With a clear understanding of AI's potential and pitfalls, nonprofits have the opportunity to shape a future where technology and human compassion work hand in hand to create positive change in the world. In the next chapter, we'll explore how to build AI fluency within your organization, ensuring that your team is prepared to navigate the AI-driven future of the nonprofit sector. This journey of AI adoption is not just about technology—it's about reimagining how we can amplify our impact and better serve our communities in an increasingly digital world.

3

AI Fluency and the Future Nonprofit Workforce

The Imperative of AI Literacy in the Nonprofit Sector

Illustrating how dependent we've become on real-time data exchange, author Chappell recently encountered a profound moment that provided a stark reminder of our reliance on a technology that has only existed for about two decades. As he recalls: "Not long ago, I found myself standing at the curb of the airport terminal, waving goodbye to the friend who had just dropped me off, when a sudden, chilling realization struck me. My phone—my trusted companion for all things logistical—was still in the car. Panic set in as the full gravity of my situation dawned on me. I had no idea how to access my boarding pass, what hotel I was supposed to stay at once I arrived, or how I would even get an Uber to leave the airport after landing. My heart began to race, my hands felt clammy, and my body broke out in a sweat. I desperately scanned the airport lobby for a payphone, only to confirm what I already knew: Pay phones have become relics of a bygone era, long replaced by the conveniences of real-time access to data.

In that moment, I felt truly stranded, alone, and, to my embarrassment, utterly debilitated. The realization was stark—my dependence on real-time data exchange had become so natural, so ingrained, that

I had forgotten how to function without it. My phone wasn't just a convenience; it was my map, my schedule, my link to the world. It was the very thing that kept my day—my life, really—running smoothly. This incident reminded me just how much technology has redefined the way we create efficiencies and steer our direction, minute by minute, throughout the day. Just as the internet became essential, AI too will become an integral layer of our lives—a technology that will quietly but powerfully reshape every aspect of our existence.

As we explored in Chapters 1 and 2, artificial intelligence (AI) has the capacity to transform the entire nonprofit landscape. Its continued adoption will undoubtedly become ubiquitous in most aspects of life itself, similar to our reliance on real-time data exchange over the Internet in our daily activities. In many ways, the Internet has become so intertwined with our existence that it's hard to imagine a time without it. The same will soon be true with AI.

From revolutionizing operations to enhancing donor engagement and amplifying mission impact, AI offers unprecedented potential. However, to realize this potential, nonprofit professionals must develop the skills needed to leverage these technologies effectively. In this chapter, we explore the concept of AI fluency, why it is crucial for the future workforce, and how nonprofits can cultivate it.

"AI moved your cheese, and it's not coming back," adapted from the popular fable *Who Moved My Cheese?* by Spencer Johnson (1998), perfectly encapsulates this shift. The original fable is about adapting to change when the comfort of familiarity is disrupted, and AI brings a similar kind of transformation, requiring us to rethink and adjust. Traditional approaches and skills that nonprofits once relied on are being disrupted, and professionals and organizations alike that don't adapt risk being left behind. But how can you adapt if you don't even recognize what has changed in the first place? In a world where the pace of change feels exponential, understanding the basics of AI, how it evolves, and how it's quickly becoming ubiquitous within most aspects of your life is the first imperative. Let's dive into the concept of AI fluency, and provide you the context that you'll need not only to navigate change more effectively, but to better understand how, and which AI tools will support your professional development and amplify your organization's mission.

What Is AI Fluency?

AI fluency is more than just a basic understanding of AI technologies. It encompasses the ability to evaluate AI solutions critically, and understand their potential applications, limitations, and how to integrate them into nonprofit operations effectively while minimizing unintended consequences. As Allison Fine and Beth Kanter wrote in *The Smart Nonprofit* (2022), AI fluency means "developing a working knowledge of AI that allows nonprofit professionals to make informed decisions about its use in their organizations."

AI fluency is not for bragging rights or impressing friends at dinner parties, although you'll get your fair share of that. Importantly, as employers are continuously looking for ways to maximize productivity, there is a new demand for nonprofit professionals who can command AI to amplify mission. Recent data highlights the financial value of AI fluency in the workforce. A 2023 AWS study shows that employees with AI skills can command up to 30% higher salaries, with similar increases across sectors such as research, marketing, finance, and business operations. This wage premium underscores the critical importance of developing AI skills, not just for personal growth, but also for organizational competitiveness and mission success.

Why AI Fluency Matters

In the nonprofit sector, the importance of AI fluency cannot be overstated. It equips professionals with the tools and understanding needed to make strategic decisions that go beyond mere adoption of technology. When a nonprofit team is fluent in AI, they are empowered to make decisions aligned with their mission and values. This enables the organization to harness AI for what truly matters: furthering their cause and enhancing their impact.

By grasping the intricacies of AI, professionals can streamline their organization's operations. They can pinpoint tasks that AI can take over—whether it's routine administrative work or data management—allowing staff to focus on the more human-centric activities, such as building relationships and planning strategically. Efficiency is no longer an abstract goal but a measurable outcome of AI integration.

Furthermore, AI fluency fosters a deeper connection with donors. Understanding AI's capacity to analyze donor behavior means nonprofits can tailor their outreach efforts with precision, crafting personalized campaigns that resonate with individuals. Instead of generic, broad-sweeping messaging, organizations can engage with their supporters in meaningful, targeted ways. With AI, nonprofits can expand their reach and deepen their impact. Whether it's identifying emerging trends in service needs or optimizing resource allocation, AI allows organizations to be proactive and responsive, amplifying their capacity to serve their communities more effectively.

However, alongside the benefits come risks, particularly ethical ones. AI-fluent professionals are better prepared to navigate these complexities, ensuring the technology is used responsibly. They can recognize biases within AI systems and address them head-on, which is crucial for maintaining the trust of donors, beneficiaries, and the public. The competitive landscape is also evolving. As more nonprofits integrate AI, those that fail to develop AI fluency risk being left behind—losing not just donors, but also valuable funding and volunteers to organizations that have embraced technology as part of their operational DNA.

Finally, AI fluency isn't just about keeping up; it's about staying ahead. AI is not a one-and-done solution. When teams understand AI's potential, they are empowered to innovate, finding additional creative solutions to many long-standing challenges. AI becomes a catalyst for new thinking, opening doors to possibilities that once seemed out of reach.

In this way, AI fluency is not just a skill—it's a mindset that propels nonprofits into the future, enabling them to thrive in an increasingly tech-driven world.

The Current State of AI Fluency in Nonprofits

Despite the increasing significance of AI in the nonprofit sector, many organizations are struggling to keep pace. A 2018 NTEN study revealed that only 23% of nonprofits actively use AI, and one of the main barriers to adoption is a lack of AI understanding and skills. This gap presents a unique challenge, but also an opportunity for nonprofits that choose to invest in AI literacy.

Several factors contribute to this lag in AI fluency. One of the most significant is resource constraints. Many nonprofits operate on tight budgets, making it difficult to allocate funds for new technologies and the necessary training. The immediate needs of day-to-day operations often take precedence over long-term investments in technology, even when those investments could lead to greater efficiency and impact down the line.

There's also a cultural resistance to AI within the sector. Nonprofits often perceive AI as being at odds with their core mission, which is deeply rooted in human connection and compassion. The concern is that AI might distance them from the personal, human-centric work that defines their purpose. In reality, AI has the potential to enhance this work by freeing up staff time and allowing for deeper, more personalized interactions with donors and beneficiaries.

A lack of technical expertise further complicates the issue. Many nonprofit professionals come from non-technical backgrounds, which can make AI feel inaccessible or intimidating. Without a clear understanding of how AI works, it's easy to view it as something better suited for tech companies rather than mission-driven organizations.

Ethical concerns also play a role in the hesitancy around AI adoption. Nonprofits are often apprehensive about the implications of AI, particularly around issues like data privacy, bias, and transparency. These concerns are valid and important, but with the right knowledge and approach, they can be navigated responsibly.

Lastly, the rapid pace of AI development can be overwhelming for nonprofits that are already stretched thin. Keeping up with the constant advancements in AI technology requires a level of agility that many organizations struggle to maintain. The fear of falling behind often leads to inaction, creating a cycle where nonprofits feel too far behind to catch up.

Yet, for nonprofits willing to invest in developing AI fluency among their teams, the rewards can be significant. As Gabe Cooper and Mckenna Bailey (2020) highlight in *Responsive Fundraising*, adopting AI doesn't mean sacrificing the human touch. On the contrary, it enables nonprofits to amplify their human impact by automating routine tasks, allowing staff to focus on building stronger relationships and engaging more meaningfully with their communities.

Ultimately, closing the AI fluency gap is not just about catching up to technological trends—it's about equipping nonprofit teams with the tools they need to thrive in an AI-driven world. By embracing AI thoughtfully, nonprofits can better fulfill their missions while remaining competitive in a rapidly evolving landscape.

Key Components of AI Fluency

Think of artificial intelligence the same way we might think about microwaves. Few people know how to build a microwave, and most of us would be lost if we had to repair one. But we know how to use it. We understand its effects, and we know when it is working properly by evaluating whether our food comes out cold or scorched. While we may not understand the engineering behind how a microwave works, we have learned to trust this tool to cook food efficiently. The same concept applies to AI, particularly in the nonprofit sector. In this same way, nonprofit professionals don't need to understand the complex architecture of large language models (LLMs) or how deep learning algorithms make predictions, but they must learn how to use these technologies effectively and recognize when they're functioning as intended. They must also be armed with critical thinking skills to evaluate when an AI is not working as intended.

As AI becomes an essential tool for scaling nonprofit missions, developing AI fluency is about understanding how to apply these systems thoughtfully, ensuring they align with organizational values and goals, and whether AI will contribute to both short-term and long-term objectives. To be clear, AI fluency doesn't require an advanced degree to build AI models from scratch; it requires knowing how to use AI tools responsibly in ways that will amplify impact and support a philanthropy ecosystem built on the currency of trust. If we may brag a little, reading this book is a fantastic start to your AI fluency journey. However, unlike microwaves, AI is an evolving technology, so you'll need to test, observe, and refine your skills regularly to get the most out of it. Nonprofit professionals should embrace a mindset of continuous learning, setting a goal of discovering one new aspect of AI each week. This perpetual curiosity ensures they stay up to date and adapt to the rapidly evolving landscape.

Creating your roadmap for AI fluency isn't just a short-term goal; it's a strategic asset that will position you as a vital part of your nonprofit's future. As AI becomes increasingly integral to how organizations operate, it's crucial for you to enhance your own fluency in AI—not only empowering your personal growth but also contributing to your organization's mission. The following steps provide a structured approach to help you navigate this journey:

- **Skill Acquisition:** To become fluent in AI, it's essential to start building your foundational knowledge. You don't need to understand every detail about how AI works, just as you don't need to know how to build a microwave to use it successfully. However, you need to learn how AI operates, how to use AI tools effectively, and how to recognize when they are functioning as intended.
  - **Start Today:** Enroll in AI courses that fit your role, whether they cover basic AI concepts or advanced data analytics. Platforms like Coursera or LinkedIn Learning offer great resources for beginners. Set a personal goal—learn one new thing about AI each week to help you feel more comfortable with this technology over time. We will cover this in more detail in Chapter 16.
- **Project Application:** Learning through doing is crucial to mastering AI fluency. Consider how AI can make your daily tasks more efficient or help you solve problems within your nonprofit. This hands-on approach allows you to apply theoretical knowledge in practical settings, increasing your fluency while contributing to your organization's success.
  - **Actionable Tip:** Try using AI in a small, manageable project first—maybe it's automating routine tasks or applying AI to better segment donors. Once you've experienced success in one area, you can scale up and apply it to larger projects or across departments.
- **Innovation and Creativity:** AI fluency is about much more than just understanding the technology—it's about thinking creatively. As you become more comfortable with AI, your goal should be to explore new ways that AI can enhance your work, whether it's improving program delivery, boosting fundraising efforts, or finding innovative solutions to existing challenges.

- **Spark Innovation:** Stay curious! Make it a habit to brainstorm AI-related ideas for your work or collaborate with others to see how AI might solve long-standing problems. Subscribe to AI newsletters, take time each week to read about the latest AI developments, and don't be afraid to experiment with new tools or concepts.
- **Ethical Awareness:** While we cover this topic in detail in Chapter 11, "Beyond AI Ethics," it can't be overstated that incorporating AI into your work comes with ethical responsibilities. As you develop your fluency, it's vital to understand the ethical dimensions of AI—how to manage bias, ensure transparency, and uphold your nonprofit's values. AI fluency isn't just about technical proficiency; it's about making responsible decisions with AI.
  - **Build Ethical Awareness:** Regularly engage with resources on AI ethics and participate in discussions about AI's ethical implications. Ensure that your AI projects are aligned with your organization's values and mission, and always think critically about the impact of your AI decisions.
- **Continuous Learning:** AI is an ever-evolving field, so your learning journey doesn't end with a few courses or projects. Developing AI fluency means committing to continuous learning—both to keep up with new advancements and to remain adaptable as the technology changes.
  - **Keep Learning:** Make it a priority to stay engaged with AI news and developments. Attend AI webinars, join AI-related networks or communities, and stay curious about how new advancements can be applied to your work. AI fluency is a journey, and keeping up with trends will ensure you remain on the cutting edge.
- **Collaboration Across Roles:** AI fluency also means being able to work effectively with others across different functions of your organization. AI adoption isn't limited to the IT team—it affects program managers, fundraisers, marketing staff, and leadership. As you build your fluency, think about how you can collaborate with others to leverage AI across different aspects of the organization.

- o **Collaborate Thoughtfully:** Make cross-functional collaboration part of your routine. Share your AI ideas with other teams, and don't hesitate to ask for input on how AI can support their work. Your ability to connect AI with different areas of the organization will make you a valuable resource.
- **Confidence in Using AI:** Just as you trust a microwave to heat your meal once you understand its basic functions, you need to build confidence in using AI systems. AI tools are powerful, but they require monitoring, adjustment, and the ability to troubleshoot when things don't work as expected.
  - o **Verify then Trust:** While many organizations build corporate values on the idea of best intention, which manifests itself in a "trust then verify" workplace culture, in the nonprofit sector where we operate on the currency of trust we have to take a more prudent approach to verify then trust. This means that you need to take time to evaluate the AI tools you're using. Are they delivering the results you need? Are there areas for improvement? Confidence comes from experience, so start by applying AI in small ways and gradually work toward using it for larger, more complex tasks.

Building AI fluency is a personal and professional investment in your future. By following this roadmap, you'll become more confident, more innovative, and more capable of leveraging AI to its full potential. Your curiosity, adaptability, and ethical awareness will ensure that you don't just keep up with the changes AI brings—you'll lead your organization through them.

AI Fluency and the Changing Nonprofit Workforce

As AI becomes a more integral part of the nonprofit sector, the skills required of nonprofit professionals are evolving rapidly. A report by the World Economic Forum (2025) emphasizes that as routine tasks become automated, skills like critical thinking, creativity, and problem-solving will become essential to navigating this new landscape. For nonprofits, this shift brings significant changes in how roles are defined, the skills required, and the overall structure of the workforce.

One major change will involve redefining job roles. As AI takes on more operational tasks, traditional roles may need to be reimagined to incorporate AI-related responsibilities. For instance, roles like AI ethics officer or data steward may emerge, focused on overseeing the ethical use of AI and managing the influx of data nonprofits rely on. Organizations will need to update job descriptions to reflect these new skill sets, ensuring that AI is seamlessly integrated into the daily workflow. This shift may also prompt new job titles, reflecting the growing importance of managing AI systems and their data-driven outputs.

Additionally, nonprofits will need to address new skill requirements. While AI and data science skills are becoming increasingly valuable, nonprofits must emphasize analytical and critical thinking across all roles, not just technical ones. Digital literacy will become essential for everyone—from development officers to program managers—enabling them to make sense of AI-generated insights and apply them strategically to enhance their impact.

Yet, while technical skills are on the rise, soft skills like empathy, creativity, and problem-solving will become more crucial than ever. AI may be capable of processing data and performing routine tasks, but it lacks the human ability to connect emotionally and solve complex, non-linear problems. Emotional intelligence will play a key role in maintaining the human touch within AI-enhanced systems, particularly in areas like donor relations, volunteer engagement, and beneficiary services. Leadership skills will also need to evolve, focusing on how to effectively manage collaboration between humans and AI, and ensuring that AI enhances rather than overshadows human contribution.

Given the pace of AI advancements, continuous learning is now a non-negotiable for nonprofit professionals. Staying current with AI developments requires ongoing up-skilling and re-skilling initiatives. Organizations will need to cultivate a culture of learning, offering regular training sessions and creating opportunities for staff to explore new technologies. Embracing a growth mindset—where learning and adaptation are viewed as continuous processes—will be vital for adapting to the rapid technological changes ahead.

Another significant aspect of AI adoption in nonprofits will be the growing need for ethical decision-making. As AI becomes more embedded in decision-making processes, staff will need to understand AI governance frameworks and be able to navigate complex ethical dilemmas that arise from AI use. Whether it's handling data privacy concerns or ensuring that AI systems remain free of bias, nonprofit professionals must be equipped to make informed, ethically sound decisions that reflect the organization's mission and values.

Nonprofits will also see a heightened demand for cross-functional collaboration. As AI transforms organizational structures, the ability to bridge the gap between technical and non-technical teams will be critical. Professionals who can work within diverse, cross-functional teams—merging IT, development, and program staff—will be instrumental in driving AI adoption. Skills in project management and change management will become essential as organizations navigate this technological shift.

Finally, integrating AI will intensify the focus on data-driven decision making. AI has the power to generate valuable insights, but nonprofits need professionals who can interpret and apply these insights in a way that aligns with their mission. Balancing data-driven strategies with a mission-driven ethos will be key to maintaining authenticity and purpose in the AI age. Nonprofit leaders must ensure that, while AI optimizes operations, it does not overshadow the core values and human connections that define the nonprofit sector.

By embracing these evolving roles and skill sets, nonprofits will position themselves not only to survive but to thrive in an increasingly AI-driven future, leveraging both technology and human capacity to achieve greater impact.

The Future of AI Fluency in Nonprofits

AI fluency is not just a future aspiration for nonprofits—it's a current necessity. By investing in AI fluency now, nonprofits can unlock the full potential of AI to drive efficiency, enhance decision-making, and amplify mission impact. The key to this success lies in recognizing that AI is not here to replace the human heart of nonprofit work, but rather to enhance it. As Lucy Bernholz (2021) reminds us in her book *Digital Technology and Democratic Theory*, "Technology should always serve as a tool for advancing social good, not an end in itself."

In the rapidly changing landscape of technology, there will inevitably be winners and losers. Nonprofits that learn to leverage AI will excel, thriving in their missions at an impressive rate compared to those that continue doing things the same way, expecting different results. The need to adapt is no longer a choice but a crucial determinant of success. Organizations that embrace AI fluency will be positioned to lead, innovate, and make a lasting impact, while those that hesitate may struggle to stay relevant.

Nonprofits willing to commit to AI fluency are poised to thrive in an increasingly digital future, embracing the transformative power of AI while remaining true to their mission. With the right approach to learning, development, and ethical use, nonprofits can navigate the complexities of the AI landscape and uncover new opportunities for creating lasting, meaningful impact.

As AI continues to reshape the nonprofit landscape, staying ahead of technological trends is essential for organizations aiming to make a lasting impact. The future of AI fluency in nonprofits will be defined by several emerging trends, each playing a crucial role in how organizations harness the power of AI for social good.

One key trend is the democratization of AI. As AI tools become more user-friendly and accessible, the barrier to entry will lower significantly, enabling organizations of all sizes to leverage these technologies. This shift will increase the importance of AI fluency as nonprofits will need to ensure that their teams are equipped to use AI responsibly and effectively, especially given the variety of tools now available to smaller organizations with limited resources. The result will be a more level playing field where even smaller nonprofits can compete technologically with larger, better-resourced organizations.

An increased emphasis on ethical AI will also define the future. As AI becomes more integrated into nonprofit operations, the need for fluency in ethical considerations will grow. Nonprofit professionals will have to navigate complex questions around bias, privacy, and fairness to ensure that AI solutions are aligned with the sector's mission to serve humanity. Understanding the ethical implications of AI use, and fostering discussions around responsible AI, will be essential as nonprofits develop AI-powered systems that interact with sensitive data and vulnerable populations.

The integration of AI across all nonprofit functions is another significant trend. AI will no longer be siloed in IT or data departments. Instead, it will be infused across functions like fundraising, program delivery, volunteer management, and communications. AI fluency will need to extend beyond data scientists to staff in all areas of the organization, requiring a broad-based approach to training that ensures everyone has the skills needed to contribute meaningfully to AI-driven initiatives.

In response to the growing demand for AI expertise, we can also expect the rise of AI specialists in nonprofits. As the sector increasingly adopts AI, new roles like AI ethics officer or AI strategy director will emerge. These positions will be critical for guiding AI adoption in ways that align with the organization's values and mission. These specialists will help bridge the gap between technology and mission-driven work, ensuring that AI serves as a force for good rather than simply a tool for efficiency.

Moreover, collaborative AI learning will become a major asset for the sector. Nonprofits will benefit from collaborating on AI initiatives, pooling resources, and sharing best practices. This collective learning will help organizations, especially smaller ones, advance their AI capabilities and stay competitive in the increasingly digital nonprofit ecosystem.

We will also see more AI-enhanced decision-making. As nonprofits grow more fluent in AI, leaders will use data-driven insights to make more informed decisions at all levels of the organization. This shift will necessitate the development of new leadership skills in interpreting AI-generated insights and balancing these with human judgment and mission alignment.

Lastly, the future will likely see the rise of personalized AI learning paths. AI itself will play a role in helping nonprofit staff develop AI fluency through adaptive learning platforms. These systems will tailor educational content and learning experiences to the needs and pace of individual learners, creating more effective and efficient paths to mastering AI-related skills.

In Chapter 4, we will explore how nonprofits can go beyond AI fluency to adopt an AI-first approach, revolutionizing their operations and impact in a way that centers on innovation and ethics.

The Road to AI Fluency Is Essential, Not Optional

Building AI fluency is no longer optional for nonprofits—it's an essential part of adapting to the future. By investing in a structured roadmap that includes assessment, training, real-world application, and continuous improvement, nonprofits can ensure that their teams are familiar with AI and fluent in its application. As AI continues to reshape the sector, those who commit to this journey will be well-positioned to lead with confidence and have an even greater impact.

In the fast-changing world of AI, perpetual curiosity will be the key to staying ahead. By integrating regular learning opportunities, nonprofits can foster a culture of innovation, where AI fluency becomes second nature to staff and stakeholders alike.

4

The AI-First Nonprofit

Reimagining Nonprofit Impact for Future Success

The nonprofit sector has always been a cornerstone of social change, tackling some of the most pressing issues in our society—from poverty alleviation and education to healthcare and environmental sustainability. Unfortunately, these challenges are growing in both scale and complexity, while the resources available to address them remain stagnant with systemic declines in the percentage of households that participate in charitable giving in most developed nations. This dilemma demands an unprecedented level of innovation and efficiency, and in this context, artificial intelligence (AI) emerges as one of the most transformative tools available. To fully harness AI's potential, nonprofits must make the leap from passive adoption to proactive strategies—becoming AI-first organizations.

While AI fluency equips nonprofit professionals with the necessary vocabulary and basic understanding to navigate the evolving digital landscape, evolving into an AI-first organization empowers them to drive significant innovation and efficiency, transforming challenges into opportunities for impactful solutions. Being AI-first is more than just an operational shift; it is a strategic evolution that demands nonprofits view AI not just as a tool, but as a cornerstone for mission delivery and ability to accelerate and maximize impact.

This chapter explores what it means to be an AI-first nonprofit, the lessons nonprofits can learn from the private sector, and how nonprofits can use AI to solve seemingly insurmountable challenges, scale their impact, and foster a culture of ongoing innovation.

From Passive AI Use to Proactive AI Strategies: A Paradigm Shift

Currently, many nonprofits are at an early stage in the AI adoption curve, using AI mainly for basic tasks—things like drafting or proofing donor communications, analyzing spreadsheets, or optimizing back-office processes such as bookkeeping and scheduling. While these applications do provide marginal efficiency gains, they are far from realizing AI's true transformative power. For nonprofits to maximize their impact, they must evolve from being reactive adopters of shadow AI platforms to proactive visionaries, integrating AI across all facets of their strategic priorities.

Being AI-first means approaching every aspect of your mission through an AI lens. It is about asking fundamental questions such as: How can AI help us predict future trends in giving and engagement? How can we personalize outreach to better engage with supporters? How can AI help us measure our impact in real time, providing transparency to our stakeholders? How can AI help accelerate and increase the chance of success of this program?

The concept of proactive AI adoption mirrors transformations that have taken place in the private sector. For instance, Google made the strategic decision in 2017 to transition from a mobile-first company to an AI-first organization, as declared by Google's CEO, Sundar Pichai. This shift signaled a commitment to embedding AI into every product and service across the company. For nonprofits, this kind of strategic clarity is essential for fully leveraging AI's potential. Being AI-first means rethinking how an organization functions at every level—from data collection and analysis to service delivery and impact measurement.

Moving toward proactive AI adoption also requires substantial investments in AI capacity-building and AI literacy by every member of the organization. This includes training staff, rethinking organizational processes, and embedding AI-driven decision-making at every level of the organization's programs and strategic priorities. The focus must be on shifting AI from a back-office efficiency tool to a consistent strategic driver that informs how nonprofits interact with their communities, engage donors, and achieve their missions.

Lessons from the Private Sector: A Comparative Analysis of AI Adoption

When comparing the nonprofit sector's adoption of AI to that of the private sector, the disparity becomes clear. Financial services companies such as JP Morgan, Morgan Stanley have declared themselves AI-first financial institutions and have already integrated AI into their core operations to enhance fraud detection, customer experience, and risk analysis. JP Morgan's COIN (Contract Intelligence) software uses AI to analyze legal documents, drastically reducing the time and costs associated with these tasks (JPMorgan Chase & Co., 2017). AI has enabled these companies to drive efficiencies, predict trends, and reduce risk—allowing them to stay competitive in a constantly evolving landscape.

In stark contrast, a recent Salesforce Nonprofit Trends Report showed that fewer than 10% of nonprofits are currently using AI, even though the vast majority recognize its potential (Salesforce, 2023). The lag in adoption is not only due to resource constraints but also a cultural hesitation with a limited appetite for things that appear to be untested. Many nonprofits perceive AI as either too expensive, too complex, too risky, or incompatible with their mission-driven focus. However, as AI tools become dramatically more accessible and affordable, those who do not adopt AI risk falling behind and becoming unable to fulfill their missions effectively.

The Royal Bank of Canada (RBC) has also demonstrated what it means to immerse AI throughout its organization. RBC uses AI-powered chatbots to manage basic customer interactions, freeing up human staff to focus on more complex customer needs. A similar approach could be highly beneficial for nonprofits: AI could handle routine donor inquiries, allowing staff to focus on deepening relationships, launching new initiatives, exploring new partnership opportunities, and solving more strategic challenges.

This disparity in AI adoption presents a major risk for nonprofits. Those that fail to adopt AI tools effectively may find themselves struggling to compete for attention, funding, and impact in an increasingly digital-first world. The World Economic Forum predicts that by 2030, AI and automation will transform the jobs of over one billion people globally (2020). Nonprofits must be prepared to embrace AI as a vital part of their mission if they want to continue thriving in this environment.

The private sector's success in leveraging AI provides important lessons for nonprofits. The key takeaway is that AI should not just be viewed as an efficiency tool. Instead, it should be seen as an innovation enabler and mission imperative—one that allows nonprofits to explore new ways to connect with their communities, create value, and expand their impact.

The Stakes Have Never Been Higher

As we discussed in Chapter 1, the stakes for nonprofits in the 21st century are incredibly high. Rising income inequality, environmental degradation, and socio-political instability all serve to intensify the demand for nonprofit services. A study conducted by the Bank for International Settlements (2023) found that AI investment correlates with a rise in income inequality across 86 countries, increasing the income share of the top decile while reducing it for the bottom decile. As inequality grows, so too does the need for nonprofit intervention. However, without AI, nonprofits will find themselves increasingly unable to meet these growing demands leading to unmet needs, staff burnout, and concerns over nonprofits' ability to survive.

Furthermore, climate change and its associated challenges are placing new pressures on nonprofits that work in environmental conservation, humanitarian aid, and disaster relief. The frequency and intensity of natural disasters are increasing, and the role of nonprofits in these efforts is more crucial than ever. AI offers a way to predict, prepare for, and mitigate the effects of climate change—whether through real-time data analysis to track changing weather patterns or using drones to deliver aid to disaster-stricken regions.

For example, during the Australian bushfires of 2020, AI-powered models were used to predict fire spread, allowing authorities and nonprofits to respond more efficiently. The ability to forecast and act on data-driven insights is an enormous advantage for nonprofits working in crisis situations.

Charity Navigator, a nonprofit that evaluates other nonprofits, also leverages AI to provide donors with real-time updates on how well different organizations are using funds. By using AI to monitor and evaluate nonprofits in real-time, Charity Navigator can help ensure that resources are being used efficiently, thereby fostering trust among donors and ensuring that help reaches those who need it most.

What It Means to Be an AI-First Nonprofit

Becoming an AI-first nonprofit is about more than just adopting a set of tools—it's about rethinking how the organization functions at every level. An AI-first nonprofit sees AI as an enabler of mission delivery and integrates it into every part of the organization. This means AI is used proactively to enhance decision-making, improve operational efficiency, and create personalized experiences for donors and beneficiaries.

Being AI-first also involves shifting organizational culture. Leadership buy-in is crucial—executive teams must see AI as a strategic investment rather than a cost. Leaders must foster a culture where experimentation is encouraged, teams are willing to fail fast and learn, and technology is embraced as a partner in the mission.

Nonprofits must also recognize that being AI-first doesn't mean replacing people with machines. Instead, it means allowing technology to handle routine, repetitive tasks so that human resources can be focused on the work that requires empathy, relationship-building, and creative problem-solving—the true essence of the nonprofit sector.

AI Can Solve Previously Unsolvable Problems

One of AI's most compelling features is its ability to solve problems at a scale that was previously unthinkable. Take, for example, environmental conservation. Measuring the populations of different animal species in remote areas was once an incredibly labor-intensive and costly endeavor. Today, AI-powered audio recognition technology can monitor species populations by analyzing sounds captured from the forest, allowing conservationists to track biodiversity in real time.

AI is also being used to understand whale communication patterns. Researchers have employed machine learning algorithms to analyze whale songs, offering unprecedented insights into their behaviors and social structures. Understanding these patterns could inform more effective conservation policies, helping to protect these majestic creatures from the numerous threats they face.

In the medical field, AI is being used to bring healthcare services to some of the world's most remote areas. For example, an AI-driven app that can diagnose eye diseases by analyzing retina photographs has the potential to revolutionize eye care in regions where access to specialists is limited. Similarly, AI is being used to diagnose early-stage skin cancer, providing doctors with the insights needed to intervene before the disease progresses.

These examples illustrate the breadth of AI's problem-solving capacity, demonstrating its potential to tackle challenges that were once seen as insurmountable. For nonprofits, this opens up opportunities not only to reach more people but also to enhance the quality and effectiveness of the services they provide.

Scalability: AI and Mission Delivery at Unprecedented Scale

A key advantage of AI is its ability to enable scalability in mission delivery. In the nonprofit sector, scaling usually means increasing the number of people served or expanding the scope of services offered—both of which traditionally require a proportional increase in resources. AI changes this dynamic by allowing nonprofits to reach more people without necessarily needing to expand their workforce or budget at the same rate.

Similarly, International Medical Corps uses AI in its emergency response operations. By leveraging predictive analytics, they can allocate resources more effectively during disasters, ensuring that aid reaches the most vulnerable populations quickly. This kind of predictive capability allows nonprofits to respond to crises not just faster, but smarter, ultimately saving more lives.

Wealth Does Not Equal Innovation: Insights from Trevor Noah

During the 2024 Microsoft Global Nonprofit Leaders Summit, author Chappell had the opportunity to ask Trevor Noah, Microsoft's Chief Question Officer, about his perspectives on technology integration in underserved regions. His response was enlightening: "Necessity is the mother of invention—there are few places where you will learn more about what a technology is capable of than a place where people need technology." He emphasized that the assumption that people in developing countries lack innovation is fundamentally misguided. Often, these communities drive the most creative uses of technology because they are driven by necessity.

As an example of this sentiment, Zipline, the drone delivery service that provides life-saving medical supplies in Rwanda, is a case in point. The drones navigate complex terrain using AI, delivering blood and vaccines to remote clinics that would otherwise be cut off. This isn't a high-tech solution that emerged from Silicon Valley—it's a response to a pressing local need, solved with the help of technology and driven by the innovative spirit of the community.

The nonprofit sector must adopt this mindset—innovation is not about wealth, it's about solving real problems. AI can help nonprofits empower the communities they serve to be co-creators in the solutions, making their impact sustainable and truly transformative.

AI Across Nonprofit Functions: Front-of-House and Back-of-House

In nonprofit operations, AI applications span front-of-house (public-facing) and back-of-house (administrative) functions. Consider the analogy of a restaurant. Front-of-house functions are all about delivering an excellent customer experience, while back-of-house functions are about operational efficiency. Both are crucial for overall success.

Front-of-house applications for AI in nonprofits include mission delivery, donor engagement, beneficiary support, and communications. AI can personalize donor outreach, provide 24/7 chat support, and even help identify potential major donors by analyzing giving patterns and engagement data. Imagine a scenario where AI identifies a donor's interests and then tailors content specifically to them—leading to deeper connections and greater trust.

Back-of-house applications, meanwhile, include finance, human resources, and logistics. AI can automate time-consuming administrative tasks, analyze financial data to predict cash flow issues, or optimize inventory in food banks to reduce waste. These efficiencies mean that staff spend less time on routine tasks and more time on activities that add value to the organization's mission.

The nonprofit Feeding America provides a compelling example of AI integration across both functions. Their MealConnect program uses AI to connect surplus food from restaurants and grocery stores with food banks that need it. On the back end, AI helps predict food supply and demand, optimizing distribution and ensuring food doesn't go to waste. On the front end, the platform provides a seamless experience for both donors and recipients, facilitating a more connected network of partners.

Encouraging a Culture of Innovation through AI

To become an AI-first nonprofit, fostering a culture of innovation is key. AI adoption isn't just about technology—it's about transforming how an organization thinks and acts. A culture of innovation means encouraging teams to experiment, take risks, and learn from failure—values that are particularly important in the evolving landscape of AI.

St. Jude Children's Research Hospital has embraced this culture of innovation by integrating AI into their treatment protocols. By analyzing massive datasets, AI has helped researchers at St. Jude develop more personalized treatment plans for children, leading to better outcomes and a more efficient use of resources. This would not have been possible without a commitment to experimentation and a willingness to embrace cutting-edge technology.

Becoming an AI-First Nonprofit

The future of the nonprofit sector will be shaped by those organizations willing to fully embrace AI and become AI-first. This shift means more than just adopting a few tools—it means fundamentally rethinking how missions are delivered, operations are conducted, and organizations engage with communities and stakeholders. The examples in this chapter illustrate the transformative potential of AI—from scaling services to personalizing donor engagement and solving challenges that were previously out of reach.

The stakes have never been higher. As the demand for services continues to grow, as inequality widens, and as new crises emerge, nonprofits must find ways to scale their impact and enhance their effectiveness. AI is not just a tool for survival; it is the key to thriving in a rapidly changing world. Becoming an AI-first nonprofit means viewing technology as an essential partner in mission delivery—a partner that allows for more creativity, more empathy, and more meaningful connections. The journey to AI adoption is a noble calling to better serve humanity, and it is a journey that nonprofits must undertake to continue making the world a better place.

5

AI for Program Development and Impact Measurement

The Power of AI in Nonprofit Operations

As artificial intelligence (AI) continues to reshape industries, its influence is increasingly being felt in the nonprofit sector. AI has become an integral part of various industries, revolutionizing how organizations operate, achieve strategic objectives, ideate new products and services, and streamline decision making. Though nonprofits have historically been cautious in adopting new technologies due to limited resources, especially funds allocated for research and development, they now have unprecedented opportunities to enhance their operations through AI. With advanced technology, nonprofits can make data-driven decisions, streamline program delivery, and significantly enhance their ability to measure the effectiveness of their initiatives.

AI allows nonprofits to tailor programs to meet community needs, predict outcomes accurately, communicate personally, and measure impact effectively. By leveraging AI, nonprofits can enhance existing programs and create new solutions for complex social challenges. The greatest limitation to leveraging AI for programmatic impact is your imagination. Throughout this chapter, we explore a few ways nonprofits can harness AI for program development and impact measurement, providing practical examples and case studies to demonstrate its transformative value. Furthermore, the chapter highlights ways AI can support organizational resilience, allowing nonprofits to adapt to changing circumstances with agility and foresight.

The utilization of AI to support nonprofit missions is nearly unlimited. Following that premise, it should be said that rather than be limited to specific use cases we've shared here, we encourage you to start with a "What if AI could _____" mindset, and have it prove you wrong.

AI for Program Development: Designing Smarter Programs

AI has the potential to revolutionize how nonprofits design, implement, and manage their programs. Whether ordering supplies, planning for enough volunteers, or determining greatest service needs, traditional program development often relies on intuition, past experiences, or outdated data, which can lead to organizations operating without effectively evaluating their impact or adapting to changes in the communities they serve.

AI empowers nonprofits to design more adaptive and responsive programs by analyzing real-time data and providing actionable insights. By leveraging AI, nonprofits can continuously refine their strategies to meet evolving needs effectively. Moreover, AI facilitates collaboration by providing data-driven insights and highlighting best practices, while also uncovering previously overlooked needs, thus expanding the impact of nonprofit initiatives.

Predictive Analytics for Program Design

Predictive AI models use vast amounts of historical data to make highly accurate predictions about future activity. For nonprofits, this means better anticipating the needs of the communities they serve and optimizing program design accordingly. AI's ability to analyze large datasets and create predictive models allows organizations to forecast trends in service demand, volunteer assignment, or program participation.

By leveraging machine learning and deep learning, predictive AI's capabilities can also help nonprofits assess risks and opportunities in their programs. For instance, predictive modeling can identify patterns that may indicate emerging challenges, such as increased demand for mental health services or shifts in volunteer engagement. By anticipating these trends, organizations can prepare and adjust their strategies to mitigate risks and capitalize on new opportunities on an ongoing basis. Predictive AI also allows for scenario planning, enabling nonprofits to model different interventions and predict their outcomes, thus allowing for a more strategic allocation of resources.

Example: Community Health Nonprofit Using AI for Disease Prevention A community health nonprofit focused on preventing the spread of infectious diseases might use AI to:

- **Forecast Disease Outbreaks:** Analyze historical health data, environmental factors, and social patterns to predict potential disease hotspots.
- **Identify At-Risk Populations:** Use machine learning to identify demographics that are more susceptible to certain diseases.
- **Optimize Intervention Strategies:** Allocate resources and design programs based on predicted areas of highest need.

By leveraging predictive AI, the organization can proactively implement preventive measures, identify vulnerable populations, allocate resources efficiently, and ultimately reduce the incidence of diseases within the community. This proactive approach improves outcomes, saves lives, and builds community trust. Predictive AI also helps engage stakeholders by demonstrating intervention effectiveness and encouraging community participation.

Personalizing Program Delivery with AI

Personalization has become a key expectation in the digital age. AI enables nonprofits to tailor their programs to individual needs by analyzing data from program participants. AI can identify trends, segment beneficiaries, and create personalized interventions, making customization feasible even for resource-constrained nonprofits.

With AI, nonprofits can create more meaningful connections with their beneficiaries by providing customized support and services. This level of personalization fosters stronger relationships and promotes deeper engagement, as participants feel that their unique needs and preferences are being understood and addressed. AI-driven personalization can also help nonprofits adapt programs as the needs of beneficiaries evolve, ensuring sustained relevance and impact.

Just as Netflix or Spotify predict your future interests and custom tailor your experiences based on past activity, AI adapts to recent behaviors by continuously updating its recommendations in real time. This ensures that interventions align with current data, making personalization dynamic and responsive. Nonprofits can analyze individual progress, preferences, and engagement to provide interventions that evolve, similar to how streaming platforms refine their recommendations with each new song you play.

Example: Educational Nonprofit Using AI for Personalized Learning An educational nonprofit focused on improving literacy rates might use AI to:

- **Assess Individual Skill Levels:** Analyze assessment results to determine each learner's reading and writing proficiency.
- **Customize Learning Materials:** Use AI to recommend reading materials and exercises tailored to individual learning styles and interests.
- **Monitor Progress:** Track each learner's improvements and adjust the program accordingly to address specific challenges.

Personalizing program delivery with AI can enhance learning outcomes, increase engagement and retention, and accelerate literacy development. Continuous monitoring with AI helps ensure participants receive timely support, while personalized feedback helps maintain motivation by highlighting progress and celebrating milestones.

Streamlining Program Management

AI can significantly enhance program management by automating routine tasks and providing real-time insights into program performance.

Program managers can use AI-powered dashboards to monitor progress, flag potential issues, and make adjustments on the fly. This increases the efficiency of program delivery and reduces the administrative burden on staff.

AI automation helps free staff to focus on strategic priorities and direct service, increasing impact. AI provides insights into program effectiveness, helping optimize approaches and allocate resources efficiently. It also integrates data from multiple sources, enabling effective cross-departmental coordination.

Example: Environmental Conservation Nonprofit Using AI for Project Coordination An environmental nonprofit focused on reforestation might use AI to:

- **Automate Task Scheduling:** Assign tasks to field teams based on real-time data like weather conditions and resource availability.
- **Manage Resources Efficiently:** Use AI to monitor inventory levels of saplings, tools, and equipment, automating procurement processes when supplies run low.
- **Improve Communication:** Automatically update stakeholders on project progress through AI-generated reports and notifications.

By streamlining program management with AI, the organization can enhance operational efficiency, reduce overhead costs, and focus more on their core mission of environmental conservation. The ability to make data-driven decisions in real-time empowers the nonprofit to achieve its goals more effectively and increase the impact of their efforts. AI-powered coordination also allows for more agile responses to unexpected challenges, such as sudden changes in weather or resource availability, ensuring that programs remain on track.

AI for Impact Measurement: Quantifying Success with Precision

Measuring impact is one of the most challenging aspects of nonprofit work. Traditional methods, such as surveys or manual data collection, can be time-consuming, costly, prone to errors, and require technical skills that might not be available with limited staff. AI has the potential to revolutionize impact measurement by automating data collection, analyzing complex datasets, and providing more accurate insights into a program's effectiveness.

AI integration within impact measurement efforts helps provide precision and insights previously unattainable, identifying subtle trends, correlations, and nuanced insights likely to be missed by even the most tenured professionals. It allows nonprofits to understand success factors and areas for improvement and facilitates efficient longitudinal studies to assess long-term program impact.

Data-Driven Impact Reporting

AI can help nonprofits generate impact reports with greater accuracy, efficiency, and personalization. By integrating AI into their monitoring and evaluation systems, organizations can analyze data from multiple sources to produce comprehensive reports showcasing the impact of their work.

AI can also enable more dynamic impact reporting, allowing organizations to provide real-time updates to stakeholders. This level of transparency helps build trust with donors, beneficiaries, and partners, as they can see the immediate results of their contributions. Furthermore, AI-driven reports can be customized to suit different audiences, from detailed analytics for internal use to simplified summaries for public communications.

Example: Housing Nonprofit Using AI for Shelter Program Effectiveness Consider a nonprofit providing emergency shelter and housing support to homeless individuals. Through AI, the organization can:

- **Monitor Occupancy and Turnover Rates:** Use AI to track shelter occupancy, average length of stay, and turnover rates to optimize space and resources.
- **Analyze Support Needs:** Apply sentiment analysis to feedback from residents to gauge satisfaction and identify areas where additional services may be needed.

- **Generate Housing Stability Reports:** Automatically compile reports on housing stability, exit outcomes, and success rates in securing permanent housing.

These insights help the nonprofit assess program effectiveness and make data-driven adjustments to enhance resident support. The ability to report on tangible outcomes enables the organization to demonstrate its impact, reinforcing credibility with funders and attracting resources for expansion.

Automating Routine Impact Measurement Tasks

Impact measurement often involves routine tasks like data entry, report generation, stakeholder surveys, and data analysis. AI can automate these tasks, freeing up staff time to focus on strategic initiatives. Nonprofits can use AI to gather and analyze data from surveys, patient reports, and program outcomes, generating detailed impact assessments with minimal human intervention.

Automation saves time, reduces human error, and ensures data accuracy. AI uncovers hidden insights, aiding nonprofits in understanding their impact, and helps visualize data effectively for stakeholders.

Example: Workforce Development Nonprofit Using AI for Job Placement Metrics Imagine a nonprofit focused on job readiness and placement for marginalized communities. AI can help the organization to:

- **Automate Participant Data Tracking:** Gather data on participant demographics, completion rates, and job placement statistics from various sources.
- **Analyze Program Success Factors:** Use AI to identify which training modules and support services contribute most to successful job placements.
- **Automate Employment Outcome Reports:** Generate routine reports showcasing job placement rates, wage increases, and participant satisfaction.

With automated data collection and analysis, the nonprofit can continuously improve its programs and adapt to participant needs. The resulting insights provide a data-backed story of impact, which helps in maintaining funder support and ensuring program sustainability.

Case Study: Stop Soldier Suicide

Stop Soldier Suicide (https://stopsoldiersuicide.org/blackboxproject) is a nonprofit organization dedicated to preventing military suicide through tailored care and continued support. The organization uses AI to analyze language patterns in communications with veterans, identifying those at risk of suicide. The AI system processes vast amounts of textual data from social media posts, emails, and other communications to detect signs of distress.

When the AI system identifies high-risk language patterns, it alerts staff members, who can then reach out proactively. This approach enables timely intervention and has been instrumental in saving lives. By harnessing AI, Stop Soldier Suicide enhances its ability to support veterans effectively. The use of AI also allows the organization to continuously refine its intervention strategies, ensuring that veterans receive the best possible care. Additionally, the insights gathered through AI analysis can be used to better understand the unique challenges faced by veterans, informing broader mental health initiatives and policy advocacy.

Recommendations for Successful AI Adoption in Program Development and Measurement

To maximize the benefits of AI, nonprofits should consider the following recommendations:

1. **Start Small:** Begin with a pilot project that addresses a specific challenge or area of need. This approach allows the organization to test AI solutions on a manageable scale, assess their effectiveness, and learn from the experience before scaling up. Starting small also helps build confidence among staff and stakeholders, making it easier to expand AI initiatives later.

2. **Gather Feedback:** Incorporate various team members into the AI project. By gathering different perspectives, the organization will be able to assess the results from many angles to achieve better outcomes. Engaging stakeholders in the process also helps build buy-in and ensures that AI tools are tailored to the specific needs of the organization. Regular feedback loops also provide valuable insights that can be used to refine AI solutions.
3. **Focus on Impact:** Use AI to enhance the ability to measure and report on program impact in real-time. By demonstrating clear results, nonprofits can build credibility with donors, beneficiaries, and other stakeholders. AI-driven insights can also help organizations communicate their impact more effectively, making a compelling case for continued support. Additionally, focusing on impact helps ensure that AI initiatives are aligned with the organization's mission and deliver tangible benefits to the community.
4. **Invest in Data Quality:** AI relies on high-quality data to produce accurate insights. Nonprofits should invest in data collection processes and ensure that their data is clean, consistent, and up-to-date. While perfect databases are not likely, always work toward improving data quality. This investment will pay off by enabling more reliable predictions and analyses, ultimately enhancing program effectiveness.
5. **Collaborate with Experts:** Partnering with AI experts, technology providers, or other nonprofits with AI experience can help organizations navigate the complexities of AI implementation. Collaboration can also lead to sharing best practices and resources, making AI more accessible and effective. Additionally, ethical considerations should be prioritized to ensure responsible AI use.

Artificial intelligence holds immense potential to transform how nonprofits design, deliver, and measure their programs. By leveraging AI, nonprofits can become more efficient, make data-driven decisions, and ultimately increase their impact on the communities they serve.

Successful AI adoption requires a strategic approach—starting with small projects, investing in data quality, and building partnerships. It also involves a commitment to ethical practices and continuous learning. As AI technologies continue to evolve, nonprofits that embrace these tools will be better positioned to achieve their missions and create lasting positive change.

The journey toward integrating AI into nonprofit operations is not without challenges. However, the potential benefits—increased efficiency, improved program outcomes, deep personalization, and enhanced impact measurement—make it an endeavor that nonprofit organizations can no longer afford to go without. By harnessing the power of AI, nonprofits can unlock new possibilities and drive social change more effectively than ever before.

AI's transformative power in the nonprofit sector is just beginning to be realized. AI is not a static technology. As we've repeated in this book, AI's ability to increase accuracy with more data and time means that the worst AI you will ever use will be today. This means that due to the exponential nature of AI, those that fail to adopt AI may never catch up. By staying informed about emerging AI technologies, collaborating with experts, perpetually experimenting, and prioritizing ethical considerations, nonprofits can navigate the complexities of AI integration and harness its potential for good. Ultimately, those organizations that adapt and innovate with AI will be at the forefront of creating meaningful, sustainable change in the communities they serve. Furthermore, as AI continues to develop, nonprofits that embrace a curiosity mindset—willing to test new tools and approaches—will be well positioned to capitalize on advancements that could further enhance their impact. The journey may be challenging, filled with both successful and failed attempts, epiphanies, and disappointments, but the reward of serving your mission in deeper, more effective, and efficient ways will pay dividends for this and future generations.

6

AI for Fundraising, Resource Development, and Donor Experience

Precision Philanthropy: The Role of Predictive AI in Fundraising

For decades, nonprofit organizations have faced the challenge of securing more philanthropic dollars amidst a shrinking pool of donors. As highlighted in *The Generosity Crisis* (Chappell, Crimmins, and Ashley, 2024), the overall decline in charitable participation has created a significant urgency for nonprofits to innovate their approaches toward resource development and donor engagement. Artificial intelligence's (AI's) emergence has fundamentally changed how nonprofits approach fundraising, offering a powerful tool to gain predictive insights into donor behavior. AI-driven fundraising isn't just about increasing efficiency; it is about precision—understanding who is most likely to give and how to engage them in the most meaningful ways. This new era of "precision philanthropy" redefines how nonprofits cultivate donor relationships.

Recent trends reflect this transformation. Nonprofits that integrate AI into their fundraising strategies are witnessing up to 50% increase in donations through predictive analytics and enriched data (Virtuous, 2024). The power of AI lies in its ability to enhance donor retention and personalize outreach, making every interaction count.

Imagine a nonprofit struggling with low response rates from their mass email campaigns. By leveraging AI, they are now able to identify the individuals who are most interested in their cause and craft messages specific to each person and send them at times when they are most likely to respond. The result is an impressive surge in donations and enhanced donor loyalty.

Our work in AI within the nonprofit context started in 2017 with a singular focus. Having become somewhat disenchanted with the lack of innovation in the nonprofit sector, and witnessing an overreliance on using wealth data to predict gratitude, we set out on a path to determine if machine learning could accurately measure the connection between a constituent and our organization on an ongoing basis. With a simple hypothesis that connection to our organization was key to measuring an individual's likelihood to make a donation, we set out to quantify the characteristics of givers and non-givers. After spending a year and a half building the first machine-learning model to measure the likelihood of giving, we learned that this effort was far more complicated than it appeared at first glance. While machine learning is very good at taking a vast data array and distilling it down into actionable intelligence, data becomes the key to unlocking its potential.

In our early evaluation of our first model, there were several epiphanies that have directed our work since then, least of which was the ratification that wealth data alone was an insufficient predictor of charitable giving. This epiphany alone set us on a course to challenge and redefine the basis by which most nonprofits use wealth to classify good or bad prospects, a process that has had tremendous negative and unintended consequences on the charitable giving sector. Armed with proof that likelihood to give is more dependent on experiences and connection than wealth, we set our path focused on understanding how ancillary data could help us more holistically identify the differences between givers and non-givers. Since those early days, our understanding and approach toward quantifying connection has become a deep and never-ending pursuit.

Since the early days of our first (rather crude) model, we have spent the last eight years working at the intersection of AI and philanthropy, and our approach and processes to derive philanthropic insights using predictive AI tools continue to evolve. In this chapter, we will explore the five key evolutions in AI for fundraising, showing how nonprofits can reimagine donor engagement through data enrichment, continual learning, differentiated models, and trust-building—all while considering the ethical implications of these advancements. We will also look at specific case studies and provide actionable recommendations for successful AI adoption in fundraising.

Evolution 1: AI-Enhanced Data Enrichment

Expanding data can result in better predictions. In the early days, nonprofits primarily relied on first-party data, such as donor names, email addresses, and giving history, to predict donor behavior. However, our working AI quickly demonstrated that first-party data was insufficient to understand in a more holistic nature the differences between those who donate and those who do not. Thus, our first evolution was in response to the understanding that when using machine learning, more data is better. While most nonprofit organizations collect basic solicitation and giving information, we quickly learned that enriching our nonprofit's first-party data with external sources provided a far more accurate and holistic view of each donor. By incorporating external data like external charitable giving, demographic, consumer, and personal interest data, your organization can significantly improve the accuracy of their predictions as it provides a more broad, and less biased perspective on your constituents.

Evolution 2: AI in Continual Learning for Fundraising Models

Dynamic Models for Evolving Donor Behavior

Dynamic models can reflect and predict donor behavior as it evolves. Prior to using AI, predictive models often remained static, offering the same predictions without accounting for changes in donor behavior. For example, many organizations relied on basic annual giving metrics and previous donation history to predict future donations, without considering recent engagement or changes in donor interests. After running our first model on the same constituents month after month, we quickly understood that a person's affinity toward an organization changed incrementally over time. Whether a donor made a gift, volunteered, filled out a survey, or attended an event changed their likelihood score. Intuitively, we know that our affinity toward a nonprofit or brand is not fixed in time; however, most predictions made in our sector up until this point would classify an individual as a "good" or "bad" on an irregular basis, whether scored annually or perhaps every several years.

Through our early exploration, using AI to predict likelihood of giving, we found that when comparing machine learning models to classic regression models the basic regression models would actually perform worse over time as they continue to compute based on data that are no longer reflective of the donors' current level of engagement.

We like to say in the AI world that you're never ready to use AI, but you're also never done. There's a lot of freedom in the settlement when you pivot from this idea that predictive models are set in time rather than cycles. In every way, the worst AI you will ever use is today because of AI's ability to retrain and improve its accuracy based on new data that it receives. Whether people make a gift or not, machine learning solves the static dilemma by continuously refining its ability to understand and more accurately predict the nuances between donors and non-donors as time goes on. Just as Amazon refines its product recommendations based on recent purchases, AI models in fundraising evolve based on new donor interactions, leading to improved accuracy over time.

Evolution 3: Differentiating Donors from Prospects

In our early days of experimenting with machine learning to predict donor behavior, our AI models failed by treating all individuals the same—donors and prospects were considered alike. We quickly realized that this seemingly subtle, but profound difference was inherently flawed because donors and prospects have distinct motivations, engagement patterns, and opportunities for connection, which require different strategies to convert and retain them effectively.

Experiences matter deeply when it comes to charitable giving. For example, within a typical healthcare fundraising environment, recent clinical encounters make up 70% of a nondonor's decision to make a first-time gift to a healthcare organization. In contrast, a current donor's recent encounters only account for 5% of their decision. This premise remains constant within every organization we've encountered, whether it be a museum, multinational membership organization, university, or petting zoo. The rest is based on recent engagement with the development office through gifts, events, and communications.

Our work in the space over the past several years has created the best practice that to accurately predict philanthropic intention, donors and non-donors should be modeled independently from one another, and nonprofits should be looking for and finding ways to capture experiential data to better quantify the depth of connection that a person has to their organization.

Evolution 4: Quality Over Quantity in Donor Relationships

Our work in machine learning has demonstrated that nurturing a smaller group of high-value donors yields better long-term results compared to acquiring a larger volume of unengaged donors. By identifying and nurturing high-value donors, nonprofits can build deeper connections, resulting in a higher lifetime value. Above all, machine learning creates tremendous efficiencies for nonprofit organizations. Nonprofits like colleges and universities, healthcare delivery networks, or membership organizations like zoos and museums have far more constituents than they have staff members to manage. While machine learning can help identify people who are likely to make a gift, the greatest efficiency comes from identifying the vast majority of prospects who are not likely to give. This insight alone allows nonprofits to focus activation efforts on individuals likely to take action, to intervene with individuals whose data shows a declining likelihood of giving, and to focus communication efforts on individuals who are earlier in their donor journey with an organization.

To be clear, AI does not have ESP; it can only make predictions based on the data that it has available to it. The goal is to purchase, find, or create enriched data using tools like surveys that help round out a donor's understanding of your organization. Too often, fundraising shops say, "We need more donors," when the real issue is that they need to better identify the right donors—those who are strong supporters but usually not hitting the typical markers to be prioritized and assigned to a portfolio.

Evolution 5: Building Trust through Transparency in AI

How can you trust something that can't be explained or interrogated? This sentiment kept us up at night when we started using machine learning to measure connection. If an AI predicted who was likely to make a gift, but we cannot look at the "math" behind the prediction, how would we know if the prediction is accurate or biased? To maintain donor trust, nonprofits must be transparent in how they use AI. While black-box algorithms are common in the private sector, they can be problematic for nonprofits that have for several decades used wealth data solely to classify "good" versus "bad" prospects or donors, which inadvertently has created biased databases that have inadvertently prioritized wealthy white males. Since trust is the currency of the nonprofit sector, AI models used to identify the best individuals to engage must take active steps to reduce bias based on data elements like wealth, race, and gender.

Just as artificial intelligence evolves, the process of building and applying AI models for philanthropy should also grow. As advanced technology becomes even more accessible, we will continue to expand on these evolutions to further identify and predict the behaviors of donors and non-donors.

Example: Arts and Culture Nonprofit Using Predictive AI to Boost Donations An arts and culture nonprofit aims to increase donations for new exhibits and outreach programs. With predictive AI, they could:

- **Identify High-Potential Donors:** By analyzing past donor behavior and demographic data, AI tools can help the organization identify individuals likely to make substantial contributions.

This includes spotting potential major donors among frequent small donors, as well as recognizing those who might be interested in supporting specific projects.
- **Forecast Donation Cycles:** Predictive models can detect seasonal patterns or events that trigger donations, such as end-of-year giving or annual gala attendance. This allows the nonprofit to plan campaigns that align with these cycles, increasing their effectiveness and ensuring they reach out at optimal times.
- **Target Personalized Outreach:** Using predictive insights, the nonprofit can tailor outreach efforts based on individual donor interests and engagement history. For example, if a donor has a history of supporting visual arts exhibits, the nonprofit could target them with a campaign related to a new art installation.

AI-Driven Personalization in Fundraising

As consumers in today's increasingly data-driven, personalized world, donors expect a personal touch. Their natural orientation is that if my local coffee shop knows my preferences, so should a nonprofit that I've donated to or volunteered at. While AI has afforded deep personalization within almost every aspect of our lives, it also allows nonprofits to tailor their fundraising approaches based on each donor's preferences, past donations, volunteerism, interests, and engagement behavior. By analyzing these data points, AI helps organizations segment supporters and craft unique outreach strategies, making personalized experiences possible even for nonprofits with limited resources.

Personalized fundraising is about building authentic relationships. When donors receive messages that speak directly to their interests—like updates on the projects they care about or appeals that match their giving history—they feel valued. This deeper connection makes them more likely to stay engaged and continue supporting the cause. AI makes it easier for nonprofits to create these experiences at scale, adapting their strategies as donors' interests evolve, ensuring appeals always feel timely and relevant.

Example: Veterans Support Nonprofit Using Generative AI to Enhance Storytelling A nonprofit supporting veterans by providing career transition services and mental health counseling could use generative AI to:

- **Create Compelling Stories of Veteran Transition Success:** AI could generate individualized stories based on veterans' experiences, showcasing their journey through the support program—such as finding new employment or achieving mental health stability. These stories can help donors understand the impact on a personal level.
- **Generate Digital Campaign Visuals and Animations:** AI can create digital artwork, animations, or even testimonials that visually represent veterans' progress. These can be used in marketing materials, social media campaigns, or donor newsletters to bring the impact stories to life.
- **Prepare Donor Presentations:** AI can assist in drafting presentation content for potential donors, automatically summarizing the program's impact and highlighting success stories, making it easier for the fundraising team to convey a powerful message in meetings.

Through generative AI, the veterans support nonprofit can elevate its storytelling, engaging donors with personalized updates and visually appealing content that resonates with them, leading to more consistent donor engagement and increased online reach.

Streamlining Fundraising with AI Automation

Fundraising involves many repetitive tasks—from managing donor records to sending follow-up emails. AI-powered automation can take over much of this administrative load, freeing up valuable time for nonprofit staff to focus on building relationships and strategy rather than logistics.

AI can automate the entire workflow of donor engagement, from onboarding new supporters to sending timely thank-you notes after a donation. This kind of automation ensures that every supporter feels acknowledged and valued without burdening staff. It also helps reduce human error and ensures consistency, meaning no donor falls through the cracks. For nonprofits, this kind of efficiency means greater focus on the bigger picture—developing impactful campaigns and building a loyal donor base.

By using AI for automation, nonprofits can increase efficiency, boost engagement, and ensure that supporters feel cared for, even as the organization grows. This blend of streamlined operations and thoughtful, consistent outreach helps nonprofits achieve their fundraising goals more effectively.

Example: Animal Welfare Nonprofit Using AI Automation for Donor Engagement An animal welfare nonprofit aiming to expand its supporter base and streamline fundraising could use AI automation for:

- **Automated Donor Welcome Journeys:** When a new donor contributes, AI can trigger an automated onboarding journey—sending a series of personalized welcome emails, sharing stories of rescued animals, and inviting them to visit the shelter. This automated sequence makes sure every new supporter feels connected and informed without requiring manual follow-up from staff.
- **Recurring Donation Reminders and Processing:** For donors interested in recurring gifts, AI can handle everything from setting up the initial contribution to sending automatic reminders or updates if a payment fails. AI ensures that the recurring process is smooth, reducing the likelihood of lost donations due to missed payments and offering an easy way for donors to adjust their giving levels whenever they want.
- **Automated Impact Reporting:** AI can compile and send automated reports that show the direct impact of donations—such as photos and stories about animals recently adopted thanks to donor contributions. By automating these updates, the nonprofit ensures timely and consistent outreach, showing donors how their support is making a tangible difference, which can encourage continued or increased support.

Case Study: Children's Healthcare of Atlanta

Children's Healthcare of Atlanta used a custom AI model to identify a highly engaged donor who had only given $5,000 cumulatively. By comparing the high AI prediction with external philanthropy, the team asked this donor for a $50,000 gift, which they closed in two weeks, paying for nearly a year and a half of the AI contract they purchased.

Additionally, by changing the metrics by which an individual was prioritized, major gift officers were able to save 70% of their time since they were focusing on engaging with donors and prospects who were interested in supporting their mission (DonorSearch, 2024).

Recommendations for Successful AI Adoption in Fundraising

To maximize the benefits of AI, nonprofits should consider the following recommendations:

1. **Define Clear Goals:** Establish specific objectives for AI adoption, such as increasing donor retention or improving campaign efficiency. Clear goals help ensure AI initiatives align with organizational priorities and provide measurable outcomes.
2. **Engage Leadership and Stakeholders:** Secure support from leadership and key stakeholders early in the AI adoption process. Their buy-in is critical for successfully implementing AI solutions, as it ensures that necessary resources are allocated and organizational culture supports the change.
3. **Invest in Staff Training:** Provide training opportunities for staff to learn about AI technologies and their applications in fundraising. This helps build confidence and understanding across the organization, ensuring that AI tools are used effectively and that staff feel empowered rather than threatened by new technologies.
4. **Leverage Existing Tools and Platforms:** Utilize existing AI tools and platforms designed for nonprofits. This can reduce the complexity and cost of implementation while providing proven solutions tailored to common fundraising challenges.
5. **Monitor and Evaluate Progress:** Establish metrics to evaluate the effectiveness of AI initiatives regularly. Monitoring progress

ensures that AI tools deliver the desired impact and allows the organization to make adjustments to maximize success. Regular evaluations help identify what is working well and what needs improvement, leading to more effective AI integration over time.

There is little doubt that AI offers nonprofit organizations a unique opportunity to understand, predict, and engage donors more effectively. The five evolutions—data enrichment, continual learning, differentiated donor models, a focus on quality relationships, and transparency—demonstrate AI's transformative potential in modern fundraising.

To fully realize AI's potential, nonprofits must use these tools ethically, with transparency to maintain trust. For organizations ready to embrace AI, starting with small, targeted pilot projects—such as predictive analytics for personalized outreach—can pave the way to more strategic and impactful fundraising. By integrating AI thoughtfully and with clear goals, nonprofits can not only increase efficiency but also foster deeper, more meaningful relationships with their donors, ensuring a sustainable future for their missions.

7

AI for Volunteer Engagement and Management

The Role of AI in Volunteer Engagement and Management

In today's digital age, AI is reshaping the nonprofit world, helping organizations overcome resource challenges and better serve their communities. Nonprofits heavily rely on the dedication of volunteers, yet managing these programs effectively can be overwhelming, especially with limited resources. In fact, nearly half (46.8%) of nonprofit CEOs cite securing volunteers as a "big problem," while 65% of nonprofits struggle with recruiting and retaining volunteers, even as the demand for their services continues to rise (Dietz & Grimm, 2023). These challenges—finding suitable candidates, keeping them engaged, and ensuring long-term retention—require innovative solutions.

Despite these difficulties, 72.2% of nonprofit leaders recognize that volunteers significantly improve the quality of their services and programs (Dietz & Grimm, 2023). The key for nonprofits is to engage volunteers effectively while maximizing efficiency and maintaining a positive volunteer experience. This is where artificial intelligence offers a transformative opportunity. AI can help nonprofits optimize volunteer management, boost engagement, and retain passionate individuals through more personalized, efficient, and strategic operations.

With AI at their disposal, nonprofits can automate tedious administrative tasks, analyze data for better decision-making, and foster personalized communication—all of which contribute to a significantly enhanced volunteer experience. By leveraging AI, nonprofits can better understand their volunteer workforce, develop more effective engagement strategies, and ultimately amplify their impact.

In this chapter we explore how AI can help nonprofits revolutionize their volunteer programs, addressing common challenges, highlighting best practices for successful adoption, and presenting real-world and hypothetical examples of its impact. The promise of AI is not only in making volunteer management more efficient, but also in creating an experience that inspires volunteers to stay engaged and continue making a difference.

Forecasting Volunteer Needs and Engagement

Nonprofits can use predictive AI models to anticipate future volunteer needs, understand the best strategies for recruiting volunteers, and identify which volunteers are most likely to stay engaged long-term. Alternatively, by tracking volunteer activity, nonprofits may preemptively identify when a volunteer is likely to withdraw from an organization before it happens. By analyzing historical data such as volunteer attendance, past event success, and demographic trends, predictive AI identifies patterns that enable nonprofits to make proactive decisions about their volunteer workforce. This allows organizations to plan with more confidence, ensuring they can meet the demands of their programs and maximize volunteer contributions.

For example, AI can identify the types of events or activities that have the highest volunteer retention rates, helping organizations design programs that are more likely to keep volunteers engaged. Additionally, AI can provide insights into volunteer demographics most responsive to specific campaigns, allowing for more targeted outreach and efficient use of resources.

Beyond recruitment, AI also plays a crucial role in volunteer retention. By understanding patterns such as how often volunteers engage, what roles they prefer, and which activities they enjoy, nonprofits can tailor their engagement strategies to keep volunteers involved long-term. AI tools might highlight that volunteers who participate in certain types of community events are more likely to stay involved, suggesting that offering more of those events could boost retention. It could also flag volunteers who might be at risk of disengaging, giving staff the opportunity to reach out with personalized messages or incentives to re-engage them.

Moreover, AI helps optimize volunteer allocation. For instance, by analyzing past events, it can forecast the number of volunteers needed for specific activities, reducing both under-staffing and overstaffing. This ensures that volunteer time is used effectively, minimizing frustration and maximizing impact. AI can also suggest which volunteers are best suited for particular roles based on their past experiences and skills, leading to better volunteer satisfaction and more successful outcomes.

Ultimately, by using these AI insights, nonprofits can proactively plan for volunteer needs, address potential engagement challenges before they become issues, and ensure their volunteer programs are running as smoothly and effectively as possible. This helps create a more resilient volunteer workforce that is prepared to meet the evolving needs of the community.

Example: Food Bank Nonprofit Using Predictive AI for Volunteer Planning A food bank nonprofit aiming to ensure that they always have enough volunteers for food distribution could use AI in the following ways:

- **Predict Volunteer Demand for Events:** By analyzing data from previous food distribution events, AI can help forecast the number of volunteers needed for upcoming events based on factors such as location, season, special initiatives, and weather.
- **Identify Volunteer Retention Patterns:** AI can also analyze historical data to identify factors that contribute to volunteer retention, such as frequency of engagement, type of activities, and feedback scores or volunteer sentiment from survey results. By understanding these patterns, nonprofit organizations can tailor engagement strategies to keep volunteers motivated and

reduce turnover, such as offering more frequent shifts or opportunities to participate in activities they find rewarding.
- **Targeted Volunteer Recruitment:** AI can help identify potential volunteer sources by analyzing data from successful recruitment campaigns. For example, it can analyze which demographic groups or neighborhoods provided the most reliable volunteers in the past and suggest targeted recruitment campaigns for future events. This way, nonprofits can better focus their efforts on areas with the highest likelihood of recruitment success.

For example, by using predictive AI a local food bank can proactively plan for volunteer needs, minimize volunteer shortages, and ensure that volunteers stay engaged and motivated over time, ultimately improving their ability to serve the community effectively.

Creating Personalized Volunteer Experiences

While predictive AI can identify the right volunteer prospects, generative AI can engage with those individuals by creating highly personalized volunteer experiences, making volunteers feel more valued and appreciated. By generating tailored messages, promotional materials, event invitations, or individualized training content, nonprofits can offer a volunteer journey that aligns closely with each individual's preferences and motivations. This type of personalized experience helps strengthen the bond between the volunteer and the nonprofit, boosting satisfaction, loyalty, and long-term commitment.

For example, AI can analyze a volunteer's history—such as the events they attended, the roles they preferred, and their feedback—and use this information to craft unique messages and opportunities that appeal directly to them. This could mean suggesting roles they're most passionate about or inviting them to similar activities based on their previous involvement. AI can also adjust communications in real time to reflect changing volunteer needs, interests, or availability, ensuring that every message feels timely and relevant.

Moreover, AI plays a key role in volunteer recognition and appreciation. It can craft highly individualized thank-you messages that reference a volunteer's specific contributions—highlighting their impact and showing genuine gratitude. AI can also create engaging social media posts or digital shoutouts to publicly acknowledge volunteers' efforts. By making each volunteer feel uniquely recognized and celebrated, nonprofits can foster a deeper sense of belonging and purpose among their volunteers, driving ongoing engagement.

AI ultimately enables nonprofits to deliver a volunteer experience that feels unique to each individual. From personalized training and communications to dynamic recognition and storytelling, AI helps ensure that volunteers feel appreciated and motivated, increasing their commitment to the organization and its mission. By leveraging these tools, nonprofits can make volunteering more rewarding, thereby boosting satisfaction and fostering long-term relationships with their volunteer community.

Example: Refugee Assistance Nonprofit Using AI for Volunteer Engagement A refugee assistance nonprofit looking to enhance its volunteer engagement could use AI in the following ways:

- **Generate Personalized Volunteer Outreach Invitations:** AI can craft customized invitations for upcoming activities such as donation drives or educational workshops. If a volunteer has previously shown interest in language tutoring, AI could send them personalized invitations to similar future sessions.
- **Create Training Content for Specialized Volunteer Roles:** AI can generate training content, such as videos or guides, for specialized roles like cultural orientation for newly arrived refugees. This tailored training ensures volunteers understand cultural nuances, making them more effective in their support roles.
- **Craft Personalized Volunteer Recognition:** AI can generate personalized messages to recognize volunteers' efforts. For instance, after an employment skills workshop, the AI could send thank-you messages highlighting a specific volunteer's contribution to helping refugees learn resume writing, making the volunteers feel appreciated and connected to the mission.

By utilizing AI, the refugee assistance nonprofit can create personalized and engaging experiences for its volunteers, from training to recognition, ensuring that they feel appreciated and are motivated to continue contributing their time and effort.

Streamlining Volunteer Coordination and Administration

AI is all about enhancing efficiency and freeing up valuable time for nonprofit staff. For nonprofits, managing volunteers often involves many administrative tasks like scheduling shifts, handling communication, and generating reports. These tasks can become overwhelming, especially as the volunteer base grows. AI automation can manage these repetitive tasks, allowing staff to focus on building relationships and improving the volunteer experience.

AI can handle tasks throughout the entire volunteer lifecycle, starting with onboarding, where new volunteers receive automated welcome messages and instructions. It also helps with ongoing engagement, such as sending reminders about shifts and adjusting schedules when conflicts arise. Furthermore, AI can generate detailed reports on volunteer contributions, enabling quick assessments of impact.

A key benefit is maintaining consistent communication, including follow-ups after events. AI can send thank-you notes, collect feedback, and share future opportunities, creating a seamless experience for volunteers. Automating these tasks improves operational efficiency and helps volunteers feel valued, boosting retention rates.

By leveraging AI, nonprofits can overcome logistical challenges, reduce administrative burdens, and maximize volunteer engagement. The result is a more agile organization that is better able to scale its programs and support both volunteers and the communities it serves. With automation, nonprofits can easily scale their volunteer programs, maintain high levels of engagement, and ensure that both volunteers and the communities they serve benefit from a more streamlined and effective approach.

Example: Community Clean-Up Nonprofit Using AI Automation for Volunteer Management A community clean-up nonprofit that organizes frequent events to clean parks and public spaces could use automation AI in the following ways:

- **Automate Volunteer Scheduling:** AI can help streamline the volunteer scheduling process. For instance, volunteers could receive automatic reminders about upcoming shifts, and the AI

could adjust schedules based on availability, weather, or any unforeseen changes. This means less manual work for staff and more accurate scheduling, ensuring that each event has the necessary number of participants.
- **Manage Volunteer Check-Ins and Tracking:** At clean-up events, volunteers can use a mobile app powered by AI to check in and log their hours automatically. This helps keep accurate records of volunteer contributions without manual data entry. The AI can also track volunteer milestones, such as hours served, and trigger automatic badges or rewards when specific goals are met.
- **Automate Event Follow-Ups:** After an event, the AI can send automated follow-up emails to thank volunteers, provide a summary of the event's impact (e.g., amount of trash collected), and offer details about upcoming opportunities. This automated communication helps maintain engagement while freeing staff to focus on larger-scale initiatives, such as community outreach or partnership building.

Through AI automation, the community clean-up nonprofit can reduce administrative burdens, improve the accuracy of scheduling and volunteer tracking, and provide seamless communication to keep volunteers informed and engaged.

Leveraging AI for Effective Volunteer Management

Incorporating AI into volunteer management allows nonprofits to tackle some of their biggest challenges—such as recruiting and retaining volunteers, managing schedules, and maintaining effective communication—with greater ease and efficiency. Predictive AI can help forecast volunteer needs and identify recruitment strategies that work, generative AI can create personalized and engaging experiences for volunteers, and automation AI can streamline day-to-day administration, reducing manual workloads and improving overall efficiency.

For nonprofits that rely heavily on volunteers, AI offers an opportunity to enhance both the volunteer experience and organizational impact. By providing personalized, efficient, and data-driven management, nonprofits can keep volunteers engaged and happy, ultimately building a stronger, more committed volunteer community that is crucial for achieving their mission.

The journey of integrating AI into volunteer management may seem daunting at first, but starting small, experimenting with AI tools, and focusing on areas with the most significant impact can set nonprofits up for success. Whether it's predicting volunteer needs, automating thank-you messages, or creating personalized training content, AI offers powerful capabilities to optimize volunteer engagement and make a difference—both for the organization and the volunteers who help bring its mission to life.

Case Study: The Trevor Project

The Trevor Project, a nonprofit focused on suicide prevention for LGBTQ+ youth, used AI to enhance volunteer training (Google, 2021). With a large network of crisis counselors, maintaining consistent, high-quality training was challenging. To address this, The Trevor Project collaborated with Google.org to create the Crisis Contact Simulator, an AI tool designed to improve volunteer preparedness.

The organization needed a solution to ensure effective crisis intervention training, which demands adaptability, empathy, and decision-making under pressure. Traditional training methods couldn't fully meet these requirements, so they sought a scalable solution capable of simulating real-world scenarios.

In partnership with Google.org, The Trevor Project developed the Crisis Contact Simulator, an AI-powered tool using natural language processing (NLP) to create realistic crisis scenarios for trainees. Volunteers practiced responding to these simulated situations, building essential skills before transitioning to live interactions. The simulator blends pre-programmed responses with machine learning algorithms to make these conversations feel dynamic and personalized, helping volunteers gain the confidence they need for real crisis situations.

The introduction of the AI-driven Crisis Contact Simulator significantly improved the effectiveness of volunteer training. Trainees felt more prepared, which reduced anxiety and increased their effectiveness in actual crisis situations. The tool also allowed The Trevor Project to scale its training program, accommodating more trainees simultaneously without compromising quality.

By utilizing AI, The Trevor Project boosted volunteer engagement and retention, providing a more supportive environment throughout the training journey. Volunteers felt empowered and supported, which reinforced their commitment to the organization's mission. This case exemplifies how nonprofits can leverage technology to enhance training quality, engagement, and scalability, ultimately supporting vulnerable communities more effectively.

Recommendations for Successful AI Adoption in Volunteer Management

To successfully integrate AI into volunteer management, nonprofits should consider the following recommendations:

1. **Identify Specific Pain Points:** Start by identifying opportunities in your volunteer management process that AI can address. This helps to ensure that AI solutions are tailored to your organization's needs and provide meaningful impact.
2. **Collaborate with Peers and Experts:** Find other nonprofits or technology experts to share best practices and gain insights into AI adoption. Learning from others' experiences can help you avoid common pitfalls and adopt strategies that have been successful for similar organizations.
3. **Allocate Budget for Maintenance:** Set aside funds for ongoing AI maintenance and updates to ensure the system remains effective over time. Proper budgeting is crucial to keep AI tools up-to-date and functioning well as technology and organizational needs evolve.
4. **Monitor AI Performance:** Evaluate the performance of AI tools regularly to identify areas of improvement and adjust accordingly. Continuous evaluation allows you to ensure that the AI is providing value and to make necessary adjustments to enhance its effectiveness.

5. **Encourage Open Communication:** Foster an open culture where staff and volunteers can provide feedback on AI implementations and suggest improvements. Encouraging open dialogue ensures that AI solutions are accepted and refined based on the real experiences of those using them, leading to better outcomes.

AI has the power to transform how nonprofits manage and engage their volunteers. By improving matching, retention, skill development, and efficiency, AI provides nonprofits with the tools they need to create more effective, personalized experiences for volunteers. AI not only reduces the burden of administrative tasks but also enables a more strategic approach to managing volunteer relationships, enhancing overall mission success.

As we conclude this chapter, we hope that we've made a case for why using AI for volunteer management is beneficial to enhance the volunteer experience. It also aims to demonstrate how nonprofits can explore AI solutions to enhance their volunteer programs, ensuring that their missions thrive in an increasingly data-driven world. There's no doubt that AI technologies will continue to evolve, and early adopters stand to gain a significant advantage by integrating these tools into their operations. As AI technology advances at an exponential pace, its role in volunteer management will only grow, offering new ways to connect, engage, and empower volunteers to support important causes. Nonprofits that leverage AI today will be better equipped to face the challenges of tomorrow and build a stronger, more resilient volunteer base that is deeply connected to their mission. By focusing on personalization, efficiency, and strategic growth within a continual feedback loop, AI can help nonprofits maximize the use of volunteers to amplify human potential and maximize social change through their efforts.

8

AI for Nonprofit Marketing and Communications

AI in Nonprofit Marketing: A Game-Changer

There is little doubt that artificial intelligence (AI) has emerged as a powerful tool that has already revolutionized industries across the globe. With the broad accessibility and affordability of generative AI, starting in late 2022 with the advent of ChatGPT, communications is likely near the top of the sectors that have begun a complete metamorphosis. In the ever-evolving digital landscape, where nonprofit organizations strive to engage donors, volunteers, and the broader public, AI offers unprecedented opportunities to optimize marketing and communication efforts. As noted by industry research, a staggering 75% of nonprofits believe that AI, specifically generative AI, can potentially transform their marketing strategies (Google for Nonprofits, 2024). The potential lies in AI's ability to generate content quickly, personalize interactions at scale, and analyze user behavior, all of which are crucial in nonprofit fundraising and advocacy campaigns.

This chapter explores how AI is reshaping nonprofit marketing and communications by improving content creation, managing social media engagement, and driving advocacy efforts. Additionally, we will examine the role of search engine optimization (SEO) and its evolution into generative engine optimization (GEO) in enhancing a nonprofit's online presence. Through various examples and practical applications, we will showcase how AI is being utilized to better communicate stories and messaging.

Content Creation: Using AI to Generate and Optimize Content

The cornerstone of any successful marketing campaign, content creation has traditionally been a labor-intensive process. Nonprofits, often working with limited resources, struggle to consistently produce high-quality content that resonates with their audience. Enter AI. By leveraging generative AI, natural language processing (NLP), and machine learning, nonprofit organizations can automate a great deal of the content creation process, allowing organizations to generate text, audio, and visual content with unprecedented speed and precision.

AI, in essence, has read every book on consumer and donor psychology, enabling it to understand what drives people to act. This capability has given rise to tools that can create tailored content based on a nonprofit's unique audience. According to a HubSpot study (2023), 85% of marketers believe generative AI will transform content creation, while 77% emphasize its ability to personalize content, thus making it more impactful.

For instance, using AI-powered text-to-video or image-to-video platforms nonprofits can generate custom videos highlighting their mission, impact, and ongoing initiatives. These tools enable organizations to personalize video content for individual donors, creating a more meaningful connection. Similarly, a national Carvana campaign, which created 1.3 million videos with personalized details about each customer's car-buying experience, is a prime example of how custom video can dramatically increase engagement (Carvana, 2023). Each video was tailored to the recipient, leading to higher increased customer loyalty and repeat business.

Social Media Management: Leveraging AI for Engagement

Social media is an indispensable tool for nonprofits aiming to raise awareness, build communities, and drive donations. However, managing multiple social media platforms can be time-consuming and overwhelming, particularly for resource-constrained nonprofits. AI can simplify social media management by automating tasks such as content scheduling, audience targeting, and performance tracking.

AI-powered social media tools offer automation features that allow nonprofits to schedule posts, monitor engagement, and adjust strategies in real-time. AI's ability to analyze user data and preferences means that nonprofits can deliver personalized content at the right time, increasing the likelihood of user interaction. Moreover, AI can identify trending topics and hashtags, helping nonprofits to stay relevant and capitalize on moments that resonate with their audience.

In addition to automating social media tasks, AI can also provide insights into audience behavior, allowing nonprofits to refine their messaging and improve engagement. For instance, by using AI analytics, organizations can identify which types of posts generate the most engagement, whether it's videos, images, or text-based content, and adjust their strategies accordingly.

Social media is a vital channel for nonprofits, allowing them to reach and engage with broad audiences. AI can help nonprofits optimize their social media strategies by automating content creation, analyzing engagement patterns, and adjusting posts to maximize visibility.

Example: Senior Assistance Nonprofit Using AI for Social Media Optimization A nonprofit supporting seniors with various assistance programs could use AI to:

- **Automate Social Media Updates:** Generate posts about senior health tips, upcoming social events, and success stories of seniors receiving assistance. AI can adapt the content based on the target audience for each platform, such as Facebook for family members or Instagram for community events.

- **Analyze Audience Engagement:** Use AI to analyze audience interaction data—such as shares, comments, and reactions—to identify what types of posts resonate most with their audience, like community success stories or educational content about senior well-being.
- **Adjust Posting Strategies:** AI can automatically adjust the frequency of posts to maximize engagement. For example, if engagement is higher during weekends, AI can prioritize weekend content scheduling.

Through AI-driven social media optimization, the nonprofit can expand its reach, connect with family members of seniors, and enhance awareness of available services.

AI-Driven Advocacy and Engagement

AI is also proving to be a powerful tool for advocacy. Nonprofits often struggle to get their message across in a crowded digital space, but AI can amplify their voice by automating the dissemination of information across multiple channels. More importantly, AI can ensure that advocacy messages are personalized and targeted to specific audiences, increasing the likelihood of mobilizing supporters.

One of the most exciting applications of AI in nonprofit advocacy is the use of custom audio and video. Generative AI tools can create personalized advocacy videos or audio messages tailored to different demographics, significantly boosting engagement. These AI-driven media forms allow nonprofits to deliver targeted messages to specific audience segments, increasing the chances of creating meaningful connections and inspiring action.

Increasingly, nonprofits are using AI-powered chatbots to engage with their audience in real time. These chatbots can answer common questions, guide users through donation processes, and even provide personalized content recommendations. By automating these interactions, nonprofits can save time and resources while providing high-quality user engagement.

For advocacy-focused nonprofits, mobilizing supporters through marketing is key to driving change. AI can assist by generating content that aligns with current trends and sentiments, ensuring that advocacy messages are both timely and impactful.

Example: A Human Rights Nonprofit Using AI for Advocacy Campaigns A human rights nonprofit advocating for refugee rights might use AI to:

- **Analyze Public Sentiment:** Use AI to track social media and news trends around refugee issues, identifying key moments when public interest is highest and tailoring advocacy content accordingly.
- **Generate Timely Content:** Automatically create social media posts, email blasts, and petitions related to breaking news stories on refugee crises, ensuring content reaches supporters when they are most engaged.
- **Optimize Outreach:** Use AI to determine the best channels for outreach (email, social media, SMS) based on supporter preferences and past engagement.

By leveraging AI, the nonprofit could ensure that its advocacy campaigns reach the right audience at the right time, driving higher levels of engagement and support.

AI for Targeted Advertising Campaigns

AI helps nonprofits manage advertising campaigns more effectively, ensuring limited budgets are well spent. By leveraging AI, nonprofits can optimize ads in real time, identifying the best platforms, times, and audiences. AI-driven insights help target demographics, interests, and behaviors, delivering messages to the right people.

AI analyzes data on potential donors, including online behavior and past giving patterns, allowing nonprofits to create targeted segments and personalized messages. This tailored content resonates more, making it compelling and engaging. For example, a wildlife supporter might see ads focused on endangered species.

AI also optimizes ad spend by analyzing campaign effectiveness. Machine learning predicts the best messaging, imagery, or calls to action, allocating funds to impactful strategies. Through A/B testing, AI scales successful campaigns and reduces underperforming ones, ensuring the best return on investment.

By making advertising smarter, AI helps nonprofits maximize reach, engage supporters effectively, and increase conversions, leading to deeper connections with those who care about their mission.

Example: Youth Development Nonprofit Using AI for Targeted Ads A youth development nonprofit promoting mentorship programs could use AI to:

- **Identify Potential Mentors:** Use AI to analyze social media activity to identify individuals who have engaged with content related to youth development or mentorship.
- **Create Tailored Ads for Recruitment:** Automatically generate ads encouraging these individuals to become mentors, with messaging that highlights the positive impact they could make and success stories from the program.
- **Improve Ad Performance:** Use AI to continuously analyze which ads yield the highest engagement, optimizing ad spend to focus on the most successful mentorship recruitment campaigns.

By using AI to create more targeted advertising campaigns, the nonprofit could attract mentorship programs, increase donations, and boost overall visibility with a limited budget.

AI for Event Promotion and Management

Events are essential for nonprofits, providing opportunities for fundraising and community engagement. Technology can streamline promotion, personalize outreach, predict attendance, and optimize participant experiences, making events more impactful and efficient.

Technology identifies the most effective outreach channels, whether email, social media, or SMS, ensuring that nonprofits reach their audience in the right way. This strategic approach maximizes engagement and minimizes wasted effort.

Predictive tools help nonprofits anticipate attendance by analyzing past behavior and preferences, allowing for informed logistical decisions such as venue size and resource allocation.

Automation handles repetitive tasks such as reminders, RSVPs, and attendee list management, freeing up staff to focus on direct, meaningful engagement. This ensures events run smoothly and leaves a positive impression on participants.

Post-event data analysis provides actionable insights to improve future events. By refining strategies based on attendee feedback and engagement metrics, nonprofits can enhance experiences and boost outcomes.

Leveraging technology helps nonprofits boost attendance, personalize experiences, and strengthen donor relationships. This fosters loyalty, deeper engagement, and increased support, ultimately contributing to long-term success.

Example: A Clean Water Nonprofit Using AI for Event Promotion
A community clean water nonprofit hosting a fundraising walkathon might use AI to:

- **Predict Attendee Interest:** AI can analyze supporter engagement history, such as previous participation in similar events or donations, to predict which individuals are most likely to join the walkathon.
- **Automate Customized Invitations:** AI can generate tailored invitations emphasizing key aspects of the event, like family-friendly activities, entertainment, or specific water-related projects that will benefit from the fundraising.
- **Monitor Campaign Performance:** AI can track engagement metrics, such as open rates and social media shares, and adjust the messaging to improve attendance, ensuring the event reaches its maximum fundraising potential.

By using AI to automate and optimize event promotion, the nonprofit could improve attendance rates and raise more funds during key events.

SEO versus GEO for Nonprofits

As the way people search for information evolves, nonprofits must adapt to remain visible in this changing digital landscape. While traditional search engine optimization (SEO) focuses on static search engines like Google, a new paradigm—generative engine optimization (GEO)—is emerging alongside AI-driven tools like ChatGPT, PerplexityAI, and Bing Chat. GEO takes a holistic approach, prioritizing user experience, personalization, and dynamic content creation, offering nonprofits a more effective strategy for engaging with their audiences.

Unlike SEO, which emphasizes keyword optimization, GEO leverages real-time data, user behavior, and content preferences to create immersive, user-centric experiences. Nathan Chappell and Brittany Shaff, CEO and Founder of Shaff Fundraising Group, highlight that nonprofits must shift their focus from just optimizing keywords to providing high-quality, relevant content tailored to user needs. GEO allows nonprofits to deliver personalized and engaging experiences, significantly enhancing digital strategies aimed at increasing donations, acquiring volunteers, or amplifying brand awareness. By incorporating AI-driven natural language processing (NLP), nonprofits can deliver content that speaks directly to users' interests, leading to higher conversion rates.

The transition from SEO to GEO represents a fundamental shift in how nonprofits engage with their supporters. GEO's emphasis on content quality, relevance, and multimodal formats—such as text, audio, video, and images—ensures that nonprofit websites are visible and engaging across various AI-driven platforms. A study by Princeton University, et al. (2023) revealed that GEO strategies led to a 30–40% improvement in visibility compared to traditional SEO, making it a critical tool for nonprofits looking to increase community engagement, donations, and overall impact.

Case Study: Furniture Bank

Furniture Bank, a Canadian nonprofit dedicated to providing furniture to those in need, leveraged AI to enhance their marketing efforts through custom image creation (Furniture Bank, 2022). By incorporating AI-generated visuals specifically tailored to their target audience's preferences, Furniture Bank was able to significantly boost their online engagement and reach a wider audience. These AI-driven images captured viewers' attention and conveyed the impactful and heartfelt stories of the individuals they serve, ensuring that these narratives were shared in a respectful and meaningful way. By avoiding the pitfalls of "poverty porn" and instead promoting dignity, empathy, and humanity, Furniture Bank was able to share stories that resonated deeply with their supporters (Furniture Bank, 2023).

This innovative approach allowed Furniture Bank to produce compelling and personalized content in a highly cost-effective manner, which was particularly important for a nonprofit operating within a limited budget. By leveraging AI technology, they were able to create visuals that truly reflected the mission and values of the organization without incurring significant costs typically associated with custom media production. Ultimately, this strategy helped them to strengthen their connection with supporters, enhance community engagement, and extend the reach of their mission. AI also empowered Furniture Bank to be more agile in their storytelling, allowing them to adapt visuals quickly based on audience feedback and preferences, thereby maximizing the impact of their outreach campaigns.

Recommendations for Successful AI Adoption in Marketing

1. **Identify Key Marketing Objectives:** Determine where AI can make the most impact, such as personalizing donor communications, optimizing campaign targeting, or automating routine marketing tasks. Focus on areas where AI can enhance both efficiency and engagement.
2. **Staff Upskilling in AI Marketing Tools:** Train your marketing team to understand AI-driven tools like content generation software, chatbots, and analytics platforms. Ensuring your team is comfortable with these tools is critical for effective implementation.
3. **Content Experimentation and Testing:** Use AI to conduct A/B testing at scale, identifying which messages, visuals, or campaigns resonate best with your audience. Encourage a culture of experimentation to find out what works for your unique community.

4. **Data-Driven Audience Insights:** Utilize AI tools to segment your audience and understand their preferences in depth. These insights can help craft more personalized marketing campaigns, ultimately leading to better engagement and donor retention.
5. **Continuous Monitoring and Iteration:** Regularly assess the effectiveness of AI-driven marketing campaigns. Analyze the outcomes and use insights to refine strategies, ensuring your marketing efforts are continuously improving and aligning with your goals.

The Future of AI in Nonprofit Marketing

The integration of AI into nonprofit marketing and communication efforts marks a new era of scale, efficiency, personalization, and engagement. Whether through content creation, social media management, SEO or GEO, AI is transforming how nonprofits interact with their audiences. By leveraging AI's capabilities, organizations can deepen donor engagement, amplify advocacy efforts, and ultimately increase their impact.

As nonprofits continue to adopt myriad AI tools, they must remember that AI is not a replacement for human connection, but rather a tool that can help facilitate and enhance it. By using AI to better understand their audience, create personalized content, and optimize their digital presence, nonprofit organizations can build stronger relationships and drive greater change. The future of nonprofit marketing is undoubtedly AI driven, and those that embrace this technology will be better positioned to thrive in an increasingly digital world.

9

AI for Administration and Human Resources

Revolutionizing Nonprofit Operations with AI

As we've shared in previous chapters, artificial intelligence (AI) has often been heralded as a game-changer for marketing and fundraising efforts, but its impact on nonprofit administration and human resources (HR) is equally significant. In 2022, 71% of nonprofit staff worked in management, professional, or related occupations—roles that often face heavy administrative burdens (U.S. Bureau of Labor Statistics, 2023). As burnout rates rise—with 95% of nonprofit leaders expressing some level of concern about burnout, both for themselves and their staff (CEP, State of Nonprofits 2024)—AI is proving to be a powerful tool for streamlining tasks and improving efficiency.

Nonprofit organizations are often tasked with delivering impactful services to their communities while navigating challenges such as limited budgets, high demands, and a small staff. To stay effective and continue making a difference, nonprofits need to work smarter, not harder. Artificial intelligence offers innovative solutions that can optimize operations, streamline administrative functions, and improve human resource management, all of which are crucial to running a successful nonprofit. Whether it's through data analysis, content generation, or automating tasks, AI can help nonprofits enhance productivity, reduce burnout, and ensure a more strategic approach to achieving their mission.

Integrating AI into nonprofit organizations is no longer a luxury but an operational imperative. While marketing and fundraising have often been at the forefront of AI adoption, its impact on operational tasks like administration and human resources is substantive, as it increases accuracy and much-needed efficiencies. With AI, nonprofits can streamline mundane processes, improve staff well-being, and free up time to focus on high-value, human-centric activities. By leveraging AI across all operations, nonprofits can reduce overhead, improve decision-making, and make more strategic use of their limited resources. Whether it's used to support HR functions or optimize administrative workflows, AI holds the potential to drive change and maximize impact in the nonprofit sector.

Recommendations for Successful AI Adoption in Nonprofit Operations

1. **Identify Areas of Impact:** Determine where AI can make the most significant difference, such as automating administrative tasks or enhancing HR functions.
2. **Staff Training:** Invest in training programs to prepare your team to work with AI technologies, ensuring everyone is comfortable and capable.
3. **Knowledge Sharing:** Collaborate with other nonprofits to exchange insights and experiences, benefiting from shared expertise and lessons learned.
4. **Monitor and Evaluate:** Continuously assess the performance and potential for biases of AI tools to ensure they are delivering value and reducing biases. Use feedback to make improvements and adapt strategies to better serve your mission.
5. **Collaborate with AI Experts:** Partner with AI experts and technology providers to ensure the proper implementation of AI solutions, leveraging their expertise to maximize effectiveness.

Streamlining Nonprofit Administration

Nonprofit organizations face significant challenges when it comes to managing administrative tasks. With limited resources, many nonprofits must juggle a wide range of responsibilities, from budgeting and scheduling to document creation and compliance tracking. Administrative work can be time-consuming, error-prone, and too often takes focus away from an organization's core mission. However, by integrating AI into administrative processes, nonprofits can streamline operations, reduce costs, and improve efficiency—allowing staff to dedicate more time to programs and services that directly impact their communities.

AI can assist in various administrative functions, from financial planning to compliance reporting. Data-driven tools can help organizations plan and allocate resources by analyzing past financial data and forecasting future trends. AI can support document creation, making it faster and more personalized, while automation tools can handle routine administrative tasks like scheduling and paperwork management. Let's dive deeper into how these technologies are transforming nonprofit administration.

Forecasting the Future with AI

AI tools can enhance administrative functions by using data to forecast future needs and trends. In the context of nonprofit administration, these tools can assist in budgeting, financial forecasting, evaluation, analysis, and resource allocation. By analyzing past spending patterns, AI can provide insights into future expenses, helping nonprofits create more accurate budgets and avoid financial shortfalls.

For example, AI can analyze historical donation trends to forecast fundraising income for the coming year. This helps organizations allocate resources more effectively, ensuring they're prepared for periods of high or low donation activity. Similarly, AI can forecast staffing needs based on program requirements or event schedules, helping HR and operations plan ahead and avoid overstaffing or understaffing.

AI can also assist with compliance and regulatory forecasting, especially for nonprofits that rely on grant funding or government contracts.

By analyzing past grant cycles and reporting requirements, AI can predict when reports are due and ensure that necessary documentation is prepared on time, avoiding delays or penalties.

Example: Domestic Violence Shelter Using Predictive AI for Resource Planning A domestic violence shelter nonprofit striving to provide safe spaces and essential services could use AI in the following ways:

- **Anticipate Shelter Occupancy Rates:** Predict future occupancy levels based on historical patterns, community reports, and seasonal factors. This allows the shelter to proactively adjust staffing, supplies, and services.
- **Identify Resource Shortages:** Use AI to analyze current inventory levels and predict when supplies like food, toiletries, and clothing are likely to run low. This helps ensure consistent stock by prompting timely reorders.
- **Predict Demand for Counseling Services:** Analyze trends in service requests and external data (e.g., local crime statistics) to anticipate increased needs for counseling services, allowing the shelter to schedule staff more effectively.

By leveraging predictive AI, the shelter can stay prepared for changing demands, better allocate resources, and ensure survivors get the support they need when they need it.

AI-Powered Content Creation

AI offers a valuable resource for nonprofits in document creation and content generation. One of the most time-consuming aspects of nonprofit administration is preparing reports, proposals, and other necessary paperwork. AI can automate much of this process by generating personalized documents based on input data, thus speeding up the creation of reports, grant proposals, and other administrative documents.

For example, AI can assist in creating budget proposals or progress reports by analyzing past data and generating drafts. This reduces the time spent writing documents from scratch and ensures that they are consistent and error-free. AI can also create personalized communications for donors, volunteers, and stakeholders, improving engagement and saving administrative staff valuable time.

Onboarding is another area where AI can make a significant impact. When new employees or volunteers join a nonprofit, there is often a considerable amount of paperwork and documentation that needs to be completed. AI can generate customized onboarding packets, including necessary forms, orientation materials, and training documents tailored to the individual's role within the organization. This reduces manual effort and ensures that all new hires have the necessary information right from the start.

Example: Public Library Foundation Using Generative AI for Internal Communication A public library foundation could use generative AI in the following ways:

- **Draft Staff Newsletters:** Create regular staff newsletters highlighting upcoming events, recent accomplishments, and staff recognitions, helping keep everyone informed and engaged.
- **Generate Meeting Agendas and Minutes:** Automatically generate meeting agendas based on previous discussions and create minutes to ensure key points are documented.
- **Develop Program Descriptions:** Use AI to create compelling descriptions for literacy programs or workshops, which can be used in promotional materials, grant applications, or community outreach.

Generative AI helps the library foundation maintain smooth internal communication, streamline documentation, and effectively describe programs to stakeholders.

Effortless Administration through Automation

Automation is one of the most impactful tools for streamlining routine administrative tasks. For many nonprofits, administrative work includes a wide range of repetitive activities such as scheduling meetings, managing volunteer hours, processing payroll, and maintaining filing systems. AI can automate these tasks, reducing the burden on administrative staff and increasing overall efficiency.

One of the most common applications of automation is in scheduling. Nonprofits often have staff members with busy calendars and numerous meetings to coordinate, including fundraising events, board meetings, and community outreach activities. AI-powered scheduling tools can automatically find available times for everyone involved, reducing back-and-forth emails and manual coordination. AI can also help with task management by automatically sending reminders for deadlines and following up on pending actions.

In addition to scheduling, AI can automate onboarding processes, including generating offer letters, completing required paperwork, and collecting necessary documentation. This allows HR departments to streamline their onboarding processes, ensuring that new hires or volunteers have a smooth and efficient entry into the organization.

Moreover, AI automation tools can handle routine documentation processes, such as generating and sending standard contracts or processing invoices. This helps ensure that the nonprofit complies with legal and financial regulations while saving time on administrative tasks.

Example: Child Protection Nonprofit Using AI Automation for Documentation and Compliance A child protection nonprofit could use AI automation in the following ways:

- **Automate Case Documentation:** Use AI to automatically fill out case forms based on previous records and input from caseworkers, ensuring compliance and reducing repetitive tasks.
- **Generate Compliance Checklists:** Automatically generate checklists for caseworkers to ensure they meet all requirements for each case, such as legal forms and necessary follow-ups.
- **Automate Status Updates to Stakeholders:** Automatically generate and send status updates to stakeholders or family members involved in cases, ensuring timely communication while keeping sensitive information secure.

AI automation helps the child protection nonprofit maintain accurate documentation, streamline compliance, and communicate important updates efficiently.

Empowering Human Resources with AI

Human resources are at the heart of nonprofit success. From recruiting passionate staff to maintaining a positive workplace culture, effective HR management is crucial for any nonprofit's longevity. However, many nonprofits face challenges related to staff retention, high turnover, and limited resources for training and development. AI offers practical solutions that can enhance nonprofit HR functions by improving hiring processes, predicting staffing needs, automating repetitive tasks, and creating personalized employee support. By leveraging AI, nonprofits can ensure they have the right talent and support to fulfill their mission more effectively.

AI-driven HR tools allow nonprofits to automate tasks that can otherwise consume considerable time and resources. Data-driven insights can help forecast staffing needs and manage employee turnover. AI helps create personalized onboarding and training content, ensuring a better experience for new hires and current staff. Automation can further support HR by handling routine administrative duties, allowing HR professionals to focus more on strategic activities that foster employee satisfaction and engagement. Let's explore how these technologies are impacting nonprofit HR.

Anticipating HR Needs with AI Insights

AI in HR can be used to anticipate workforce trends and behaviors. In the nonprofit world, these tools can help anticipate staffing needs, identify turnover risks, and support staff proactively. By analyzing historical HR data, AI tools can provide insights that guide decision-making and optimize staffing levels and employee satisfaction.

For example, AI can forecast staffing needs during specific times of the year when nonprofits are most active. This ensures the organization has enough resources to manage peak activities, such as fundraising events or major campaigns. It can also help identify factors that lead to employee turnover, allowing HR to intervene before valuable staff members decide to leave. These data-driven insights are particularly valuable in reducing the costs and disruptions associated with high turnover rates, a common issue in the nonprofit sector.

AI can also support employee well-being by identifying early signs of burnout or disengagement. By analyzing factors such as workload, attendance, and engagement scores from employee surveys, AI can alert HR managers to employees who might need additional support. This allows nonprofits to take timely action, offering flexible work options, additional training, or wellness initiatives to prevent burnout and increase overall job satisfaction.

Example: LGBTQ+ Support Nonprofit Using Predictive AI for Employee Engagement An LGBTQ+ support nonprofit could use predictive AI in the following ways:

- **Predict Employee Burnout:** Use AI to analyze workload, overtime hours, and survey responses to predict which employees are at risk of burnout, allowing HR to implement preventative measures.
- **Forecast Engagement Trends:** Predict changes in employee engagement levels based on historical survey data, allowing HR to plan initiatives that boost morale during low periods.
- **Identify Factors Affecting Retention:** Analyze data from exit interviews and engagement surveys to predict factors that contribute to employee turnover, helping HR make changes to increase retention.

With predictive AI, the LGBTQ+ support nonprofit can enhance employee engagement, reduce burnout, and maintain a motivated workforce.

Tailoring HR Content with AI

AI plays a key role in content creation, which is highly beneficial for HR departments focused on communication, training, and onboarding. Nonprofits often lack the resources to provide individualized attention during onboarding or create customized training materials for each employee. AI can fill this gap by creating tailored onboarding documents, employee handbooks, training content, and personalized career development plans.

For instance, AI can draft personalized welcome letters and tailored onboarding content for new hires, providing them with key information about the organization, its culture, and their specific role. It can also help HR create customized training modules based on the new hire's skills, ensuring that training is relevant and engaging. This capability ensures that every employee receives the information and support they need to succeed, even when HR resources are stretched thin.

AI can also be used to keep employees informed and engaged through personalized newsletters and updates. By analyzing employee interests and job roles, AI can generate content that resonates with staff members, helping them feel more connected to the organization's mission and current initiatives. This enhances overall engagement and helps foster a culture of inclusivity and involvement.

Example: An Anti-Poverty Nonprofit Using Generative AI for Training Materials An anti-poverty nonprofit could use generative AI in the following ways:

- **Create Training Manuals:** Generate role-specific training manuals for new hires, helping streamline the onboarding process and ensure consistency.
- **Produce Soft Skills Training Content:** Use AI to develop content focused on soft skills such as empathy, communication, and teamwork, tailored to the needs of working with vulnerable populations.
- **Generate Onboarding Checklists:** Create personalized onboarding checklists for new employees, helping them navigate their first days at the organization smoothly.

Generative AI helps the anti-poverty nonprofit provide consistent and tailored training materials, making onboarding efficient and impactful.

Automating HR Tasks for Greater Impact

Automation in HR focuses on streamlining repetitive tasks such as payroll processing, benefits administration, leave management, and performance reviews. For nonprofit HR teams that often work with limited resources, automation can significantly reduce administrative burdens, allowing them to dedicate more time to strategic initiatives, like talent management and fostering a positive work environment.

Automating payroll and benefits processing ensures that these tasks are handled accurately and consistently, reducing the risk of human error. This is especially important for nonprofits where staff compensation may be tied to complex funding structures or grant stipulations. Automation also allows HR to handle requests for leave or vacation time automatically, improving efficiency and making the process smoother for employees.

Moreover, AI-powered automation tools can simplify the process of performance tracking and reviews. By collecting and analyzing performance data, AI can help HR teams conduct timely and objective evaluations. Facilitated by human leaders, these evaluations can be further enhanced with personalized feedback generated by AI, offering constructive guidance that supports employees in their professional development.

Example: An Addiction Recovery Nonprofit Using AI Automation for Human Resources An addiction recovery nonprofit could use AI automation in the following ways:

- **Automate Employee Surveys:** Automatically schedule and send employee feedback surveys, collecting data on job satisfaction, work environment, and morale.
- **Analyze Survey Results:** Use AI to automatically analyze survey results and generate reports with insights into areas that need attention.
- **Trigger Follow-Up Actions:** Automate follow-up actions based on survey results, such as scheduling meetings for employees who indicate concerns or recommending actions for improvement.

AI automation helps the addiction recovery nonprofit gather valuable feedback, analyze employee sentiment, and ensure HR can address issues efficiently.

Case Study: Education Resource Strategies

Education Resource Strategies (ERS), a nonprofit dedicated to helping school districts become more strategic with their spending, is leveraging AI to transform how school budgets are analyzed. Historically, school districts have struggled with inconsistent reporting standards, making it challenging to categorize expenses such as transportation, teacher salaries, and facilities. These discrepancies often led to lengthy manual efforts, taking analysts months to sort through over 100 different spending categories for each district (Lipstein, 2017).

By using AI trained on examples of previously labeled budgets, ERS can now automate this categorization process. The AI predicts the appropriate spending category for each new budget item and ranks its confidence in each prediction. This automation significantly reduces the workload, saving up to 75% of the time analysts previously needed to classify financial data (DrivenData, n.d.). Rather than getting bogged down by manual data sorting, analysts can now focus on interpreting budget insights and advising schools on best practices.

ERS's use of AI also enhances the accuracy and reach of its services. In a recent data science challenge, ERS partnered with DrivenData to develop an algorithm capable of tagging budget data with over 90% accuracy (DrivenData, n.d.). This solution not only accelerates the coding of financial files, but also makes it possible for ERS to serve more school districts efficiently and at a lower cost.

Ultimately, this AI-driven approach allows ERS to offer deeper insights into resource allocation, empowering school districts to make smarter financial decisions. Freed from the tedious task of categorizing line items, ERS staff can focus more on collaboration with schools—helping them optimize spending in ways that directly improve educational outcomes for students. By pairing technology with human expertise, ERS is creating a smarter, more strategic foundation for school budgeting practices.

Conclusion

AI is no longer a futuristic concept—it's a practical tool that can profoundly enhance nonprofit operations today. By automating tasks, preventing burnout, streamlining HR, and ensuring legal compliance, AI empowers organizations to focus on their core missions. However, ethical considerations like data privacy must be addressed proactively to ensure AI complements human efforts rather than replacing them. Embracing AI enables nonprofits to operate more efficiently, make data-driven decisions, and ultimately serve their communities better.

Infusing AI within operations provides a pathway to unlocking new possibilities in how nonprofits serve communities, engage employees, and make strategic decisions. AI's power lies not only in the automation of routine processes but also in its ability to generate insights that can shape future programs and initiatives. It has the potential to bring about a new era of innovation and effectiveness in the nonprofit sector.

Embracing AI doesn't mean losing the human touch; instead, it amplifies our capacity to make a difference by offloading mundane tasks and freeing time for high-touch, high-yield human efforts. Nonprofits are uniquely positioned to leverage AI for operational efficiency, deepening their impact, innovating solutions, and inspiring change on a global scale. By proactively prioritizing ethical considerations and making deliberate choices about how to implement AI, nonprofits can lead the way by amplifying their human potential to better serve their important missions.

10

AI Transformation Is a Journey, Not a Destination

CHANGE IS AN inevitable part of progress, particularly when it comes to technology. Over the past decade, artificial intelligence (AI) has rapidly evolved, reaching far beyond theoretical applications into the daily operations of companies and organizations across the globe. AI is no longer a futuristic concept—it is here, it is real, and it is changing the way we work, communicate, and participate as citizens of the world. AI has also brought with it an incredible amount of change. In a sector typically stigmatized for its lack of desire for change, this period of exponential technological growth can be inherently challenging. If you're a nonprofit leader, professional, volunteer, or advocate, there's one undeniable fact: AI has moved your cheese, and it's not coming back.

Drawing from the popular business parable *Who Moved My Cheese?* by Spencer Johnson (1998), this chapter will explore how AI has already reshaped the landscape of nonprofit work, much like the metaphorical cheese in the story. However, unlike in the story, where the cheese could eventually be relocated, AI represents a permanent shift in how organizations function more nimbly and adaptably. The traditional approaches that nonprofits once relied on for donor engagement, fundraising, service delivery, and operations have already been displaced, which is evidenced in the changes in charitable participation over the past two decades. The new paradigm, driven by AI, requires nonprofits to adapt, innovate, and embrace change—or risk being left behind.

The AI genie is out of the bottle, and it's not going back in. But with this change comes tremendous opportunity. As we gain efficiencies, personalization, and precision through AI, we can free time to amplify missions in innovative and powerful ways. AI transformation sheds light on the importance of managing change during AI adoption, strategies for successful implementation, and how to foster a mindset of curiosity, continuous learning, and adaptability within your nonprofit organization.

In *Who Moved My Cheese?* characters Hem and Haw discover that the cheese they had depended on for nourishment has disappeared. While Hem refuses to move forward, clinging to the hope that things will return to normal, Haw learns to adapt, search for new opportunities, and embrace change. For nonprofits, the cheese represents the familiar and traditional ways of working—manual processes, repetitive tasks, and dependence on human-driven decisions and interactions.

However, AI has disrupted these established systems, offering nonprofits new opportunities to improve efficiency, personalize outreach, and scale their impact. The cheese is no longer where it used to be, and organizations must realize that the old ways are not coming back. AI has permanently altered the landscape, and waiting for the traditional methods to work again will only lead to frustration and missed opportunities.

Artificial intelligence is already transforming industries ranging from healthcare to finance to entertainment. In the nonprofit sector, AI tools are revolutionizing everything from donor management to service delivery to data analysis. Nonprofits must recognize that this change is not temporary; it is part of an ongoing, irreversible transformation.

But why does this shift matter so much for nonprofits specifically? Unlike for-profit businesses, where profit maximization drives technological innovation, nonprofits are mission-driven, and the stakes are higher. The needs that nonprofits address—poverty, education, healthcare access, human rights just to name a few—are increasingly complex and urgent. AI offers nonprofits the potential to scale their impact like never before. The challenge, however, lies in understanding how to leverage this technology while managing the inevitable changes it brings to humanity's greatest challenges and the nonprofits that exist to support this and future generations through love.

The Importance of Change Management in AI Adoption

Change is difficult. That's a universal truth, but it is especially true in the nonprofit sector, where resources are often limited, and organizations rely on deeply entrenched processes. The introduction of AI technologies represents a monumental shift in how nonprofits operate. AI changes the way people work and make decisions, and how organizations engage with their communities. If this shift isn't managed properly, it can lead to confusion, resistance, and even failure.

Too often, the nonprofit sector operates with a scarcity mindset. Staff are overworked, resources are stretched thin, and many organizations are hesitant to invest in new technologies, especially those that appear to be experimental. Given the confluence of these and other factors, effective change management is absolutely imperative for AI adoption to succeed. It's not just about integrating AI tools—it's about transforming the culture of the organization to embrace AI as a core part of its mission.

In our experience deploying AI solutions for the past eight years, we've come to the simple conclusion that 70% of AI transformation efforts fail primarily due to poor change management practices. This statistic is not surprising. AI transformations are often viewed as purely technical projects, but they are, at their core, human endeavors. The key to successful AI adoption lies not just in the technology itself, but in how well the people within the organization are prepared for the change.

Nonprofits, in particular, must focus on change management strategies that address the human side of AI adoption. AI will undoubtedly change workflows, roles, and expectations within the organization. Leaders must proactively manage this change by communicating openly, providing training and support, and fostering a culture of innovation and curiosity.

In a 2024 online article titled "The Curiosity Code," author Chappell discusses the importance of fostering curiosity in the face of technological change. AI adoption requires nonprofits to nurture a mindset of curiosity and exploration, where staff are encouraged to ask questions, experiment with new tools, and seek out innovative solutions. This culture of curiosity is essential for overcoming resistance and ensuring that AI is embraced as a partner in the organization's mission.

Strategies for Successful AI Implementation

Implementing AI in a nonprofit organization is not a one-size-fits-all process. Every organization has unique needs, goals, and challenges. However, there are proven strategies that can help ensure successful AI integration, regardless of the organization's size or mission. Let's discuss the essential elements of change management to increase your organization's chance of success when adopting and integrating AI into various capacities.

1. **Set Clear, Impact-Driven Goals:** AI adoption should always begin with a clear understanding of what the organization hopes to achieve. Nonprofits must identify specific pain points that AI can address. For example, if donor retention is a challenge, AI tools can help predict which donors are most likely to give again and offer insights into how to engage them more effectively. If program impact measurement is a priority, AI can analyze data from service delivery efforts to identify trends and outcomes. We've already discussed the myriad ways in which AI can support nonprofits in the previous chapters. Identify the problem, then evaluate which AI solution is best equipped to fill that gap. Having clear goals ensures that AI is applied strategically, and that its impact is measurable.
2. **Start Small and Scale Over Time:** Over the past several years, we have seen our fair share of successes and failures when it comes to AI adoption. One of the ways to guarantee

AI failure would be to take on too much at once. Perhaps counterintuitively, one of the most effective approaches to AI adoption is to start with small, manageable pilot projects before scaling. Nonprofits can begin by using AI for a specific task—such as automating donor communications or analyzing programmatic data—then gradually expand AI use across the organization as they become more comfortable with the technology. This iterative approach allows organizations to learn from their experiences and make adjustments along the way.

3. **Build a Multidisciplinary AI Team:** AI adoption is not just an IT project—to be successful it requires collaboration across departments. Nonprofits should assemble a multidisciplinary team that includes program managers, operations staff, fundraisers, leadership, and even supporters and volunteers. Each AI team member brings a unique perspective on how AI can be used to support the mission. Fundraisers may focus on using AI to personalize donor outreach, while program managers might explore how AI can optimize service delivery. Donors and volunteers will highlight ways that AI can be used to improve their engagement experience. The key is to involve all relevant stakeholders in the AI adoption process to ensure the technology aligns with the organization's overall priorities and goals.

4. **Invest in AI Training and Up-skilling:** According to the *2024 AI Skills Report*, 95% of executives and 94% of IT professionals agree that AI initiatives will fail without skilled teams that can effectively use AI tools (Pluralsight, 2024). Nonprofits must invest in ongoing training and up-skilling programs for their staff. AI is constantly evolving, and the skills needed to leverage it will continue to change over time. Training should focus not just on the technical aspects of AI, but also on how it can be used to enhance mission delivery. Leaders should foster a mindset of continuous learning, encouraging staff to stay curious and engaged with new developments in AI.

5. **Encourage a Culture of Experimentation:** AI is an iterative technology, meaning it improves over time as it processes more data and gains experience. Nonprofits should embrace a culture of experimentation, where staff feel empowered to test AI tools, gather insights, and iterate on their approaches. As in *Who Moved My Cheese?*, those who are willing to adapt, experiment, and embrace change are the ones who thrive. AI adoption is not a linear process—it requires flexibility, curiosity, and a willingness to learn from failures.
6. **Communicate Openly and Transparently:** One of the biggest barriers to AI adoption is fear. Many nonprofit staff worry that AI will replace their jobs or make their roles redundant. Leaders must communicate openly about the role AI will play in the organization. Staff need to understand that AI is a tool to help them be more effective, not a threat to their employment. Transparent communication can alleviate concerns, build trust, and foster buy-in from staff.
7. **Align AI with Mission Impact:** For nonprofits, success is measured not by profit margins but by mission impact. AI should be used to advance the organization's mission, whether that means reaching more beneficiaries, improving program outcomes, or increasing donor engagement. AI tools should be aligned with the organization's core values and goals. When AI is seen as a partner in mission delivery, staff are more likely to embrace it and integrate it into their workflows.

Setting Up a Multidisciplinary Team for Success

We cannot over-emphasize that AI adoption is not solely an IT function. In large part, due to the distributed and iterative nature of AI, the purchase and assimilation of AI within a nonprofit organization should look very different from other static hardware or software solutions that change only incrementally through systematized updates. The iterative nature of AI, which is a direct result of the exponential nature in which AI improves itself, is a foundational change from how most organizations have used and evaluated solutions for the past several decades. AI adoption in nonprofits requires a collaborative, cross-functional approach that ensures the technology is integrated thoughtfully and strategically. Again, it's not just the responsibility of IT or data specialists but a holistic effort that involves key players across various roles. By creating a multidisciplinary team, nonprofits can harness the strengths of diverse skill sets to maximize the impact of AI while ensuring it aligns with the mission. Each role within the team brings unique expertise and is vital to the overall success of leveraging AI.

Every organization is different, and size will determine the number of stakeholders included. Here's a breakdown of some of the key roles and their expected contributions in a multidisciplinary AI team for nonprofits:

- **Fundraisers**

    Role: Fundraisers are at the forefront of donor engagement, and their role in the AI team is to explore how AI can enhance donor outreach, segmentation, and retention. AI allows fundraisers to personalize communications and predict donor behavior using data-driven insights. AI-driven models can help identify potential major donors, automate thank-you messages, and tailor campaigns based on donor preferences and history.

    Contribution: By leveraging AI, fundraisers can work more efficiently, focusing on high-value relationships rather than repetitive tasks. Their expertise ensures AI tools are applied in ways that nurture donor trust and deepen engagement, ensuring the organization's long-term financial health.

- **Program Managers**

    Role: Program managers play a crucial role in ensuring the alignment of AI with service delivery and program outcomes. They can use AI to optimize resource allocation, improve program effectiveness measurement, and predict future service needs. AI tools such as predictive analytics can help program managers identify trends, monitor progress in real time, and refine service delivery strategies.

Contribution: Program managers provide insights into how AI can streamline operations, improve beneficiary outcomes, and scale services. Their involvement ensures that AI projects directly contribute to the organization's mission and service goals, making the adoption of AI more mission-aligned and impactful.

- **Operations Staff**

    Role: Operations staff ensure that day-to-day processes run smoothly. In the AI team, their role is to explore how AI can automate administrative and logistical tasks, from scheduling and resource management to supply chain optimization and inventory tracking. AI can help operations teams streamline workflows, reduce costs, and increase overall efficiency, freeing up time for staff to focus on more strategic activities.

    Contribution: Operations staff help identify areas where automation can create the greatest efficiencies. They ensure that AI is seamlessly integrated into existing processes, reducing redundancy and improving resource management—key elements in scaling nonprofit operations effectively.

- **IT Professionals**

    Role: IT professionals are essential for implementing, maintaining, and securing AI systems. Their role in the team is to ensure that AI tools integrate seamlessly with existing technology infrastructure, meet security and privacy standards, and are continuously optimized for performance. IT professionals are responsible for data management, system updates, troubleshooting, and ensuring that AI tools comply with data governance policies.

    Contribution: With their technical expertise, IT professionals ensure that AI systems are not only functional but also secure, reliable, and adaptable to future needs. They ensure AI tools are designed for longevity and scalability, minimizing disruption to organizational operations while supporting the growth of AI capabilities.

- **Leadership (Executive Directors/Board Members)**

  Role: Leadership plays a strategic role in overseeing the organization's vision for AI adoption. Executives provide the vision, direction, and priorities for AI projects to ensure they align with the nonprofit's overall mission and goals. They must balance innovation with sustainability, ensuring that AI is used responsibly and ethically while fostering a culture of innovation within the organization.

  Contribution: Leaders provide the guiding principles that ensure AI is implemented thoughtfully and strategically. They are responsible for approving resources for AI initiatives and ensuring that ethical considerations, such as data privacy and fairness, are at the forefront of every AI decision. Their involvement helps the organization navigate the complexities of AI while focusing on its human-centered mission.

- **Data Scientists/Analysts**

  Role: While this role might overlap with IT, data scientists or analysts bring specialized expertise in working with large datasets, building AI models, and analyzing data to produce actionable insights. They can develop predictive models, analyze trends, and create algorithms that drive the organization's AI strategies.

  Contribution: Data scientists translate raw data into valuable insights that drive decision-making across all departments. Their expertise ensures that AI solutions are based on rigorous data analysis, enhancing accuracy and effectiveness. They ensure AI tools are built on ethical and reliable data practices.

- **Volunteers and Frontline Workers**

  Role: Often overlooked, volunteers and frontline workers provide practical insights into the day-to-day challenges that AI could help address. Their firsthand experience with beneficiaries and on-the-ground operations can inform the design and deployment of AI tools, making them more user-friendly and effective.

Contribution: By including volunteers in the AI adoption process, nonprofits can ensure that AI solutions are grounded in real-world challenges and needs. Volunteers can offer feedback on how AI tools impact their work and suggest improvements to enhance efficiency and engagement.

Why a Multidisciplinary Team Is Essential

The success of AI adoption in nonprofits hinges on the involvement of a multidisciplinary team, where each role contributes a unique perspective. This ensures that AI integration benefits all aspects of the organization, from optimizing donor outreach to improving program outcomes. The complexity of AI requires input from various departments—technical, operational, ethical, and strategic—allowing nonprofits to tailor AI tools to their specific needs.

A multidisciplinary approach prevents the formation of silos, encouraging collaboration across departments. For example, fundraisers can leverage AI for personalized donor engagement, while program managers can use it to track and measure the effectiveness of services. Operations teams ensure AI tools streamline logistical and administrative tasks, and IT professionals guarantee that AI systems are implemented securely and effectively. By aligning these roles with the organization's mission, nonprofits ensure that AI is a tool for amplifying impact rather than just an upgrade to existing processes.

Moreover, cross-functional collaboration fosters organizational buy-in, which is crucial for overcoming resistance to AI adoption. When everyone—from frontline workers to leadership—understands how AI can enhance their role and contribute to the overall mission, it builds momentum and encourages more strategic and thoughtful use of AI throughout the organization. This holistic integration of AI leads to more sustainable and impactful outcomes.

In summary, setting up a multidisciplinary AI team helps nonprofits leverage AI as a technological tool and a catalyst for positive change. By combining diverse skills and insights, nonprofits can maximize the potential of AI, ensuring that it aligns with their mission and fosters long-term, meaningful impact.

Failing Fast: AI Is Iterative by Design

By now you're understanding that due to its recursive and exponential nature AI is not a set-it-and-forget-it technology. AI is iterative by design, meaning it improves over time as it processes more data and gains experience. This iterative nature of AI means that nonprofits need to adopt a mindset of learning and experimentation. In many cases, AI initiatives will require multiple attempts, adjustments, and refinements before they yield the desired results.

The concept of failing fast is particularly important when it comes to AI adoption. Failing fast doesn't mean accepting failure as an outcome—it means learning quickly from mistakes and using those insights to improve. For nonprofits, this can involve testing AI tools in small-scale projects, gathering data on their effectiveness, and making adjustments based on what works and what doesn't. Organizations that adopt a "fail fast, learn fast" approach will be more agile and better positioned to leverage AI's full potential.

For example, a nonprofit might start by using AI to analyze donor data and predict future giving patterns. The initial implementation may not provide the expected results, but by examining the data, tweaking the algorithm, and testing new approaches, the organization can refine the tool and ultimately achieve better outcomes. This iterative process allows nonprofits to continuously improve their AI strategies and adapt to changing conditions.

Investing in Philanthropic R&D

One of the keys to successful AI adoption is investing in philanthropic research and development (R&D). Nonprofits must be willing to allocate resources to explore new AI tools, experiment with different approaches, and develop strategies for long-term success. Just as corporations invest in R&D to innovate and stay competitive, nonprofits must invest in R&D to advance their missions.

Philanthropic R&D doesn't necessarily require a significant financial investment. Nonprofits can start small by dedicating time for staff to experiment with AI tools, partnering with technology providers to pilot new solutions, or collaborating with other nonprofits to share insights and best practices. The key is to create a culture where experimentation and innovation are encouraged, and where AI is seen as a tool for advancing the mission.

Over the past several years, hundreds, if not thousands, of nonprofit organizations have invested in machine learning capabilities to support their operations and the efficiency of their program delivery. For example, charity: water has invested in AI-driven predictive analytics to monitor and maintain the wells it builds in developing countries. By analyzing data from sensors placed in the wells, the organization can predict when a well will likely fail and send a repair team before the issue becomes critical. This proactive approach reduces downtime, ensures that communities have continuous access to clean water, and maximizes the impact of the organization's work. This innovative use of AI would not be possible without a commitment to philanthropic R&D.

The Need for Perpetual Adaptation: Lessons from History

Throughout history, major technological advancements have always required adaptation. The shift from steam power to electricity took decades, as industries gradually learned to harness the new technology. The same was true for the adoption of automobiles, telephones, and the internet. AI is no different. While it is being adopted at a faster pace than many previous technologies, the transition will still take time, and organizations will need to stay in a perpetual state of adaptation.

AI is evolving rapidly, and the tools and techniques that work today may not be effective tomorrow. Nonprofits must be willing to continuously learn, experiment, and adapt to new developments in AI. The organizations that succeed in this new landscape will embrace change, foster a culture of curiosity, and remain open to new possibilities.

AI Is Here to Stay—Adapt or Get Left Behind

By now, we hope that you've come to the stark realization that AI has moved your cheese, and it's not coming back. Nonprofits that fail to adapt will find themselves left behind in a world where AI is driving innovation, efficiency, and impact. But those who embrace AI, manage change effectively, and foster a culture of curiosity will not only survive—they will thrive.

The future belongs to AI-first organizations willing to take risks, experiment, and continuously learn. By setting clear goals, building multidisciplinary teams, and investing in training and R&D, nonprofits can harness the power of AI to amplify their missions and create lasting change.

11

Beyond AI Ethics: The Nonprofit Sector's Imperative for Responsible and Beneficial AI

Artificial intelligence (AI) for nonprofits, at its core, must prioritize humanity over utility. It must lift up the most vulnerable, not further entrench their struggles. It must be guided by principles of fairness, transparency, and respect for the dignity of all people for this and future generations.

The nonprofit sector faces a unique and heightened responsibility in this AI revolution. Unlike the private sector, where profit and market share take precedence by design, nonprofit organizations must take proactive steps that prioritize efforts that extend far past ethical frameworks to promote and protect their most valuable asset: trust.

Maintaining trust, transparency, and fairness in AI is paramount for nonprofits. By aligning AI practices with core values and ethical standards, organizations can ensure meaningful stakeholder engagement and mission alignment.

Upholding Ethical Standards: AI Aligned with Values

Maintaining trust, transparency, and fairness in AI is paramount for nonprofits. By aligning AI practices with core values and ethical standards, organizations can ensure meaningful stakeholder engagement and mission alignment.

It's crucial to understand AI not just as a technological tool, but as a socio-technical system. This means that AI is shaped by, but also shapes social contexts, human behaviors, and organizational structures. As Afua Bruce and Amy Sample Ward (2022) emphasize in "The Tech That Comes Next," technology doesn't exist in a vacuum—it's deeply intertwined with social systems and human values.

For nonprofits, this understanding is paramount. Implementing AI isn't just about adopting new software; it's about rethinking processes, redefining roles, and often, reshaping organizational culture around the use of data to assist in creating efficiencies and making decisions. It requires careful consideration of how AI will interact with existing systems, both technological and human.

Consider, for example, a nonprofit implementing an AI-driven donor segmentation tool. The tool might provide valuable insights, but its effectiveness will depend on how well it integrates with existing CRM systems, how easily staff can interpret and act on its recommendations, and how it aligns with the organization's overall fundraising strategy.

This socio-technical perspective also highlights the importance of considering the broader implications of AI adoption. Questions that nonprofits must begin to grapple with include:

1. How will AI impact the roles and responsibilities of our staff?
2. What new skills will our team need to develop to effectively work with AI?
3. How might AI change the way we interact with our beneficiaries and donors?
4. What ethical considerations do we need to address in our use of AI?
5. What is the impact AI will have in promoting or diminishing trust?
6. What might be the unintended consequences on our mission, community, and sector that this AI may present?

By viewing AI through this socio-technical lens, nonprofits can ensure that their AI initiatives are not just technologically sound, but also organizationally and ethically aligned.

Maintaining trust, transparency, and fairness in AI is paramount for nonprofits. By aligning AI practices with core values and ethical standards, organizations can ensure meaningful stakeholder engagement and mission alignment.

In Chappell's 2023 article "Beyond AI Ethics: The Nonprofit Sector's Imperative for Responsible AI," it's argued that nonprofits must take on a leadership role in defining and implementing responsible AI. Unlike corporations, whose incentives are often driven by profit and efficiency, nonprofits are in the business of trust. Trust is hard to earn but easily lost, and nonprofits must hold themselves to the highest level of accountability regarding AI adoption.

As the AI Equity Project Report (Das & Vryn, 2024) highlights, many nonprofits struggle with outdated or fragmented data systems that make it challenging to implement AI responsibly. The report found that nearly 65% of nonprofits still rely on siloed data collection methods like Excel, which limits their ability to integrate AI meaningfully and equitably. This makes it all the more critical for nonprofits to invest in data equity practices—such as developing comprehensive data governance frameworks, standardizing data collection protocols, and training staff on AI ethics and responsible usage. By doing so, nonprofits can close the gaps that may unintentionally disadvantage the very communities they aim to serve.

Responsible AI is not just about preventing harm—it's about proactively ensuring that AI systems enhance trust, transparency, and fairness.

Currency of Trust: The Nonprofit Sector's Most Valuable Asset

The AI Equity Project Report also underscores the risk that poorly implemented AI systems pose to nonprofits' most valuable asset—trust. A key finding from the report showed that when AI systems are built on biased data, they can reinforce existing inequalities and erode stakeholder confidence. Nonprofits must ensure that their AI models are effective, representative, and fair. This is particularly important when engaging with marginalized groups or underserved populations. Trust is fragile, and once broken, it can have a lasting negative impact on an organization's ability to raise funds, deliver services, or fulfill its mission.

The nonprofit sector must recognize that trust is the foundation of its success, and trust can be easily lost if AI is not implemented responsibly. Nonprofits must approach AI with the mindset that they are not just adopting a new technology—they are redefining their relationship with their stakeholders. They must prioritize accountability, transparency, and fairness in every AI initiative they undertake.

This is particularly important because nonprofits often deal with sensitive data, including data on constituents, benefactors, financial records, and personal details about the beneficiaries they serve. The misuse of this data, even unintentionally, can have devastating consequences. Nonprofits must ensure that their AI systems are designed and deployed in ways that protect data privacy, minimize biases, and ensure that AI decisions are explainable and accountable.

As nonprofits embrace the transformative potential of AI, they must tread carefully, mindful of their responsibility to act ethically and maintain the trust that defines their relationships with donors, beneficiaries, and the public. AI offers powerful tools, but those tools must be wielded with intention, always in alignment with the organization's mission and values. For nonprofits, ethical AI adoption is not simply a matter of compliance—it is about living up to their core purpose of fostering equity, social justice, and community well-being.

Afua Bruce and Meena Das, two prominent voices in AI ethics, underscore the necessity of a balanced and thoughtful approach to AI. Bruce, in her work on public interest technology, advocates for the alignment of technological innovation with human-centered values, ensuring that AI systems promote fairness and equity. Das, with her focus on data governance and ethical data practices, highlights the critical importance of not perpetuating inequalities through unexamined data use. Their insights help shape a framework for nonprofits to engage with AI in a way that reflects the highest ethical standards.

At the core of this approach are several key considerations that must be central to any AI adoption strategy. These considerations ensure that AI serves the organization and actively promotes its stakeholders' well-being, ensuring both technological advancement and social responsibility.

The risk of bias in AI systems is one of the most pressing ethical concerns. Algorithms, while neutral in theory, are built on data that may reflect societal inequalities. For nonprofits, this could mean that AI systems unintentionally prioritize or exclude certain groups, reinforcing existing disparities. It is imperative that organizations continuously monitor and audit their AI systems for fairness, ensuring that marginalized communities are not disproportionately impacted. Das's advocacy for equitable data practices offers guidance on how nonprofits can structure their AI tools to mitigate bias and promote inclusiveness.

Nonprofits handle a significant amount of sensitive information, from donor profiles to the personal details of beneficiaries. As AI systems process this data, the importance of safeguarding it cannot be overstated. Nonprofits must go beyond basic compliance with regulations such as the General Data Protection Regulation (GDPR) or California Consumer Privacy Act (CCPA), adopting a proactive approach to data protection. Transparency about how data is collected, stored, and used is essential in maintaining trust. Privacy, much like equity, should be a central pillar of any AI initiative within the nonprofit sector.

AI systems can often seem like black boxes—complex, opaque algorithms that produce results without easily understood explanations. For nonprofits, transparency is not just a technical issue but a moral one. Stakeholders, particularly donors and beneficiaries, must understand how AI systems work, how decisions are made, and why certain outcomes are produced. Nonprofits should strive to use AI tools that offer explainability, allowing them to demystify AI processes for their communities. Bruce's work stresses the importance of transparency in public-facing technologies, emphasizing that trust can only be maintained when users feel they are not being left in the dark.

AI offers incredible efficiencies, but automation should never replace the human judgment at the heart of nonprofit work. While AI can analyze data and predict outcomes at remarkable speed, it is the human touch—compassion, empathy, and ethical reasoning—that ensures decisions align with an organization's mission. Nonprofits must establish clear guidelines for human oversight, ensuring that AI augments rather than overrides the expertise and intuition of staff. This ensures that AI remains a tool of support, not a replacement for the human element that is so central to nonprofit work.

Nonprofits must be prepared to take responsibility for the outcomes of their AI systems. This includes establishing clear lines of accountability within the organization and designating who is responsible for the maintenance, monitoring, and ethical use of AI tools. Just as with any decision-making process, there must be mechanisms for addressing errors or unintended consequences. Bruce highlights the importance of building accountability into the design of AI systems, ensuring that organizations are not only responsive to issues as they arise, but also proactive in preventing harm.

AI should never be implemented simply for the sake of innovation. Every AI tool a nonprofit adopts must serve a purpose that aligns with the organization's core mission. Whether enhancing donor engagement or optimizing program delivery, AI must be used to amplify the social impact of the nonprofit. This mission-centric approach ensures that AI remains a tool for good, helping organizations achieve their goals in a manner consistent with their values.

Maintaining trust, transparency, and fairness in AI is paramount for nonprofits. By aligning AI practices with core values and ethical standards, organizations can ensure meaningful stakeholder engagement and mission alignment.

The ethical adoption of AI in the nonprofit sector is not just a technological issue—it is a matter of trust, responsibility, and mission. As Bruce and Das remind us, the choices we make today about how we use AI will shape the future of philanthropy and social good. Nonprofits, as stewards of trust and equity, must lead the way in ensuring that AI serves as a force for positive change, reinforcing the values that define the sector.

Ethical According to Whom?: Measuring AI Perceptions from an End User's Perspective

Another recommendation from the AI Equity Project Report is the importance of actively engaging with end-users to better understand their attitudes toward AI technologies. By checking in with stakeholders, nonprofits can gain valuable insights into their perceptions of transparency, fairness, and privacy in AI use. This approach not only fosters greater acceptance of AI systems but also helps organizations identify and address concerns before they become larger issues.

One of the most significant concerns highlighted in the report is transparency. For many end-users, AI can seem like a mysterious and opaque technology—something that works in the background but remains poorly understood. This lack of clarity can breed suspicion and erode trust. When appropriate, nonprofits should take proactive steps to explain when and how AI systems are being used within various functions of their operations. Whether AI is employed for automating donor segmentation, predicting fundraising outcomes, or enhancing service delivery, stakeholders deserve to understand what role AI plays and how it aligns with the organization's mission.

Providing clear, accessible explanations of AI-driven processes helps demystify the technology and strengthens trust. By being upfront about the presence and purpose of AI, nonprofits can ensure that their stakeholders feel included in the journey of digital transformation. In an era where data privacy is top of mind, it is particularly important to ensure that donors and beneficiaries are aware of how their personal information is being used and protected.

To mitigate these risks, nonprofits must actively work to ensure that their AI systems are representative, ethical, and just. This requires ongoing auditing and monitoring of AI models to identify and correct any biases that may arise. Engaging end-users in this process—by asking for their feedback on AI-driven decisions—can also provide critical insights into how these systems are perceived and whether they are functioning equitably.

Privacy remains a cornerstone of trust in AI adoption. According to the report, one of the most important steps nonprofits can take to safeguard trust is to give end-users control over their personal data. Donors and beneficiaries want to know that their data is being handled with care, and they expect the ability to opt out of AI-driven personalization or data collection if they choose.

Nonprofits should implement robust data governance policies that clearly define how personal information will be used by AI systems. Offering clear consent options and ensuring that stakeholders have the right to review or delete their data are important steps in maintaining trust. When individuals feel empowered to make decisions about their personal information, they are more likely to trust that the organization is acting in their best interests.

While AI can automate many processes, it is critical that nonprofits maintain a level of human oversight in their AI implementations. According to the report, one of the most effective ways to build trust in AI systems is to ensure stakeholders understand how AI-generated decisions are made. Explainability—providing clear, easy-to-understand explanations of AI outputs—is crucial in fostering transparency and accountability (see Chapter 12).

Additionally, human oversight should be a non-negotiable aspect of any AI-driven process, particularly when it involves decisions that directly impact people's lives. Nonprofits must ensure that AI systems augment human decision-making rather than replace it entirely. This balance between automation and human judgment helps reassure stakeholders that AI is being used ethically and responsibly.

To maintain and enhance trust in AI, nonprofits must take a proactive approach to transparency, fairness, and end-user engagement. The report offers several key recommendations to help organizations safeguard trust while adopting AI:

- **Engage stakeholders early and often:** Involve donors, beneficiaries, and volunteers in discussions about AI initiatives. Regular check-ins and feedback loops ensure that end users' concerns are heard and addressed.
- **Provide clear and accessible explanations:** Explain AI-driven processes in simple, non-technical language. Make sure stakeholders understand how AI is being used and why.
- **Offer opt-out mechanisms:** Give end users control over their data by offering clear options to opt out of AI-driven personalization or data collection.
- **Conduct ongoing AI audits:** Regularly evaluate AI models to ensure they are fair, transparent, and aligned with the organization's values. Continuous monitoring helps catch and correct biases early on.

Maintaining trust, transparency, and fairness in AI is paramount for nonprofits. By aligning AI practices with core values and ethical standards, organizations can ensure meaningful stakeholder engagement and mission alignment.

The Unique Role of the Nonprofit Sector in AI Governance

Nonprofits cannot rely solely on governments or corporations to set the standards for AI governance. Governments, even when they are involved, tend to create broad and general regulations that apply to all sectors, leaving little room for the unique challenges faced by nonprofits. Corporations, on the other hand, are often driven by incentives that prioritize scale over safety, meaning they may be more focused on rapid AI deployment than on ensuring that AI is used ethically and responsibly.

Standards organizations, while important, are often too slow to keep up with the rapid pace of AI development. This leaves the nonprofit sector in a unique position: it must take matters into its own hands and develop frameworks for responsible AI tailored to its specific needs and values.

This is the genesis of the Fundraising.AI initiative, a global volunteer effort dedicated to the responsible and beneficial use of AI in the nonprofit sector. The initiative is built on the belief that AI can be a force for good, but only if it is guided by a framework that prioritizes trust, fairness, and accountability.

At the heart of Fundraising.AI is an open-source framework that guides nonprofits in adopting AI responsibly while ensuring long-term positive impact. This framework, developed with insights from nonprofit leaders, technologists, and ethicists, lays out 10 key tenets to help organizations navigate the complexities of AI adoption. These tenets not only emphasize trust and accountability but also provide a comprehensive roadmap for ethical and effective AI use in the nonprofit sector.

Nonprofits must ensure that AI systems are transparent in their operations, making it clear how decisions are made and what data is used. This transparency fosters trust between the organization and its donors, beneficiaries, and stakeholders. Openly communicating about AI's role in decision-making ensures that stakeholders feel informed and confident in the technology's use.

AI systems should be designed and deployed in ways that promote fairness and reduce biases. Nonprofits must ensure that their AI tools do not inadvertently perpetuate discrimination or inequality, especially when working with vulnerable communities. This means continuously assessing AI models to ensure they provide equal opportunities and outcomes across all demographics.

Protecting the privacy of donor and beneficiary data is paramount. Nonprofits must prioritize the security of personal information in AI systems, adhering to strict data protection standards. Data used for AI must be securely stored, processed, and anonymized where necessary, minimizing the risk of data breaches or misuse.

AI systems should be accountable to human oversight. Nonprofits must have clear governance structures in place that define who is responsible for AI decisions. This includes setting up protocols for reviewing and addressing issues arising from AI use, ensuring that AI actions are traceable and correctable when errors occur.

AI initiatives should directly align with the nonprofit's mission and values. Nonprofits must ensure that AI is used to enhance their social impact, rather than merely for operational efficiency. Every AI deployment should be mission-driven, reinforcing the organization's commitment to serving its community rather than just optimizing processes.

AI should augment human decision-making, not replace it. Nonprofits must retain a human-in-the-loop approach, where AI complements human judgment and ethical considerations remain at the forefront. This ensures that AI outputs are interpreted through a human lens, particularly in sensitive areas like donor relations and program delivery.

Nonprofits must adopt AI technologies with a focus on long-term sustainability, ensuring that they can maintain, update, and ethically govern AI systems over time. This includes planning for the ongoing financial and technical resources needed to sustain AI initiatives and prevent them from becoming obsolete or harmful due to lack of oversight.

AI adoption should involve input from diverse stakeholders, including staff, beneficiaries, and community members. By engaging a broad range of perspectives, nonprofits can ensure that AI systems serve the entire community equitably. Inclusivity also helps identify blind spots that may not be apparent to a limited group of decision-makers.

AI should be a force for good, driving innovation that benefits the communities nonprofits serve. Nonprofits must prioritize AI projects that have a direct, positive impact on society rather than simply adopting trendy technologies. This means focusing on AI initiatives that address real-world problems and create lasting social value.

AI is constantly evolving, and nonprofits must commit to continuous learning and adaptation. Organizations should regularly update their AI knowledge, reassess their systems, and adapt to new ethical standards and technological advancements. Building an organizational culture that embraces ongoing education ensures that AI is used responsibly and remains aligned with the nonprofit's mission.

Maintaining trust, transparency, and fairness in AI is paramount for nonprofits. By aligning AI practices with core values and ethical standards, organizations can ensure meaningful stakeholder engagement and mission alignment.

By adopting and internalizing these tenets, nonprofits demonstrate their commitment to ethical leadership in the AI space. This framework offers more than just guidelines—it provides the foundation for using AI as a force for good, amplifying mission-driven work while preserving the human element at the heart of social change. When trust is prioritized and upheld, nonprofits can confidently harness the potential of AI to create long-lasting, meaningful impact, ensuring that their missions flourish in a rapidly evolving technological landscape.

AI Advances Exponentially: Keeping Your AI Framework Adaptable

Advances in AI are measured in cycles, not time. One of the unique differences between AI and other static technology is that AI is most often trained to have self-improvement capabilities which dramatically increases the pace at which AI advances happen—often exponentially—rather than incrementally. For nonprofits, this means they must adopt frameworks for responsible and beneficial AI that are adaptable and capable of evolving alongside the technological breakthroughs.

This type of recursive self-improvement means that without a doubt, the worst AI you will ever use is today, and that the AI tools that nonprofits use in the present will likely be outdated in just a few years, if not months. As such, a key for nonprofits to leverage AI technology is to create systems and cultural processes that allow them to remain agile and flexible in their approach to AI governance.

Adaptability is also crucial because the risks and challenges associated with AI will change over time. Today, the primary concerns may be data privacy and bias, but as AI becomes more integrated into more of our daily decision-making processes, new risks will certainly emerge. Nonprofits must be prepared to anticipate and address these risks, rather than reacting to them after the fact.

One way to ensure adaptability is through continuous learning and monitoring. Nonprofits must stay informed about the latest developments in AI in terms of terminology, technology, usability, and governance. This includes participating in industry forums like Fundraising. AI, engaging with experts on pros and cons, having evaluation metrics for purchasing and deploying, and regularly reviewing their own AI systems to identify areas for improvement.

The Responsible and Beneficial AI Framework

While an AI governance framework should be designed and adopted in accordance with organizational values, there are 10 key tenets at the heart of a responsible and beneficial AI framework to help organizations navigate the complexities of AI adoption while remaining malleable as technology changes. These tenets emphasize trust and accountability and provide a comprehensive roadmap for ethical and effective AI use in the nonprofit sector.

The tenets include:

1. **Transparency**

    Nonprofits must ensure that AI systems are transparent in their operations, making it clear how decisions are made and what data is used. This transparency fosters trust between the organization and its donors, beneficiaries, and stakeholders. Openly communicating about AI's role in decision-making ensures that stakeholders feel informed and confident in the technology's use.

2. **Fairness and Equity**

    AI systems should be designed and deployed to promote fairness and reduce biases. Nonprofits must ensure their AI tools do not inadvertently perpetuate discrimination or inequality, especially when working with vulnerable communities. This means continuously assessing AI models to ensure they provide equal opportunities and outcomes across all demographics.

3. **Privacy and Security**

    Protecting the privacy of donor and beneficiary data is paramount. Nonprofits must prioritize the security of personal information in AI systems, adhering to strict data protection standards. Data used for AI must be securely stored, processed, and anonymized where necessary, minimizing the risk of data breaches or misuse.

4. **Accountability**

    AI systems should be accountable to human oversight. Nonprofits must have clear governance structures that define who is responsible for AI decisions. This includes setting up protocols for reviewing and addressing issues that may arise from AI use, ensuring that AI actions are traceable and correctable when errors occur.

5. **Purpose Alignment**

    AI initiatives should directly align with the nonprofit's mission and values. Nonprofits must ensure that AI is used to enhance their social impact, rather than merely for operational efficiency. Every AI deployment should be mission-driven, reinforcing the organization's commitment to serving its community rather than just optimizing processes.

6. **Human Oversight**

    AI should augment human decision-making, not replace it. Nonprofits must retain a human-in-the-loop approach, where AI complements human judgment and ethical considerations remain at the forefront. This ensures that AI outputs are interpreted through a human lens, particularly in sensitive areas like donor relations and program delivery.

7. **Long-Term Sustainability**

    Nonprofits must adopt AI technologies focusing on long-term sustainability, ensuring that they can maintain, update, and ethically govern AI systems over time. This includes planning for the ongoing financial and technical resources needed to sustain AI initiatives and prevent them from becoming obsolete or harmful due to lack of oversight.

8. **Inclusivity**

    AI adoption should involve input from diverse stakeholders, including staff, beneficiaries, and community members. By engaging a broad range of perspectives, nonprofits can ensure that AI systems serve the entire community equitably. Inclusivity also helps in identifying blind spots that may not be apparent to a limited group of decision-makers.

9. **Innovation for Good**

    AI should be a force for good, driving innovation that benefits the communities nonprofits serve. Nonprofits must prioritize AI projects that have a direct, positive impact on society, rather than simply adopting trendy technologies. This means focusing on AI initiatives that address real-world problems and create lasting social value.

10. **Continuous Learning and Adaptation**

    AI is constantly evolving, and nonprofits must commit to continuous learning and adaptation. Organizations should regularly update their AI knowledge, reassess their systems, and adapt to new ethical standards and technological advancements. Building an organizational culture that embraces ongoing education ensures that AI is used responsibly and remains aligned with the nonprofit's mission.

Human Oversight: Keeping Humans in Control of AI Decisions

It can't be overstated that the key tenet of responsible and beneficial AI is ensuring that humans remain in control of AI decisions. This is particularly important in the nonprofit sector, where decisions about donor engagement, service delivery, and resource allocation can have significant societal implications that impact this and future generations. AI systems, while powerful, should never be allowed to make critical decisions without human oversight, evaluation, and careful management.

In practical terms, this means that nonprofits must establish clear protocols for AI's intended goals, how the AI systems are being used, who is responsible for overseeing them, and how decisions are made. AI should be seen as a tool that supports human decision making, not a replacement for human judgment. From a fundraising perspective, while AI can analyze constituent data and make recommendations for engagement strategies, the final decision about how to approach a donor should always be reviewed and made by a human.

When AI is deployed for the determination or delivery of services, the stakes and need for AI governance are immeasurably greater. This is particularly important in areas where AI decisions could have a direct impact on people's lives. For instance, in organizations that provide social programs related to education, health, or human services, AI might be used to assess eligibility for programs or prioritize service delivery. When AI is used in ways that determine the social determination of benefits, it becomes imperative that humans systematically review these decisions to ensure that they are fair, ethical, and aligned with the organization's mission.

Ethical versus Legal Considerations: Navigating the Gray Areas

One of the most pressing challenges in AI governance is navigating the intersection of ethical and legal considerations. While laws provide a baseline for compliance, they are often slow to evolve and may fail to address the rapid pace of technological innovation and the unique challenges posed by AI. For nonprofits, this gap is particularly significant, given the vulnerable populations they serve and the moral imperative to protect them.

Data Privacy and Security: Protecting Sensitive Information

Nonprofits often handle highly sensitive data, including personal information about donors, beneficiaries, and volunteers. Ensuring that this data is protected is a critical component of responsible AI. AI systems rely on vast amounts of data to function, and without proper safeguards, that data can be vulnerable to breaches, misuse, or exploitation.

Nonprofits must implement robust data privacy and security measures to protect the sensitive information they collect. This includes ensuring that AI systems comply with data protection laws, encrypting sensitive data, and regularly auditing AI systems to identify and address vulnerabilities. Additionally, nonprofits should be transparent with their stakeholders about how data is being used, who has access to it, and what steps are being taken to protect it.

Bias and Fairness: Ensuring AI Systems Are Fair and Unbiased

One of the most well-documented challenges of AI is the risk of bias. AI systems are only as good as the data they are trained on, and if that data is biased, the AI will produce biased outcomes. For nonprofits, this is particularly concerning because biased AI systems can perpetuate inequalities and harm the very communities they are meant to serve.

Ensuring fairness in AI systems requires a proactive approach to identifying and mitigating biases. This includes regularly auditing AI systems to detect biases, using diverse datasets to train AI models, and involving a diverse group of stakeholders in the design and implementation of AI tools. Nonprofits must also be vigilant about ensuring that AI systems do not disproportionately benefit certain groups while disadvantaging others.

In the nonprofit sector, where trust is paramount, transparency is critical. AI decisions must be explainable and understandable to stakeholders, including donors, beneficiaries, and regulators. This means that nonprofits must be able to clearly articulate how their AI systems work, how decisions are made, and what steps are being taken to ensure fairness and accountability.

Nonprofits should adopt transparent AI practices, which include providing stakeholders with clear explanations of how AI systems are used, what data is being collected, and how decisions are being made. Additionally, nonprofits must establish clear lines of accountability for AI outcomes, ensuring that there is always a person responsible for overseeing AI systems and addressing any issues that arise.

The Role of Legislation: Navigating the Regulatory Landscape

AI governance is not just about ethics—it's also about complying with existing and emerging laws. As AI becomes more prevalent, governments around the world are introducing legislation to regulate its use. Nonprofits must stay informed about these legal developments and ensure their AI systems comply with relevant laws.

Nonprofits operating in the United States must be mindful of the layered nature of legal requirements, which can vary significantly between local, state, and federal levels. For example:

- **Local Laws:** These often regulate community-specific issues, such as data collection for fundraising events or zoning restrictions for AI-powered services like drone deliveries. Compliance at this level may also include privacy ordinances in cities with stricter regulations than state or federal laws.
- **State Laws:** State legislation often addresses data privacy and security standards, such as CCPA, which establishes stringent guidelines for collecting and using personal information. States may also enact their own AI-specific regulations, creating a patchwork of laws that nonprofits must navigate depending on where they operate.
- **Federal Laws:** Federal regulations tend to set broader frameworks, such as the Children's Online Privacy Protection Act (COPPA) or the Americans with Disabilities Act (ADA), which can directly impact how nonprofits use AI tools like predictive analytics or chatbots. However, federal laws often lack the specificity needed to address AI's unique ethical dilemmas, leaving nonprofits to interpret how existing frameworks apply to their use of emerging technologies.

As nonprofits increasingly work across borders, they must also know how different countries are establishing their own AI regulations. Some key examples include:

- **European Union:** The EU's General Data Protection Regulation (GDPR) is one of the most comprehensive privacy laws globally, directly impacting how nonprofits collect and store data from

EU residents. The proposed EU AI Act goes a step further by categorizing AI systems into risk levels, requiring organizations to meet stringent requirements for "high-risk" systems.
- **Canada:** Laws like the proposed Artificial Intelligence and Data Act (AIDA) aim to regulate how AI systems are developed and deployed, emphasizing accountability and transparency.
- **Asia:** Countries like Singapore and Japan are adopting progressive AI frameworks, focusing on ethical guidelines and government oversight to ensure AI is used responsibly across sectors, including nonprofits.
- **Global Standards:** International organizations, such as UNESCO, are also introducing guidelines for ethical AI use, encouraging global alignment on principles like fairness, transparency, and human oversight.

While laws vary widely across jurisdictions, ethics remain a universal consideration for nonprofits. AI systems can amplify bias, exploit sensitive data, or unintentionally harm the communities they aim to serve. Therefore, nonprofits must proactively establish their own ethical frameworks, often going beyond what the law requires, to ensure responsible AI use.

Nonprofits must comply with these laws and be proactive in shaping the regulatory landscape. As trusted institutions, nonprofits have a unique opportunity to advocate for laws and policies that promote responsible AI while protecting vulnerable populations.

This dual approach—adhering to legal requirements while prioritizing ethical responsibility—requires significant effort and expertise. Nonprofits must balance the complexities of compliance with their mission to act as stewards of public trust, ensuring that AI serves as a tool for empowerment rather than harm.

A Higher Standard to Promote and Protect Trust

AI offers immense potential to transform the nonprofit sector, enabling organizations to scale their impact, optimize operations, and deliver more personalized services. But with this potential comes great responsibility. Nonprofits must lead the charge in adopting responsible and beneficial AI, ensuring that AI is used in ways that are fair, transparent, and aligned with their mission.

The journey from ethical to responsible AI is not just about complying with laws or preventing harm—it's about embracing AI as a tool for social good and ensuring that it enhances, rather than undermines, the trust that nonprofits have built with their stakeholders. By adopting frameworks like the Fundraising.AI tenets, investing in continuous learning and adaptation, and prioritizing transparency and accountability, nonprofits can harness the power of AI to create lasting, meaningful change.

As the AI revolution continues to unfold, the nonprofit sector has a unique opportunity to lead by example, demonstrating how AI can be used to build a more just, equitable, and trustworthy world. The stakes have never been higher, but with the right approach, the nonprofit sector can ensure that AI is not just a technological advancement—but a force for good.

The nonprofit sector holds a unique position in guiding responsible AI adoption. By embracing frameworks like Fundraising.AI and fostering trust through transparency, nonprofits can leverage AI as a transformative force while staying aligned with their mission to serve humanity.

By leading the charge in responsible AI adoption, nonprofits can build a future where technology serves humanity, ensuring equity, trust, and lasting impact in every community they touch.

12

Evaluating AI for Nonprofits

As we have discussed throughout this book, the integration of artificial intelligence (AI) holds the potential to transform nonprofit missions by streamlining operations, amplifying fundraising efforts, and creating efficiencies in how programs are delivered. However, as powerful as AI can be, selecting the right tools requires a thoughtful evaluation process. Nonprofits need to balance operational efficiency with ethical standards, ensuring that the AI solutions they choose align with their mission and values. In this chapter, we'll explore key evaluation criteria and best practices that ensure AI technologies are leveraged effectively without compromising the integrity of nonprofit work.

Criteria for Evaluation: Key Factors for AI Selection

Nonprofits must take a holistic approach when evaluating AI tools. The decision to adopt AI should be based not only on operational benefits but also on the technology's ethical implications and long-term viability. It is important to consider how well the technology integrates with existing systems, whether it can adapt to the organization's specific needs, and what broader impacts it may have on all stakeholders involved. Below are the critical factors nonprofits should assess when selecting AI tools.

Data Security and Privacy

A majority of nonprofits handle sensitive data on the populations they engage with, which must be safeguarded with the highest degree of care in order to protect and preserve trust between benefactors, advocates, and beneficiaries. Data breaches can lead to significant consequences, including the loss of trust, legal implications, and reputational damage. AI tools should prioritize robust data security measures, including encryption, secure data storage, and adherence to privacy regulations like GDPR and HIPAA.

As addressed in the Fundraising.AI framework, the importance of transparent data practices that are auditable and fully compliant with privacy laws is paramount for nonprofits adopting AI. A comprehensive approach to data privacy ensures that both donors and beneficiaries are confident in how their information is used. This is especially critical as nonprofits work to build a culture of trust and integrity within the community.

In addition to adhering to legal standards, nonprofits should assess the AI vendor's track record in handling data breaches and security incidents. An AI partner with a solid history of safeguarding information and proactively mitigating risks can help ensure that sensitive data is managed effectively and responsibly.

Nonprofits should also consider how the AI tool manages data storage and retention. Proper management of the data life cycle, including timely disposal of outdated or unnecessary information, is a key part of maintaining privacy. The AI solution should provide customizable data retention policies, allowing nonprofits to ensure that no excess data is stored longer than needed. Furthermore, AI vendors should offer regular vulnerability assessments to identify potential security weaknesses before they can be exploited.

- **Good AI:** Has comprehensive, auditable privacy protocols and complies with all relevant regulations, ensuring that data is protected at every stage.
- **Bad AI:** Provides vague assurances about privacy and may have a history of data breaches or poor data management, potentially putting sensitive information at risk.

Transparency and Explainability

AI systems that operate as black boxes can undermine trust by making decisions difficult or impossible to explain. This is particularly problematic for nonprofits, where stakeholders need to be assured that decisions are fair and equitable. Explainability in AI allows users to understand how decisions are made and provides confidence that the system is acting in the organization's best interest.

Nonprofits should favor AI tools that offer transparency in their processes, allowing stakeholders to understand the reasoning behind decisions. Non-proprietary models should be fully explainable, especially in critical areas like program development, donor segmentation, and campaign optimization. Explainable AI tools are easier to justify to boards, donors, and beneficiaries alike, making it possible to maintain accountability and trust.

Transparency is not just about understanding how decisions are made, but also about having clear documentation and reporting mechanisms that detail the underlying data, algorithms, and processes. This level of transparency helps with internal accountability and strengthens relationships with external stakeholders who may be concerned about the implications of using AI.

Additionally, nonprofits should evaluate whether the AI tool offers visualizations or other user-friendly interfaces that make it easier for staff to interpret model outputs. By providing clear and accessible information, AI vendors can help nonprofits make informed decisions and communicate these decisions effectively to their stakeholders. AI tools that use visualization methods, such as flowcharts or decision trees, can make complex AI processes more comprehensible.

- **Good AI:** Provides detailed, transparent reporting on how decisions are made, offering clear explanations for model outputs, which enhances understanding and trust.
- **Bad AI:** Operates opaquely, making it difficult to track or understand the logic behind its decisions, which can lead to skepticism and mistrust from stakeholders.

Donor-centricity and Relationship Focus

For nonprofits focused on fundraising, AI tools must enhance donor relationships rather than treating donors as transactional entities. AI tools that fail to prioritize relationships may alienate donors, leading to a decrease in donor retention over time. Nonprofits should utilize AI models that focus on long-term donor engagement through personalized communication and predictive insights.

This donor-centric approach can foster stronger relationships and increase donor retention rates by making every interaction more meaningful. For instance, AI can help identify what types of communication each donor prefers, allowing nonprofits to send personalized messages that resonate more deeply.

AI tools should also offer insights into donor motivations and behaviors, allowing nonprofits to understand what drives donor loyalty and engagement. By tailoring communication based on these insights, nonprofits can create more meaningful connections with donors, ultimately improving retention and increasing lifetime donor value.

In addition to personalized messaging, AI tools should enable predictive analytics that help nonprofits understand donor intent and engagement potential. Predictive models can provide insights into when a donor is most likely to contribute or how they prefer to be engaged, which can help organizations design more effective campaigns. This personalized and proactive engagement fosters stronger relationships by ensuring donors feel understood and valued.

Moreover, nonprofits should evaluate whether AI solutions provide tools for monitoring and assessing donor sentiment over time. Sentiment analysis can help nonprofits detect shifts in donor attitudes and take preemptive steps to address concerns before they escalate, contributing to a positive donor experience.

- **Good AI:** Prioritizes highly engaged individuals, customizes donor engagement strategies, focuses on long-term relationships, and uses insights to personalize interactions, enhancing the overall donor experience.
- **Bad AI:** Solely focuses on immediate donations and wealthy individuals or pushes aggressive strategies that do not consider donor preferences, potentially harming long-term engagement.

Bias Mitigation

AI systems can inadvertently perpetuate biases in decision-making, especially when dealing with donor segmentation or program delivery. Bias in AI can lead to unfair outcomes, such as excluding certain groups from targeted campaigns or overlooking potential donors. It is essential that nonprofits choose AI tools with safeguards in place to detect, monitor, and correct bias.

AI models for nonprofits should include bias reduction measures to ensure fairness, particularly when dealing with diverse donor bases or vulnerable populations. An AI tool that is biased not only risks making flawed decisions but also poses ethical challenges that can damage the nonprofit's reputation.

To effectively mitigate bias, nonprofits should consider implementing regular audits of their AI tools, focusing on data quality and diversity. Ensuring that training data represents the entire community the nonprofit serves can significantly reduce the risk of unintentional biases. Additionally, nonprofits should work closely with AI vendors to develop and refine ethical guidelines for responsible and beneficial AI use.

AI vendors should provide nonprofits with tools to assess bias at every stage of data collection, model training, and deployment. These tools should include bias detection metrics and adjustment mechanisms that help maintain fairness. Furthermore, nonprofits should inquire about the diversity of the AI vendor's own team, as diverse teams are often better equipped to identify and address potential biases.

Nonprofits can also benefit from using AI models that are designed to undergo iterative refinement. AI solutions should have not only initial bias detection but also the ability to learn from past outcomes and improve with more diverse data inputs. This iterative approach helps ensure that the AI system evolves to become more equitable over time, adapting to changes in the donor landscape.

- **Good AI:** Proactively identifies and mitigates biases, ensuring equitable treatment across all segments, thus promoting fairness in decision-making.
- **Bad AI:** Fails to address bias, leading to skewed decisions that may harm marginalized communities or donor groups, potentially causing reputational damage.

Real-Time Insights and Continuous Rescoring

AI tools should provide real-time insights, allowing nonprofits to act quickly on dynamic beneficiary or donor behavior, engagement trends, and other key metrics. Static models that do not adapt to changing data may become less effective over time, essentially wasting resources that could be utilized elsewhere. AI solutions should be capable of continuously rescoring records and analyzing new data.

This ensures that nonprofits are working with the most up-to-date information to improve decision-making for great program development and fundraising effectiveness. For example, if a donor's giving pattern changes, a dynamic AI tool can quickly reassess the donor's profile, allowing the nonprofit to adjust its engagement strategy accordingly.

Real-time insights can also help nonprofits identify and capitalize on emerging opportunities, such as community needs that arise unexpectedly or increased engagement trends during certain times of the year, like end-of-year giving drives. By leveraging continuously updated data, nonprofits can optimize their outreach efforts, resulting in higher engagement and better fundraising outcomes.

Moreover, real-time analytics can support resource allocation by allowing nonprofits to focus on high-potential donors and campaigns. By analyzing engagement metrics in real time, AI tools can identify which outreach methods are most effective, enabling nonprofits to allocate resources to the channels that provide the best return on investment.

Nonprofits should also consider AI tools that integrate with other platforms and data sources in real time, providing a comprehensive view of engagement activity across all channels. Seamless integration between CRM systems, social media platforms, and AI analytics can help nonprofits develop a unified understanding of constituent engagement.

- **Good AI:** Offers near-real-time updates, allowing nonprofits to adjust their strategies based on current donor and beneficiary behaviors and maximize impact.
- **Bad AI:** Only provides periodic updates, leading to outdated insights that may no longer be relevant, which could hinder fundraising efforts and program effectiveness.

Customization and Scalability

Nonprofits vary widely in size, focus, and operational needs, and AI tools should reflect this diversity by offering customization and scalability. AI models should be tailored to the nonprofit's specific data and operational goals. Customizable AI solutions will provide more meaningful insights and allow for better alignment with the organization's mission.

Scalability is also crucial, as nonprofits grow and change over time. AI tools that scale with an organization can help maintain continuity in data analysis and meet the organization's evolving needs. Additionally, nonprofits should consider whether the AI vendor can support their growth with continued software updates, new features, and ongoing technical support.

Customizable AI tools should allow nonprofits to adjust parameters, add new data sources, and modify their engagement strategies. This flexibility ensures that the AI solution remains relevant and effective, even as the nonprofit's priorities evolve.

Scalable AI tools should also offer modular features, allowing nonprofits to add or remove functionalities based on their current needs and budget. This modularity ensures that nonprofits do not have to invest in an entirely new system as they grow but can instead build upon the existing platform. Additionally, customizable dashboards and reporting tools help nonprofit staff easily access the necessary information without unnecessary complexity.

Nonprofits should also evaluate the support structure provided by the AI vendor, including training resources, customer service, and technical support. Robust support is essential for ensuring that nonprofit staff can fully utilize the AI tool's features and scale its use effectively over time.

- **Good AI:** Is highly customizable and able to scale with the nonprofit as it grows, ensuring it continues to meet the nonprofit's unique needs.
- **Bad AI:** Offers a generic solution that fails to meet the specific needs of the organization, leading to ineffective decision-making and limited growth potential.

Customized versus Generic Models

Nonprofits should be wary of AI vendors that offer one-size-fits-all models or tools. Nonprofits should select tools that allow deep customization and transparency, tailoring AI models to their specific operational needs. A tailored approach ensures that the AI aligns with the nonprofit's mission, increasing its overall effectiveness.

Customized models also allow nonprofits to input specific variables that are important to their mission, such as local community data, program metrics, or donor engagement trends. This level of customization ensures that the insights generated are not only relevant but also actionable, empowering nonprofits to make data-driven decisions that align with their goals.

Additionally, customized AI tools should enable organizations to conduct A/B testing of different approaches, helping them determine the most effective engagement strategies. This capability provides further personalization, allowing nonprofits to refine their strategies based on empirical data and make adjustments that resonate more with their target audience.

Nonprofits should also consider the availability of a sandbox environment—a safe space to experiment with AI tools before full deployment. This environment helps nonprofits understand how different configurations might impact outcomes, enabling them to better align the AI models with their organizational goals.

- **Good AI:** Allows nonprofits to use their unique data, such as community demographics and donor behaviors, to generate mission-aligned insights that improve targeted outreach and engagement.
- **Bad AI:** Uses generic data points that fail to adapt to the nonprofit's unique needs, resulting in broad recommendations that miss key engagement opportunities.

Client Involvement in Model Building

Nonprofits should be actively involved in the model-building process. This ensures that the AI system is tailored to their mission and values and that key stakeholders understand how the tool operates. Nonprofits must be able to collaborate closely with AI vendors to co-create effective and ethical models.

Collaboration during model development can also provide valuable insights that improve the overall quality of the AI solution. By involving key stakeholders, nonprofits can ensure that the AI tool is practical, relevant, and ethical, while also building internal capacity to understand and manage the technology effectively.

Client involvement also ensures that specific cultural and contextual factors are incorporated into the AI model, leading to better outcomes. For example, a local nonprofit may have unique donor behaviors that differ significantly from national averages. By collaborating with AI vendors, nonprofits can include these local insights in the model, ensuring that it provides tailored recommendations.

Nonprofits should also ask vendors about the tools and training they provide to help organizations make informed decisions about AI use. A strong focus on training empowers nonprofit staff, helping them gain confidence in using AI, interpreting results, and adjusting models to better fit their needs.

- **Good AI:** Involves nonprofit stakeholders in the model-building process, ensuring that the AI is tailored to their unique mission and incorporates local insights for practical, ethical use.
- **Bad AI:** Develops models without input from the nonprofit, leading to solutions that lack cultural and contextual relevance, reducing their overall effectiveness and alignment with the nonprofit's mission.

Does the AI Prioritize, Protect, and Promote Trust?

Trust is a foundational element of nonprofit work, especially regarding donor relations, volunteer coordination, and beneficiary services. AI tools should not only enhance operational efficiency, but also strengthen the organization's trustworthiness. AI systems should reinforce this trust by protecting sensitive data, offering transparent decision-making processes, and ensuring that all interactions with donors and stakeholders are conducted ethically.

Consider a nonprofit using AI to segment its donors for a new fundraising campaign. If the AI tool is unable to explain why certain donors are targeted while others are not, or if it inadvertently excludes key demographics, this could erode trust with the donor base. Trustworthy AI tools provide clear rationales for decision-making and ensure that all segments are treated fairly.

Likewise, imagine a nonprofit using AI to decide which health initiatives to expand. If the AI cannot explain why some programs, like mental health, are prioritized over others, it risks losing community trust. Ignoring vulnerable subgroups can also create service gaps. Trustworthy AI must provide clear insights and ensure inclusivity to effectively address all community health needs.

To promote trust, AI solutions should be designed with user feedback in mind. By incorporating stakeholder input at various stages of the AI life cycle—from data collection to model training and implementation—nonprofits can help ensure that the technology remains aligned with the needs and values of the communities they serve. This collaborative approach can lead to stronger relationships and increased trust among all stakeholders.

Nonprofits should also consider the ethical implications of using AI and how these systems can be designed to promote inclusivity and prevent harm. This includes having guidelines that outline acceptable AI usage and providing transparency reports that highlight how data is being used, who is involved in data management, and how decisions are being made.

Regular training and education programs on AI ethics for nonprofit staff are also crucial for fostering trust. Staff members should be well-versed in understanding AI outputs, questioning potential biases, and explaining AI-driven decisions to donors and other stakeholders. Transparency and education work hand-in-hand to create an environment of trust and accountability.

Red Flags: Warning Signs of Potentially Harmful AI Solutions

While AI can provide significant benefits, nonprofits should remain cautious of several red flags that may indicate an AI tool is not suitable:

- **Lack of Transparency:** AI systems that cannot explain how decisions are made or that operate as black boxes should be avoided. Nonprofits must have clear insights into how their AI tools function, particularly in critical areas like donor targeting. A lack of transparency can lead to unintended negative consequences, such as alienating key donor groups.
- **Insufficient Data Privacy Protections:** If an AI tool does not have strong data privacy protocols or has a history of data breaches, it is not suitable for nonprofits, particularly those handling sensitive information. The cost of a data breach goes beyond fines and legal fees—it can severely damage the organization's reputation and donor relationships.
- **Unrealistic Promises:** AI vendors that overpromise—claiming massive increases in donations or guaranteed outcomes—should be approached cautiously. While AI can improve efficiency and results, it is not a magic solution. Unrealistic expectations can lead to disappointment and wasted resources.
- **Limited Customization Options:** AI tools that offer little flexibility or customization are unlikely to deliver the tailored insights nonprofits need. A generic model that fails to account for the unique characteristics of the nonprofit's operations and donor base is unlikely to be effective. Customization ensures that AI tools can provide meaningful value.

The Ever-Evolving Nature of AI: Why Evaluations Must Be Reassessed Frequently

AI is a fast-moving and ever-evolving field. Technologies that are state-of-the-art today may be outdated in a matter of months. The algorithms, models, and data sets that power AI systems are constantly evolving. New ethical concerns, such as algorithmic bias or data privacy, may arise as AI systems become more sophisticated. This rapid pace of change makes it essential for nonprofits to regularly reassess the AI tools they use.

A tool that was perfectly suited to a nonprofit's needs when it was first adopted may no longer be the best fit as both the technology and the organization's needs evolve. Nonprofits should build periodic reviews of their AI systems into their operations, ensuring that they continue to meet ethical standards and operational goals. This is particularly important as new data privacy regulations come into force, new biases are uncovered, and new AI capabilities become available.

Regular reassessment also allows nonprofits to stay informed about new developments in AI. For example, recent advancements in natural language processing might offer new opportunities for engaging donors more effectively. By staying up-to-date and integrating new features, nonprofits can leverage AI tools to their fullest potential, ensuring a consistent impact.

Furthermore, continuous reassessment helps identify gaps or shortcomings in the existing AI implementation. Nonprofits should consider seeking feedback from both internal and external stakeholders during these reviews, as their insights can provide valuable perspectives on how the AI tools are performing and whether they are meeting the intended objectives.

Nonprofits should adopt a proactive approach by setting up regular training sessions to inform staff of new AI features and enhancements. Training programs should be designed to help staff stay current on AI trends, ethical considerations, and the latest tools available. This helps ensure that staff are equipped with the necessary skills to make the most of AI technologies and are aware of any potential challenges that need addressing.

In addition, nonprofits should consider forming partnerships with other organizations using AI tools. These partnerships can be valuable for sharing insights, best practices, and lessons learned about AI implementation. Collaborating with peers who face similar challenges and opportunities can lead to better-informed decisions and the development of innovative strategies for AI use.

Evaluating AI for nonprofits is not a one-time task but an ongoing process that requires careful consideration of operational and ethical factors. By utilizing frameworks like Fundraising.AI, nonprofits can assess AI tools for transparency, bias reduction, privacy, and donor-centricity. Given the rapid pace of AI development, regular reassessments are crucial to ensure that the tools remain aligned with the organization's mission and continue to serve their purpose effectively.

To fully harness the power of AI, nonprofits should also invest in educating their staff and stakeholders about AI technologies, ensuring that everyone involved is well-informed about the capabilities, limitations, and ethical considerations of the tools in use. By staying vigilant and proactive, nonprofits can leverage AI responsibly, enhancing their impact while maintaining the trust and support of their donors, volunteers, and communities.

As AI continues to evolve, nonprofits have the opportunity to shape the responsible use of these powerful tools within the sector. This means going beyond technology adoption and actively advocating for ethical AI standards, collaborating with other organizations, and contributing to the ongoing conversation about AI's role in nonprofit work. By doing so, nonprofits can help ensure that AI is used to uplift communities and support the greater good, creating a positive impact that is both measurable and meaningful.

13

Humanity or Utility? New Questions for a New World

ARTIFICIAL INTELLIGENCE (AI) is revolutionizing industries, solving complex problems at a scale and speed previously unimaginable. From analyzing vast datasets to predicting human behavior, AI has become an indispensable tool for nonprofits seeking to optimize operations and maximize impact. However, as with all powerful technologies, AI presents a profound philosophical dilemma: Do we prioritize humanity or utility?

This is not a new question. The tension between what we can do and what we should do has echoed throughout history, shaping the moral frameworks by which we operate. AI, however, brings this age-old debate into sharper focus. Nonprofit professionals, perhaps more than any other group, must confront this tension head-on. Nonprofits operate at the intersection of compassion, equity, and social good, and they are uniquely positioned to address the profound questions that AI raises about the balance between technological efficiency and human dignity.

As author Chappell (2024) explored in his article, "Humanity or Utility, or Humanity over Utility? It's Your Choice," we are facing a pivotal moment in history where the decisions we make about AI's role in society could shape the very fabric of how we relate to one another. In this chapter, we will expand on this idea, explore provocative questions, and highlight case studies that challenge nonprofit professionals to prioritize humanity over utility in their use of AI. We will also reflect on the future implications of trading privacy for convenience in an increasingly digital world. Together, we'll dive into the ethical considerations, the potential for harm, and the urgent need to ensure that AI serves human values rather than reducing people to data points in a relentless pursuit of efficiency.

Humanity over Utility: A Moral Imperative

AI presents a central dilemma for nonprofits: balancing its potential for driving utility—through automation, prediction, and optimization—with the need to preserve the human element at the heart of their missions. While AI can be a powerful tool for resource-constrained organizations, there is a risk that over-reliance on its utility could lead to a loss of focus on the deeper ethical and emotional connections that are core to nonprofit work. Nonprofits must carefully evaluate how AI aligns with their values and the impact it has on the communities they serve, ensuring that technology enhances, rather than diminishes, their human-centered mission.

AI, by its very nature, is designed to maximize utility. It is programmed to identify patterns, optimize outcomes, and increase efficiency. But nonprofits do not exist to optimize financial returns or operational processes alone. They exist to improve human lives, foster relationships, and create a more just and equitable world. If AI is used solely for utility—such as reducing staff workload, streamlining communications, or increasing donations—it risks commodifying the very individuals nonprofits are designed to serve.

Consider the question: Just because we can optimize donor engagement with AI, should we? Given advances in predictive AI in the past decades, it's relatively easy for AI to predict when a donor is most likely to give, but with this power we must continually assess the point at which a human relationship is traded for a transactional event fostered by technical automation. We must evaluate at which point the convenience of AI-driven engagement erodes the deep, authentic connections that foster genuine, long-term donor relationships. These are questions that nonprofit professionals must grapple with regularly as AI continues to grow in its ability to predict and then act upon those predictions autonomously.

Trading Privacy for Convenience: A Faustian Bargain?

In recent years, individuals have increasingly traded privacy for the convenience digital tools provide. From accepting cookies on websites to allowing apps to track their location, people often sacrifice personal information in exchange for seamless experiences. While this tradeoff has become a hallmark of the digital economy, the nonprofit sector faces unique moral challenges when navigating this terrain.

When individuals give, volunteer, or advocate for a nonprofit, they are not just offering their individual support—they are extending their trust. They trust that their personal information will be kept secure, their privacy will be respected, and their generosity will be used to advance the nonprofit's mission, not exploited for ulterior motives. As nonprofits adopt AI systems to analyze donor behavior or personalize engagement, they must be especially mindful of the ethical implications of collecting and using this data.

More than ever, nonprofit professionals must ask themselves: At what point does the quest for convenience compromise our commitment to privacy and trust? Just because AI can gather data on a donor's giving patterns, social media activity, or personal preferences, does that mean it should? There is a delicate balance between using AI to enhance engagement and crossing the line into invasive data collection that can make donors feel uneasy or exploited.

Furthermore, as AI systems evolve, there is a growing risk that data collection practices will become more opaque. Donors may not even be aware of the full extent of the data nonprofits gather and use to inform AI-driven decisions. Nonprofits must, therefore, be committed to fostering trust through transparency, ensuring that their stakeholders are appropriately informed about how their data is being used, and providing options to opt out when appropriate. This is critical for maintaining the trust that is the foundation of nonprofit work.

Provocative Questions for the Nonprofit Sector

The key to navigating AI's complexities lies in asking the right questions—questions that force us to think beyond the immediate benefits and consider the long-term implications of our actions. In this new world shaped by AI, here are a few provocative questions that nonprofit professionals should be asking:

- **How do we ensure that AI enhances, rather than diminishes, human dignity?**

    AI can be incredibly efficient in managing tasks such as donor management, service delivery, and data analysis. But if it removes the human element from these processes, what is lost in the transaction? For example, when AI is used to automate responses to donor inquiries, does it enhance the donor experience or make it feel impersonal?

- **When does AI cross the line from assisting humans to replacing them?**

    One of the most pressing fears around AI is that it will replace jobs. In the nonprofit sector, where the human touch is so vital, how do we ensure that AI supplements human labor rather than replaces it? In fields such as healthcare or social services, for example, AI might help caseworkers manage client data, but it should not replace the compassionate, human interactions that define those roles.

- **Can AI ever truly understand human needs and emotions?**

    AI can analyze past behaviors and predict future actions, but can it ever truly understand the depth of human emotions, motivations, or desires? Nonprofit professionals must critically assess the limits of AI's ability to connect with people on a meaningful, emotional level. When we rely too heavily on AI to engage with beneficiaries, are we sacrificing empathy for efficiency?

- **Are we using AI to reinforce existing power dynamics, or are we leveraging it to promote equity?**

    AI systems can inadvertently reinforce societal inequalities if they are not designed with inclusivity in mind. For example, predictive analytics tools may prioritize wealthier donors because they are seen as more valuable to the organization. How can nonprofits ensure that their AI systems do not perpetuate systemic biases?

These questions do not have easy answers, but they are essential to the responsible and beneficial use of AI in the nonprofit sector. Nonprofits must continually challenge themselves to think critically about **how** and **why** they are using AI and what impact it will have on the people they serve.

Humanity as the Guiding Principle

Technology, including AI, must be developed and implemented with the needs of marginalized communities at its core. Nonprofits have a responsibility to ensure that their adoption of technology does not reinforce systems of oppression or inequity but rather works to dismantle them. To achieve this, organizations should prioritize approaches that amplify the voices of those often excluded from decision-making processes, using technology as a tool to empower communities rather than reduce their agency or commodify their experiences.

Key questions for nonprofit professionals to consider are: Whose needs are served by this technology? Is AI being leveraged to make processes more convenient for the organization's staff or to drive meaningful and positive change for the people they serve? This distinction is critical because, without intentional oversight, AI can easily shift focus toward organizational utility rather than advancing human well-being.

It is also essential for nonprofits to include the communities they serve in decisions about how AI and other technologies are utilized. This involves holding open dialogues, listening to beneficiaries' concerns, and ensuring that AI systems are designed with equity and inclusivity as guiding principles. By centering these practices, nonprofits can use technology to enhance humanity and promote a more equitable future.

The Need for Deliberation: Prioritizing Humanity in AI

The rapid pace of AI development often pressures organizations to adopt new technologies without fully considering the long-term consequences.

In many cases, AI tools are deployed before organizations have had the opportunity to reflect on whether they align with their mission or the values they seek to uphold.

In her 2020 TED talk, Zeynep Tufekci, a sociologist and AI ethicist, warned of the dangers of rushing headlong into AI adoption without taking the time to fully understand the risks (Tufekci, 2017). She explained that AI can create a false sense of progress—optimizing systems and processes in ways that look efficient on the surface but may hide deeper, systemic harms. Her warning to slow down and be deliberate in how we integrate AI technologies resonates powerfully for nonprofit leaders.

Nonprofits must avoid the temptation to adopt AI simply because it offers convenience or promises to improve operational efficiency. Instead, they must take a more deliberative approach, ensuring that every AI decision is grounded in the organization's mission to serve human needs. This requires a shift in mindset—one that prioritizes long-term ethical considerations over short-term gains.

A key aspect of this deliberation is the recognition that human leadership must remain at the forefront of nonprofit work, even as AI systems become more integrated into daily operations. AI can assist in data analysis, predictive modeling, and even decision-making, but the final decisions about how to serve beneficiaries, engage donors, and fulfill the mission must always lie with human leaders who are guided by empathy, ethics, and a commitment to social good.

Case Study: The Dangers of Over-optimizing for Utility

One powerful case study that illustrates the dangers of over-prioritizing utility comes from the world of healthcare. In 2019, a major AI-driven healthcare system was found to be significantly biased against Black patients (Obermeyer et al., 2019).

The system was designed to optimize patient care by predicting which individuals most needed follow-up care. However, the AI's predictive model relied heavily on cost-related data, which disproportionately prioritized wealthier (and often white) patients over poorer patients, including many from Black communities.

In this case, the AI system was built to maximize utility—to increase efficiency and reduce costs. However, by focusing solely on cost as a marker for need, the AI system neglected to consider the underlying human context—the systemic barriers to healthcare access faced by minority groups. This case is a cautionary tale for nonprofits. AI systems designed to maximize efficiency or cost-effectiveness may unintentionally perpetuate the very inequities that nonprofits exist to dismantle.

In response to this incident, healthcare organizations and AI developers took steps to redesign their systems, incorporating a broader range of data points to ensure more equitable outcomes. The key lesson here is that AI is not neutral—its decisions are shaped by the data and values that inform it. Nonprofits must carefully evaluate whether the data they feed into AI systems is representative and whether their algorithms align with the mission of promoting social good.

Analogies in the Nonprofit World: The Hammer and the Hand

One of the most useful analogies to illustrate the tension between utility and humanity is the hammer analogy—a concept that I often reference in discussions about AI and its ethical implications. A hammer is a tool, and like any tool, it can be used to build or destroy. In the hands of a skilled carpenter, a hammer can create structures that provide shelter, safety, and comfort. In the wrong hands, the same hammer can cause harm and destruction.

AI, like the hammer, is a tool. It has the potential to drive social good, streamline operations, and extend the reach of nonprofit missions. But in the wrong hands or with the wrong intentions, it can also harm—by reinforcing biases, making decisions that dehumanize individuals, or optimizing for efficiency at the expense of compassion.

Nonprofits must continually ask themselves: How are we using AI? Are we building something meaningful with it, or are we inadvertently causing harm by prioritizing utility over humanity?

Human Oversight: The Need for Continuous Human Control

A crucial element of this debate is ensuring human oversight in AI systems. AI should never be allowed to operate autonomously in ways that affect people's lives without the involvement of human decision makers. Human oversight ensures that AI systems align with an organization's values and mission.

In nonprofit contexts, where decisions about donor engagement, service delivery, or resource allocation can have far-reaching consequences, maintaining a human-centered approach is critical. For instance, while AI can recommend the most effective fundraising strategies, it should be up to human fundraisers to make final decisions on how to engage donors, ensuring that relationships remain personal and genuine.

Moreover, AI systems should always be monitored for unintended outcomes. As with the case of the healthcare AI bias, nonprofits must have mechanisms in place to regularly audit their AI systems, ensuring they remain fair, transparent, and aligned with their mission.

Humanity over Utility—A Moral Imperative

As AI continues to evolve and reshape the nonprofit sector, the tension between humanity and utility will become increasingly difficult to navigate. AI can offer immense benefits, enabling nonprofits to serve more people, raise more funds, and deliver services more efficiently. But these benefits come with significant risks if they are not managed carefully.

Nonprofit professionals must continually ask themselves whether they are using AI in ways that enhance human dignity, or whether they are sacrificing humanity for the sake of efficiency. This tension—between optimizing outcomes and ensuring that AI remains a force for good—will define the future of AI in the nonprofit sector.

The choice is ours: Will we use AI to serve humanity, or will we allow it to reduce people to mere data points? As nonprofit professionals, we have a moral responsibility to ensure that humanity always comes first.

14

Overcoming Challenges in AI Adoption

As NEW TECHNOLOGIES continue to reshape industries, AI is emerging as a major force of change. For nonprofits, the prospect of integrating AI sparks a mix of excitement and fear. Will AI replace jobs? Make nonprofits irrelevant? The truth is, nonprofits that fail to adopt AI will not be able to compete against those that jump in. This shift highlights how nonprofits must adapt to stay relevant, efficient, and impactful in an ever-evolving landscape.

Integrating AI isn't without challenges—both cultural and technical. Nonprofits must tackle these obstacles to fully unlock AI's potential. In this chapter, we'll explore the cultural and technical barriers to AI adoption and provide practical recommendations to help nonprofits thrive in the AI era. We'll dive into the complexities involved, offer actionable solutions, and share examples to illustrate the journey of adopting AI effectively. Nonprofits that are proactive in their approach to AI adoption will be better positioned to achieve greater impact, improve efficiency, and foster deeper engagement with stakeholders.

Cultural Challenges: No Vision versus Too Much Vision

Nonprofits can fall into two camps when adopting AI: those with no vision and those with too much vision. The no-vision group often adopts AI out of fear of missing out, without a clear understanding of its purpose. They choose tools based on trends, often leaving them underutilized and causing frustration. This often leads to wasted time and resources as the organization struggles to see tangible benefits from the technology. Without a clear roadmap, these nonprofits are left confused, not knowing how to integrate AI effectively into their workflows.

On the other hand, those with "too much vision" have unrealistic expectations, believing AI will solve all their problems overnight. They fail to define goals or measure success, leading to ineffective use of the technology. This enthusiasm can lead to a rushed implementation, where AI is thrown at every problem without understanding its true capabilities or limitations. The result is often disappointment, as AI fails to meet expectations that were never clearly defined in the first place. These organizations may become disillusioned with AI altogether, abandoning it before they can realize its true value.

The no-vision group is like embarking on a road trip without a map—aimlessly hoping to stumble upon something great. Meanwhile, the too-much-vision group expects a fancy car alone will guarantee the perfect journey. Both end up frustrated because they lack the necessary planning and understanding to make the trip successful.

To truly benefit from AI, nonprofits need to strike a balance between ambition and practicality. They need a roadmap that defines clear goals, realistic milestones, and a thorough understanding of how AI can support their mission. Organizations should start by asking themselves why they want to use AI, what specific problems they want AI to address, and how success will be measured. By approaching AI with clarity and intention, nonprofits can align their efforts with their broader strategic goals. A well-defined vision helps ensure that AI initiatives are purposeful and that all stakeholders are on the same page, reducing the likelihood of misaligned expectations and wasted resources.

In addition, nonprofits must also recognize that AI adoption is an iterative process. Goals and milestones should be reviewed and updated regularly to ensure continued alignment with the organization's evolving needs. This means maintaining flexibility in the AI strategy and adapting to new challenges and opportunities. The key takeaway: AI adoption starts with a realistic, well-defined vision. AI isn't a magic solution, and understanding its potential and limitations is essential for success.

Jumping into the Deep End

Even nonprofits with a clear vision can falter by trying to implement AI everywhere from the outset. Like any major change, AI adoption should be phased. Start small by identifying areas where AI can add immediate value, such as donor segmentation or automating routine tasks, and scale up as success is demonstrated. This phased approach not only reduces risk, but also allows the organization to build confidence in AI gradually.

Consider the example of a nonprofit that decides to implement AI across multiple departments simultaneously. They envision transforming their donor management, volunteer coordination, and service delivery all at once. However, the lack of focused effort leads to confusion, employee burnout, and system inefficiencies. By contrast, nonprofits that start with a targeted use case can build a foundation for broader AI adoption, ensuring that each step is well-supported and delivers measurable results.

The importance of starting small cannot be overstated. Nonprofits should identify a specific, manageable project where AI can provide value quickly. This could be as straightforward as automating data entry or improving donor engagement through personalized messaging. Once the organization sees success in these smaller initiatives, they can expand AI adoption more confidently and effectively. By demonstrating quick wins, nonprofits can create momentum, build internal support, and lay the groundwork for more ambitious AI projects.

Moreover, starting small provides valuable learning experiences. AI is not just about deploying technology—it's about understanding how it integrates into existing workflows, how employees interact with it, and how it can enhance the organization's overall mission. Nonprofits that rush to adopt AI without this foundational knowledge will likely face setbacks. A phased approach helps mitigate these risks, providing opportunities for reflection, adjustment, and growth.

Another benefit of starting small is gathering feedback from employees and stakeholders. Understanding how AI impacts day-to-day activities, identifying areas for improvement, and making iterative changes based on feedback can lead to a more successful and sustainable AI implementation. Nonprofits that take a measured approach can leverage early successes to gain buy-in from leadership and staff, making the broader adoption of AI more seamless and effective.

Cassie Kozyrkov, Google's pioneering Chief Decision Scientist, asserts that the true hallmark of an AI-first organization is, paradoxically, being AI-last (2024). She explains that the most successful organizations in AI adoption don't begin with the question, "How can we use AI?" Instead, they start with the fundamental question, "What challenges do we need to solve?" By prioritizing the problem over the solution, these forward-thinking organizations create a more thoughtful and strategic approach. This mindset allows them to assess whether AI is the right tool for the job and to implement it in a way that aligns with their broader goals, ensuring a more effective and sustainable integration.

Cultural Resistance

Resistance to change is a significant barrier. Employees may fear that AI will replace their jobs or devalue their contributions. To overcome this, leadership must foster open conversations about AI, educating staff on its benefits and reassuring them that AI is here to enhance their work, not replace it. Building a culture that views AI as a collaborative tool is crucial for success.

Creating a sense of ownership among employees can help mitigate resistance. Involve staff in the planning and implementation stages of AI adoption. Offer training sessions to build skills and demonstrate how AI can make their work more impactful. Including employees in the process makes them more likely to view AI as a resource that supports their efforts rather than a threat to their roles.

Change is often met with fear, especially when it involves new technologies that are not fully understood. Nonprofits need to address this fear head-on by providing education and transparency. Leadership should communicate clearly about how AI will be used, what it means for employees' day-to-day responsibilities, and how it aligns with the organization's mission. Encouraging an open dialogue where employees can voice concerns and ask questions helps build trust and acceptance. This approach can turn skeptics into advocates, creating a more positive environment for AI adoption.

AI adoption should be framed as an opportunity for growth, both for the organization and for individual employees. Emphasizing how AI can eliminate mundane tasks and allow staff to focus on more meaningful work can help shift perceptions. Additionally, providing ongoing support and resources to learn about AI will empower employees to feel more confident using these new tools. When employees understand that AI is meant to augment their capabilities rather than replace them, they are more likely to embrace the change.

Another strategy to overcome cultural resistance is to celebrate successes and recognize contributions. Acknowledge the efforts of employees who have contributed to successful AI implementations and highlight AI's positive impact on their work. By celebrating these achievements, nonprofits can foster a culture that is more open to technological change and more willing to engage with AI as a valuable asset.

Technical Challenges

Wrong Tools for the Job

AI is not a one-size-fits-all solution. Nonprofits must choose the right tool for the right task—predictive AI for forecasting behaviors, generative AI for content creation, and so on. Understanding the specific problem to solve is key to selecting the appropriate tool. A mismatch between the tool and the problem can lead to inefficiencies and frustration, ultimately undermining confidence in AI.

For example, a nonprofit may decide to use a generative AI tool to predict which donors are likely to give again, without fully understanding the difference between predictive and generative AI. While generative AI is a great tool for creating new content and personalizing outreach to individuals, it is not built for making predictions of what will happen in the future. By not understanding which tools are designed for which purposes, an organization is not likely to see success.

Nonprofits should conduct a needs assessment before adopting any AI solution. This involves identifying specific challenges, understanding the data available, and determining the type of AI that is best suited to address those challenges. By taking a strategic approach to tool selection, nonprofits can avoid common pitfalls and ensure that AI adds real value. Additionally, organizations should stay informed about the evolving landscape of AI technologies to make informed decisions about which tools to adopt and when.

Another consideration is scalability. A tool that works well for a small pilot project may not be suitable for broader implementation across the organization. Nonprofits must consider how AI tools will scale as their needs grow. Ensuring that the chosen tools can adapt and integrate with existing systems is essential for long-term success. Scalability also means considering whether the tools can handle increased data volume, more complex workflows, and broader use cases as the organization grows.

It is also important for nonprofits to think about customization and flexibility. Off-the-shelf AI tools may need to be tailored to meet the unique needs of a nonprofit, and understanding how easily a tool can be customized can make a significant difference in its effectiveness. Organizations should consider the level of support available from vendors and whether internal expertise will be needed to adapt the tools to fit their specific requirements.

Garbage In, Garbage Out

AI relies on data, and without clean, relevant data, it won't deliver meaningful results. Nonprofits must assess their data quality and establish governance practices to ensure secure, ethical use. Data management should be ongoing, allowing for continuous improvement rather than delaying AI adoption in pursuit of perfection. Building good data habits is essential for the long-term success of any AI initiative.

Nonprofits, particularly smaller ones, often struggle with limited resources for data collection and management. However, even with modest efforts, data quality can be significantly improved. Implementing data validation practices, regularly cleaning up data, and training staff on proper data entry can help create a more reliable data foundation. A proactive approach to data management enables nonprofits to get the most out of their AI investments.

Moreover, data governance is not just about quality; it's also about ensuring data is used ethically. Nonprofits should develop policies that address privacy concerns and ensure compliance with relevant regulations. This is particularly important when dealing with donor information or sensitive beneficiary data. Transparency about how data will be used helps build trust with stakeholders, which is vital for successful AI adoption. Donors, volunteers, and beneficiaries must feel confident that their information is handled responsibly.

To maintain data quality over time, nonprofits should establish processes for regular data audits and updates. AI systems require fresh and relevant data to remain effective, and outdated or incorrect information can lead to inaccurate predictions or recommendations. By embedding data quality practices into the organization's culture, nonprofits can ensure that their AI initiatives continue to deliver value.

Nonprofits should also be aware of the risks associated with data biases. Biases in data can lead to AI systems making inaccurate or unfair predictions, which can undermine the trust of stakeholders and harm the organization's mission. By regularly reviewing data for biases and working to mitigate them, nonprofits can make their AI tools more equitable and effective. Establishing data ethics guidelines and promoting diversity in data collection practices are critical steps in minimizing the impact of bias.

Under-resourced and Overworked

Nonprofits often face budget constraints and limited staff capacity. AI can still be accessible by starting small with low-cost, off-the-shelf tools or collaborating with other nonprofits to share resources. Gradual adoption and leveraging free tools can help overcome resource limitations. By focusing on incremental improvements, nonprofits can make meaningful progress without overwhelming their teams or budgets.

One strategy for under-resourced nonprofits is to partner with technology providers or universities that offer AI tools and expertise. Many academic institutions have programs that support community organizations through student projects or grants, providing an opportunity to experiment with AI in a low-risk environment. Additionally, nonprofit alliances can create shared services that allow organizations to pool resources and benefit collectively from AI technologies.

Another approach is to seek out grants or funding opportunities specifically aimed at technology adoption. Many foundations recognize the importance of technology in driving nonprofit success and offer funding for digital transformation initiatives. Nonprofits can also look to corporate partners for in-kind donations of software or consulting services, which can help bridge the gap between ambition and available resources.

It's also important for nonprofits to manage expectations regarding AI implementation. While AI has the potential to create efficiencies, the initial stages require investment in time and learning. Nonprofits that approach AI adoption with patience and a willingness to iterate are more likely to see positive outcomes without overwhelming their staff. By setting realistic expectations and celebrating small wins, nonprofits can build momentum and demonstrate the value of AI to stakeholders.

In addition to external support, nonprofits can look internally to build capacity for AI. This could include training staff on AI basics, encouraging a culture of innovation, and fostering partnerships across departments to share knowledge and resources. Cross-functional teams can be particularly effective in integrating AI, as they bring diverse perspectives and skills that can help maximize the benefits of AI initiatives.

External Factors

Here Today, Gone Tomorrow

AI tools evolve rapidly, and nonprofits must remain flexible. Avoid overreliance on any single tool by exploring different options and adopting a forward-thinking mindset. AI is not static, and nonprofits must be ready to adapt to new developments. This adaptability will ensure that the organization can continue to leverage AI effectively, even as the technology landscape shifts.

The dynamic nature of AI also means that nonprofits need to stay informed about new trends and emerging tools. Establishing a dedicated team or point person to monitor AI developments can help nonprofits stay ahead of the curve. As we've stated previously, the worst AI you will ever use is today's. Regularly assessing the tools being used and considering alternatives, as well as keeping an eye open to new applications of AI, can prevent an organization from becoming too dependent on a solution that may quickly become outdated.

Additionally, nonprofits should cultivate relationships with AI vendors that prioritize innovation and customer support. Vendors that are committed to continuous improvement and provide regular updates to their tools can help nonprofits stay on the cutting edge of technology. Having an open line of communication with vendors also allows nonprofits to provide feedback and influence product development to better meet their needs.

Nonprofits should also consider the long-term viability of AI tools and vendors. The rapid pace of innovation means that some tools may become obsolete or that vendors may pivot away from supporting certain products. Developing a contingency plan that includes alternative tools or approaches can help nonprofits stay prepared for unexpected changes. This type of forward-thinking approach helps ensure that AI adoption is sustainable and resilient to technological shifts.

Navigating Trust in the AI Marketplace

With numerous AI companies vying for attention, nonprofits need to carefully evaluate partners. Using trusted frameworks and seeking peer recommendations can help identify reliable vendors. Asking tough questions about track record, data security, and long-term viability is essential. Vetting AI vendors thoroughly reduces the risk of investing in tools that may not meet the nonprofit's needs or that could pose ethical concerns.

In addition to evaluating vendors, nonprofits should also consider the broader ecosystem in which they operate. Joining networks like Fundraising.AI or collaborating with similar organizations can provide insights into effective AI practices and reliable tools. Leveraging these networks can also facilitate collective learning, allowing nonprofits to share successes, challenges, and strategies for overcoming common obstacles.

Trust is a crucial component of AI adoption. Nonprofits need to feel confident that the vendors they work with are aligned with their values and mission. This means evaluating not only the technical capabilities of a tool but also the ethics and sustainability of the vendor. Nonprofits should be proactive in asking questions about how data is handled, what safeguards are in place, and how the vendor plans to support the organization in the long term. By doing their due diligence, nonprofits can reduce the risk of working with vendors that may not have their best interests at heart.

Nonprofits should also consider vendor partnerships as long-term relationships rather than transactional engagements. Building a collaborative partnership with AI vendors can lead to better support, more customized solutions, and a shared commitment to achieving the nonprofit's mission. Establishing trust and a clear understanding of expectations at the outset helps lay the foundation for a successful and productive partnership.

Recommendations

- **Clear Vision and Expectations:** Define how AI fits into your strategy, set realistic goals, and understand what success looks like. A clear roadmap is crucial to avoid wasted effort and to align everyone in the organization toward common objectives. This vision should be revisited regularly to ensure alignment with evolving needs.
- **Proper Use Cases and Tools:** Identify specific challenges and select the right AI tools to address them. Matching the right tool to the right problem increases the likelihood of success and ensures efficient use of resources. Conduct a needs assessment to determine the best tool for your organization's needs.

- **Leadership and Staff Buy-in:** Encourage both leadership and staff to embrace AI, providing training and education to foster support. When staff understand AI's value and how it will enhance their roles, resistance decreases and adoption becomes more seamless. Leadership should champion AI initiatives and model a positive attitude toward technological change.
- **Phased Approach:** Start with pilot projects and gradually expand AI use, ensuring careful testing and iteration. A phased approach helps manage risk, build expertise, and create a track record of success that can be built upon. Document lessons learned from each phase to inform future AI initiatives.
- **Define Success Metrics:** Establish how to measure AI's impact, whether through increased donor retention, improved efficiency, or time saved. Clearly defined success metrics provide a way to evaluate progress and adjust as needed. Success metrics should be communicated across the organization to maintain focus and momentum.
- **Ongoing Education and Support:** Ensure staff have access to training and resources to continuously improve their understanding of AI. Providing opportunities for learning helps build a culture of innovation and keeps employees engaged with AI as it evolves.
- **Collaborative Partnerships:** Cultivate strong relationships with AI vendors and technology partners. These relationships can provide valuable support, customized solutions, and opportunities for joint innovation, ensuring that AI adoption is sustainable and aligned with the organization's mission.

AI won't replace nonprofits or their employees—it's a powerful tool that can help organizations enhance their operations and achieve greater impact. By addressing cultural, technical, and external challenges strategically, nonprofits can harness AI to stay competitive and relevant in a rapidly changing world. The journey of AI adoption is ongoing, requiring adaptability, education, and a clear vision. Nonprofits that approach AI thoughtfully and incrementally are best positioned to thrive, achieving greater efficiency, stronger engagement, and increased mission impact.

AI is not just a technology; it's a catalyst for transformation. Nonprofits that take the time to understand its capabilities, align it with their mission, and empower their teams to use it effectively will find themselves at the forefront of innovation in the sector. By embracing AI as a partner in their work, nonprofits can unlock new possibilities, drive greater impact, and continue to serve their communities in meaningful ways.

As the AI landscape continues to evolve, nonprofits must remain committed to learning, iterating, and adapting. The organizations that succeed will be those that view AI not as a one-time project, but as an ongoing journey of growth and improvement. By fostering a culture of curiosity and resilience, nonprofits can ensure that they are not only keeping pace with technological advancements but also leveraging AI to achieve their missions more effectively than ever before.

15

Building an AI Strategy for Your Nonprofit

The Role of AI in Nonprofit Strategy

Artificial intelligence (AI) has the potential to drive transformative change in the nonprofit sector, enabling organizations to streamline processes, optimize fundraising, and enhance program delivery. As nonprofits tackle increasingly complex challenges, AI can improve decision-making, reduce inefficiencies, and maximize limited resources. By leveraging AI, nonprofits can better understand donor behavior, identify trends in their programs, and enhance the effectiveness of their outreach efforts. AI also allows nonprofits to explore new possibilities for personalization, strategic planning, and operational efficiency that can ultimately lead to a larger and more sustained impact.

Crafting an AI strategy that aligns with your mission-driven objectives is key. A well-planned AI strategy provides a roadmap for achieving organizational goals while making the most of available resources. This chapter will guide you through setting realistic AI goals, assessing readiness, developing implementation roadmaps, allocating resources effectively, and ensuring sound governance. By thoughtfully planning AI integration, nonprofits can unlock opportunities for growth, innovation, and greater community impact.

AI integration is not a one-size-fits-all solution; it requires careful alignment with an organization's mission, ensuring that AI efforts truly advance the goals of the nonprofit.

Setting AI Goals

The first step in building an AI strategy is to define clear, achievable goals that align with your organization's needs and long-term vision. In resource-constrained environments, AI initiatives should target high-impact areas where they can deliver the most value. Setting strategic goals provides a sense of direction and purpose, ensuring that AI projects are aligned with your nonprofit's mission. These goals should serve as a foundation for every AI-related decision, guiding the implementation process and helping prioritize resource allocation. Effective AI goal setting also ensures that the technology serves the community rather than becoming an end in itself.

Start by assessing your existing data, processes, and technological capabilities. AI can automate routine tasks, enhance predictive analytics, and provide valuable insights—but only if goals are well-defined. Vague or overly ambitious goals can lead to frustration, wasted resources, and, ultimately, a loss of confidence in AI initiatives. Instead, focus on identifying specific problem areas where AI can make a tangible difference.

Make sure your goals are SMART (specific, measurable, achievable, relevant, time-bound). For example, a nonprofit might aim to improve donor retention by personalizing communications using AI to analyze donor history and preferences. Another goal could be to increase volunteer engagement by using AI-driven scheduling tools that match volunteers with activities based on their interests and availability. Prioritizing these goals helps nonprofits focus on the most pressing needs first, gradually building AI capabilities without overwhelming resources. Setting realistic and achievable goals creates momentum that can lead to greater organizational buy-in and ongoing support for AI initiatives. Clear goals align efforts and provide a benchmark to measure the success and impact of AI initiatives.

In addition, consider creating a phased approach to goal setting. Begin with smaller, more manageable AI projects that can demonstrate quick wins and build momentum. Once initial successes are achieved, you can expand your AI initiatives to address more complex challenges. This phased approach helps to minimize risks and ensures that your organization remains adaptable throughout the AI implementation journey. For instance, a phased approach could start with a pilot program focused on donor retention and expand to incorporate AI across all areas of donor management and outreach. By dividing the process into phases, you can build confidence among staff and stakeholders, making it easier to tackle larger and more complex AI projects in the future.

Developing Your AI Adoption Plan

Before implementing AI, assess your organization's potential for success through an AI Adoption Plan that evaluates infrastructure, data management, and staff capabilities. This framework consists of three phases: readiness, maximization, and immersion. Each of these phases plays a crucial role in ensuring that AI is successfully adopted and integrated into your nonprofit's operations. Readiness is about laying a solid foundation. Maximization involves enhancing current systems with AI. Immersion is about achieving full integration. Understanding where your organization stands in each of these phases is essential for creating a tailored approach to AI adoption.

- **Readiness:** Ensure you have quality data, appropriate tech infrastructure, and a willing staff. AI relies on large volumes of data, so it's crucial that your data is organized, accessible, and high quality. Evaluate if your technological infrastructure—servers, software, IT resources—is sufficient to support AI tools. Assess staff skills and openness to AI tools; investing in training and development may be necessary to build confidence and competence in using AI. For example, if your organization's data is scattered across multiple platforms, consolidating and cleaning the data should be a top priority before implementing any AI solution. AI tools are only as good as the data fed into them, and ensuring that you have a solid data foundation is essential for AI success.

Nonprofits should also evaluate their culture and mindset. AI adoption requires openness to change, experimentation, and learning from failures. If your organization has a risk-averse culture, leadership must work on fostering an environment that encourages innovation and accepts the learning curve that comes with adopting new technologies. Engaging staff in the vision of how AI can make their work more impactful can help overcome resistance and build enthusiasm for AI initiatives. The more inclusive and communicative the leadership is about the benefits and changes AI will bring, the more likely the staff will embrace it. Creating a culture of innovation and adaptability is crucial, and leadership must actively promote this mindset to facilitate successful AI integration.

- **Maximization:** Integrate AI into existing systems to enhance, not replace, them. This phase focuses on using AI to complement current workflows and processes, making them more efficient and effective. Automate repetitive tasks, improve data analysis, and personalize outreach—gradually incorporating AI without disrupting core activities. AI should be seen as an enabler, helping your team to work smarter and freeing up time for higher-value activities. The goal is to leverage AI to enhance productivity without overwhelming your workforce. For example, using AI to automate routine administrative tasks allows staff to focus on building relationships and engaging with stakeholders.

  By building on what already works, nonprofits can ensure that AI implementation is sustainable and aligned with their strategic priorities. Maximizing existing systems involves finding the right balance where AI supports and amplifies human expertise rather than replacing it. AI tools can be implemented to support decision-making by providing data-driven insights, ultimately helping staff make more informed choices.

- **Immersion:** Embed AI fully into your operations so that it becomes a core part of workflows. Long-term success depends on continuous learning, adaptation, and regular evaluations to ensure AI tools remain effective. In this phase, AI should be fully integrated into daily activities, and staff should feel comfortable using AI to support decision-making and program delivery. Immersion means that AI becomes a natural component of the organizational culture and workflows. When AI becomes fully integrated, it is no longer viewed as an experimental or separate initiative but as an essential part of the nonprofit's strategy.

Achieving immersion requires ongoing support and training, as well as a commitment to continuous improvement. AI technologies evolve rapidly, and staying informed about new developments is essential. Organizations should establish mechanisms for regular evaluations and updates to ensure that AI systems continue to deliver value. Nonprofits should also consider dedicating resources to keeping staff updated on the latest AI trends and practices, fostering a culture of continuous learning and adaptation. AI should not be static; it should evolve with your organization, continuously improving and adapting to better meet the needs of the people and communities you serve.

Creating an AI Roadmap

An AI roadmap provides a step-by-step plan for implementation, outlining key milestones, responsibilities, resource allocation, and timelines. A clear roadmap helps to align efforts across departments, manage expectations, and track progress toward achieving AI goals. It serves as a guide to keep all stakeholders focused and coordinated, ensuring a unified approach to AI adoption. An effective roadmap provides clarity and helps prevent miscommunication, keeping everyone on the same page throughout the implementation process.

Break down AI goals into smaller, manageable tasks, such as selecting tools, preparing data, and training staff. Assign clear roles—cross-department collaboration is crucial—and allocate resources carefully, including budgeting for both direct and indirect costs. For example, the IT department might oversee vendor security analysis and deployment, while the fundraising team works on integrating AI-driven insights into donor outreach strategies. Creating cross-functional teams ensures that different perspectives are considered, leading to better integration of AI solutions. This approach can also foster a deeper understanding of AI across the organization, as each department becomes engaged in the process.

A realistic, flexible timeline will keep your organization on track while allowing room for adjustments as needed. Regular progress reviews should be built into the roadmap to assess whether milestones are being met and if any changes are required. This iterative approach helps ensure that the AI journey remains aligned with organizational goals and that any roadblocks are addressed promptly. A roadmap with clearly defined milestones also helps communicate progress to stakeholders, keeping everyone informed and engaged. It provides an opportunity to celebrate achievements and learn from challenges, fostering an ongoing culture of improvement.

Budgeting for AI Implementation

Careful budgeting is critical for AI adoption. Consider costs like software, data storage, initial onboarding, ongoing maintenance, and continual training. AI initiatives often require significant upfront investment, but they also have the potential to deliver long-term savings through increased efficiency and effectiveness. Understanding short-term and long-term financial implications is key to successful AI integration. Nonprofits should conduct a cost-benefit analysis to determine whether the expected benefits justify the investment and identify areas where costs can be optimized.

Some philanthropic organizations provide grants for digital transformation projects, which can be a funding avenue. Consider partnering with technology providers or seeking grant opportunities supporting innovation in the nonprofit sector. Budgeting should include contingency planning, as unexpected costs may arise during implementation. Ensuring you account for long-term expenses, such as system updates and staff training, is essential for sustaining AI initiatives over time. Proactively seeking funding opportunities and building strong partnerships can alleviate some of the financial pressures associated with AI adoption. Leveraging funding opportunities and collaborations can significantly reduce the financial barriers to implementing AI.

In addition, nonprofits should consider the opportunity costs of AI implementation. Allocating resources to AI projects may mean that other initiatives need to be delayed or deprioritized. Careful planning is needed to balance the organization's overall priorities and ensure that AI initiatives are strategically aligned with mission-critical goals. This kind of strategic budgeting helps minimize disruptions and ensures that AI initiatives are integrated smoothly into the organization's broader activities. Creating a comprehensive budget that accounts for various scenarios, including possible setbacks, helps ensure the sustainability of AI projects.

Building a Multi-Disciplinary AI Team

AI adoption requires a multidisciplinary team involving IT, operations, fundraising, marketing, and program delivery. Each team member brings a unique perspective that helps ensure AI is integrated effectively across the organization. This collaborative approach ensures alignment with the overall mission and maximizes the potential impact of AI. A diverse team with members who have different skill sets can more effectively address the complexities of AI integration. Including diverse voices is also critical to ensuring that AI tools are equitable and free of biases that might otherwise be overlooked.

Senior leadership involvement is an absolute necessity to securing support and aligning AI with broader strategic goals. Leadership must champion AI initiatives, allocate resources, and foster a culture of innovation. In addition to senior leadership, consider designating AI champions within different departments to help drive adoption and address any challenges that arise. These champions can serve as role models, demonstrating the value of AI tools and encouraging others to adopt new technologies. They can also help create momentum by sharing success stories, building enthusiasm, and providing ongoing support to colleagues.

Team members should be equipped with the necessary skills to work with AI tools. Training programs, workshops, and continuous learning opportunities can help staff build confidence and expertise. The goal is to create a team that is comfortable using AI and capable of leveraging it to advance the organization's mission. Providing opportunities for staff to upskill also helps increase buy-in and mitigates fears about AI replacing jobs. When staff see AI as a tool that makes their work easier and more impactful, they are more likely to embrace it. Upskilling staff ensures that the organization can continue to innovate without needing to rely solely on external expertise.

AI Governance to Support Adoption

Effective governance ensures responsible and ethical AI use. Establish clear principles around data privacy, transparency, and minimizing bias. Nonprofits must be mindful of the ethical implications of AI, especially when dealing with sensitive data or vulnerable populations (see Chapter 11). Establishing governance structures that align with your organization's values is essential for maintaining trust and accountability. Ethical AI use is not just about compliance, but also about fostering trust among stakeholders, including donors, beneficiaries, and the public. Maintaining ethical standards is crucial for ensuring that AI benefits rather than harms the communities that nonprofits aim to serve.

Oversight structures—like ethics committees or designated staff—can monitor AI initiatives to ensure they are implemented responsibly. Regular audits should be conducted to assess the effectiveness of AI tools, identify potential biases, and make necessary adjustments. Transparency is key; stakeholders, including donors and beneficiaries, should be informed about how AI is used and how decisions are being made. Engaging stakeholders in conversations about AI can help build trust and ensure that AI use aligns with community values and expectations. Transparent communication about AI initiatives also helps dispel misunderstandings and build confidence among stakeholders.

Governance should also include a framework for addressing unintended consequences. For instance, if an AI tool inadvertently exhibits bias, there should be mechanisms in place to quickly identify and correct the issue. This proactive approach to governance helps ensure that AI is used ethically and that any issues are addressed before they can cause harm. Regular training and education on AI ethics for staff involved in AI projects can also help maintain high ethical standards. Creating a culture of accountability and responsibility is essential for ensuring that AI is used for the greater good.

Measuring Impact and Continuous Improvement

AI adoption is an ongoing process. Set key performance indicators (KPIs) to track success, establish feedback loops for continuous refinement, and learn from failures. Measuring the impact of AI initiatives helps determine whether they are delivering the expected benefits and informs future decisions. KPIs can help quantify the return on investment and justify further AI initiatives. By regularly evaluating the performance of AI tools, nonprofits can ensure that they continue to align with and support their mission.

KPIs might include metrics like increased donor retention, reduced administrative costs, or improved program outcomes. Tracking these metrics over time provides insights into the effectiveness of AI tools and helps identify areas for improvement. Feedback loops are also crucial—staff members who use AI tools should be encouraged to provide feedback on their experiences, which can be used to refine systems and processes. Engaging staff in the evaluation process ensures that AI tools are user-friendly and effective, ultimately leading to higher adoption rates. Staff feedback is invaluable for identifying practical challenges and ensuring that AI tools are tailored to meet real-world needs.

Learning from failures is an important part of the AI journey. Not every AI initiative will succeed, and that's okay. By viewing setbacks as learning opportunities, nonprofits can foster a culture of innovation and resilience. For example, if an AI-driven marketing campaign does not yield the desired results, analyze what went wrong and use those insights to improve future campaigns. Encouraging a growth mindset where experimentation is valued can lead to a more innovative and adaptive organization. A culture that views challenges as opportunities to grow will ultimately be more successful in navigating the complexities of AI.

Continuous improvement should also involve staying informed about the latest developments in AI technology. AI evolves rapidly, and new tools and techniques are continually emerging. Nonprofits should allocate resources to research and development, attend conferences, and engage with the AI community to stay abreast of the latest advancements. This commitment to learning ensures that your organization remains competitive and can leverage the most effective AI solutions available. Keeping an eye on the evolving landscape of AI allows nonprofits to continuously refine and enhance their AI strategies to remain impactful.

AI has the power to revolutionize the nonprofit sector by enhancing efficiency, decision-making, and impact. However, successful AI adoption requires careful planning, readiness assessments, and strong governance. By setting SMART goals, building a multidisciplinary team, and establishing sound governance practices, nonprofits can harness AI to further their mission and create meaningful social change. AI offers the potential to deepen engagement with stakeholders, maximize resource allocation, and enable data-driven decision-making that ultimately benefits the communities served.

The journey to AI integration is ongoing, and staying adaptable and open to learning is key. With a strategic approach and a focus on continuous improvement, AI can become an invaluable tool that helps nonprofits navigate the complex challenges they face, enhance their impact, and make a positive difference in the communities they serve. Embracing AI is not just about adopting new technology—it is about creating a culture of innovation, resilience, and learning that will drive the nonprofit sector into a more impactful future. Nonprofits that embrace AI with a clear strategy and commitment to ethical practices are poised to lead the way in addressing societal challenges and delivering sustained positive outcomes. By committing to a journey of continuous learning, ethical governance, and strategic alignment, nonprofits can fully unlock the transformative potential of AI and pave the way for lasting change.

16

Training and Capacity Building

Building Capacity for AI Adoption in Nonprofits

AI adoption is a powerful lever for increasing the impact and efficiency of nonprofit organizations. However, to make this a reality, nonprofits must invest in training, skill development, and capacity building. This chapter provides a comprehensive guide for nonprofit leaders on approaching AI training and capacity building, with practical resources, skill-building advice, and strategies for making AI adoption both accessible and effective.

Nonprofits face unique challenges, including limited budgets, a lack of technical expertise, and competing priorities. Despite these challenges, AI has the potential to transform how nonprofits operate, enabling them to amplify their impact and streamline processes. The key is to make AI adoption an organization-wide priority that includes clear planning, effective training, and sustained support. By investing in the right tools and resources, nonprofits can set themselves up for success in this evolving landscape.

AI Training Programs: Available Resources and Courses for AI Training

Nonprofits need accessible and affordable resources to upskill their staff on AI technologies. By offering practical training options, nonprofits can bridge the knowledge gap and empower their teams to make the most of AI. Here are several platforms that offer AI-related courses and programs:

- **Coursera:** Coursera offers a wide range of AI-related courses, including partnerships with renowned universities such as Stanford and industry leaders like Google. Their "AI for Everyone" course by Andrew Ng is particularly accessible for beginners. This course helps staff understand the basic concepts of AI, its capabilities, and its limitations—an ideal introduction for nonprofits. Additionally, Coursera offers advanced programs for those interested in developing deeper technical skills.
- **LinkedIn Learning:** LinkedIn Learning hosts various courses on AI and data science, focusing on practical applications in a business context. For nonprofit staff, these courses can provide insight into how to integrate AI into day-to-day operations like donor outreach, program management, and impact assessment. LinkedIn Learning's emphasis on real-world scenarios makes it a valuable resource for nonprofits looking to understand the practical implications of AI.
- **Udemy:** Udemy offers affordable AI courses ranging from beginner to advanced levels. Many of these courses are focused on practical applications, such as using AI for data analytics, automating routine tasks, or creating predictive models. Nonprofits can leverage these to understand how AI can help streamline internal processes, enhance efficiency, and free up staff time for mission-critical work. Udemy's frequent discounts make it a cost-effective option for nonprofits with limited budgets.
- **YouTube:** There are numerous free tutorials on YouTube offered by AI enthusiasts and educators. Channels such as "3Blue1Brown" provide excellent content on understanding complex concepts visually, while channels like "Tech With Tim" offer

practical coding tutorials. YouTube is a great starting point for nonprofits that want to provide flexible learning opportunities for their teams. Additionally, YouTube playlists can be curated to create tailored learning paths for different skill levels within the organization.
- **EdX:** EdX offers advanced courses from institutions like MIT and Harvard that focus on AI, machine learning, and data science. These courses are particularly suitable for staff who want to deepen their technical understanding of AI and consider developing in-house AI solutions. EdX also offers professional certificate programs that can help nonprofit staff demonstrate their expertise in AI, which can be useful for future funding and partnership opportunities.

The key to effective AI training is providing resources that match the skill level and needs of the staff while maintaining a sense of neutrality and avoiding endorsements of specific individuals. Nonprofits should also consider blending formal learning with practical, hands-on experience to reinforce knowledge and build confidence in AI usage.

Skill Development: Key Skills Needed to Leverage AI Effectively

To leverage AI effectively, nonprofit staff need to cultivate specific skills that will enable them to understand, implement, and manage AI projects. Here are the key skill areas to focus on:

- **AI Mindset:** Developing an AI mindset involves fostering a culture of curiosity and experimentation. Nonprofits should encourage their teams to be open to learning, experimenting with new technologies, and making data-driven decisions. It also involves understanding the ethical implications of using AI—such as data privacy, fairness, and avoiding bias—which is particularly important in the nonprofit sector. An AI mindset means approaching challenges with a solutions-oriented perspective and being willing to iterate and adapt based on new information.

- **Data Literacy:** Data literacy is crucial for AI adoption. Nonprofits need to train their staff on how to collect, analyze, and interpret data effectively. Data literacy will help organizations feed accurate information into AI systems, improving outcomes and ensuring AI projects are grounded in high-quality data. This includes understanding data types, cleaning data, and knowing how to evaluate the reliability of data sources. Enhanced data literacy can also help staff better communicate insights derived from AI, making it easier to gain stakeholder buy-in.
- **Problem Solving and Critical Thinking:** The ability to identify operational or strategic challenges where AI can provide a solution is key. AI is most effective when applied to solve well-defined problems, such as improving fundraising efficiency or volunteer management. Nonprofit teams should develop a problem-solving mindset that allows them to identify AI opportunities and think critically about the implications and potential solutions. This includes understanding the limitations of AI and recognizing when a non-AI solution may be more appropriate. Encouraging a culture of inquiry and exploration can help staff become more adept at pinpointing AI use cases that align with organizational goals.

Building AI Literacy: Strategies to Increase AI Fluency Among Staff

Increasing AI literacy within nonprofit organizations involves fostering a culture where staff feel comfortable exploring and experimenting with AI. Here are several strategies to increase AI fluency:

- **Internal AI Workshops:** Hosting in-house training sessions or workshops can help demystify AI for staff across different departments. These sessions should break down AI concepts into manageable parts, making them relatable and applicable to the nonprofit's mission. Encouraging staff to ask questions and discuss real-world use cases can help build confidence. Nonprofits can bring in external trainers or collaborate with partner organizations to facilitate these workshops, which can make the learning process more engaging and provide diverse perspectives.

- **Partnering with AI Experts:** Engaging with external AI experts, volunteers from tech companies, or university partnerships can provide nonprofits with opportunities for hands-on learning. Bringing in experts allows staff to learn from professionals who understand how to apply AI in various contexts. Additionally, partnering with universities or tech companies may open up opportunities for nonprofits to pilot new AI technologies, providing learning experiences and tangible benefits to the organization. Building mentorship relationships with AI professionals can also provide ongoing support beyond initial workshops.
- **AI Literacy Resources:** Creating a shared repository of AI learning resources, such as articles, videos, and guides, can encourage staff to continue learning at their own pace. This repository could include case studies on AI projects within nonprofits, success stories, and practical tools that can be adopted internally. By centralizing resources and making them easily accessible, nonprofits can foster a culture of continuous learning. Resources can be grouped by skill level, enabling staff to progress from beginner to more advanced materials as their confidence grows. Additionally, sharing success stories of how AI has positively impacted similar organizations can inspire staff and make the potential benefits of AI more tangible.

These strategies, when combined, help create an environment where learning and experimenting with AI becomes a natural part of the organization's culture. Building AI fluency helps reduce resistance to technology, promotes a data-driven culture, and equips staff with the skills they need to drive impactful change. By emphasizing practical applications and providing ongoing support, nonprofits can empower their teams to embrace AI as a tool for advancing their mission.

Financial Resources for Nonprofits to Adopt AI: Programs Offering Financial Assistance for AI Adoption

Adopting AI technology can be financially challenging for nonprofits. However, several programs and initiatives provide financial support, grants, or discounted services to nonprofits to lower the cost barrier to AI adoption:

- **Google.org Accelerator:** Generative AI: Google.org offers a program to help nonprofits integrate generative AI tools. This accelerator provides mentorship, technical training, and pro bono support for selected organizations. By utilizing Google's resources, nonprofits can explore and implement generative AI solutions for tasks like automating donor communication. Nonprofits participating in this program also gain access to a network of peer organizations and experts, providing a community of support throughout the AI adoption process.
- **OpenAI for Nonprofits:** OpenAI provides discounted access to its tools, such as GPT-4o, enabling nonprofits to leverage advanced AI models for tasks like grant writing, donor outreach, and chatbot services. These tools help nonprofits streamline communications and free up time for more strategic activities. OpenAI's resources can be particularly valuable for small nonprofits that lack the capacity for full-time technical staff but still want to benefit from AI's capabilities.
- **Microsoft AI for Good Program:** Microsoft offers cloud and AI credits to nonprofits through its AI for Good program. This includes access to Azure services and other AI tools for social impact projects. Nonprofits can use these credits to build AI-powered solutions, such as predictive analytics for better program management. Additionally, Microsoft provides training and support to help nonprofits make the most of these tools, ensuring that organizations have both the financial and technical resources needed to succeed.
- **Amazon Web Services (AWS) Nonprofit Credit Program:** AWS offers credits and free tiers to nonprofits to explore their machine learning and AI platforms. Their AWS Imagine Grant also funds technology-driven nonprofit projects, including AI. This helps nonprofits develop innovative solutions without incurring high initial costs. AWS also offers technical support and training for nonprofits, helping them overcome common barriers to cloud and AI adoption. The AWS credits and training can be instrumental

in building proof-of-concept AI projects that demonstrate value before committing to larger-scale implementation.

- **IBM and Salesforce:** IBM provides AI tools at reduced costs for social impact initiatives, while Salesforce integrates AI with its CRM platform, offering discounts to nonprofits. These solutions can be used to enhance donor engagement, improve service delivery, and gain valuable insights through AI-driven analytics. IBM's AI offerings include tools for natural language processing and predictive analytics, which can be particularly useful for program evaluation and stakeholder reporting. Salesforce's AI capabilities, such as Einstein, allow nonprofits to automate donor follow-up and personalize communication, improving engagement rates.

By leveraging these programs, nonprofits can minimize financial barriers to AI adoption and invest in building impactful, technology-driven solutions. Taking advantage of financial support helps offset the cost of AI tools and enables nonprofits to explore innovative projects that can enhance their overall mission effectiveness. Nonprofits should actively seek out these opportunities and integrate them into their strategic planning to maximize their return on AI investments.

Building Capacity for AI Adoption

To make AI adoption successful, nonprofits need to make strategic investments in training, upskilling, and culture-building. Here are the core takeaways from this chapter:

- **Invest in Training and Upskilling:** AI training should be a priority across the organization. Make use of accessible platforms such as Coursera, LinkedIn Learning, and YouTube to provide tailored learning opportunities for your staff. Develop an AI mindset that encourages curiosity, data literacy, and problem-solving. Continuous training ensures that staff at all levels remain informed about the latest AI advancements and can apply them effectively in their roles.

- **Leverage Financial Support:** Make the most of available grants and discount programs from companies like Google, Microsoft, AWS, OpenAI, IBM, and Salesforce. These resources can help minimize the financial burden of AI adoption, making the technology more accessible. Nonprofits should also consider collaborating with funders and stakeholders who are interested in supporting technology and innovation, thereby creating a broader base of financial support for AI initiatives.
- **Foster an AI-Friendly Environment:** Encourage a culture of experimentation, data-driven decision-making, and cross-functional learning. Create opportunities for staff to participate in AI workshops, partner with AI experts, and access a shared repository of resources. Building AI literacy across the organization will ensure that everyone is comfortable with the new technologies. Nonprofits should promote cross-departmental collaboration to maximize the potential benefits of AI, ensuring that insights from AI projects are shared and applied throughout the organization.

In summary, nonprofits have an opportunity to harness the power of AI to amplify their impact. With the right cultural mindset, training, and financial support, AI adoption can become both accessible and highly effective. By fostering an AI-friendly environment, investing in staff development, and seeking financial assistance, nonprofits can take full advantage of AI's transformative potential and continue to thrive in a rapidly changing world.

17

The Future of AI for Nonprofits

IN HIS 2023 BOOK, *The Coming Wave*, Mustafa Suleyman shares: "This is going to be the most productive decade in the history of our species, but we need to learn how and when to say no—collectively."

Suleyman's sentiment summarizes the crossroads at which the nonprofit sector finds itself today. The AI revolution, which promises to be the most transformative force since the Industrial Revolution, presents nonprofits with unprecedented opportunities to increase productivity, enhance their social impact, and tackle some of humanity's most pressing issues. But with this wave of technological innovation comes a host of ethical, operational, and strategic dilemmas. Nonprofits must harness AI's power to compete in an algorithmic world while remaining mindful of its potential pitfalls—knowing when and how to say no to practices that undermine trust, privacy, or the human element at the heart of their missions.

To fully grasp the pace and scale at which AI is advancing, it helps to consider the concept of exponential growth. Imagine folding a standard piece of paper in half. On the first fold, the paper's thickness doubles, but it's still imperceptibly small—just twice as thick as before. By the time you fold it 10 times, the paper is about as thick as your hand. At 20 folds, it reaches a height comparable to that of a house. By 42 folds, the paper would stretch all the way to the moon.

This simple thought experiment illustrates how exponential growth starts deceptively small but quickly accelerates to incomprehensible proportions.

AI, as an exponential technology, follows a similar trajectory. Its advancements are not linear but compound rapidly, often outpacing our ability to fully comprehend their implications. This is why nonprofits must approach AI with both urgency and caution. The opportunities to enhance mission-driven work through predictive analytics, personalized engagement, and optimized operations are immense, but so are the risks of misapplication, bias, and erosion of trust.

As we move deeper into the AI age, this chapter will explore a few emerging trends in AI, offer a long-term vision for how AI will continue to shape the nonprofit sector, and provide actionable steps for nonprofits to stay ahead in this rapidly evolving landscape. Crucially, nonprofits must strike a delicate balance between leveraging AI for innovation and ensuring that humanity, ethics, and purpose remain central to their work.

Agentive AI: A Step toward Autonomous Operations

One of the most anticipated advancements in AI is agentive AI, a technology that takes automation to the next level by not only performing tasks proactively but also creating its own AI workers to complete tasks in parallel. Think of agentive AI as a manager delegating responsibilities, except instead of assigning tasks to people, it generates additional AI systems—virtual assistants, if you will—to work simultaneously toward achieving goals. This approach allows for a level of speed and efficiency that humans or traditional reactive AI systems simply cannot match.

For example, imagine an AI system tasked with organizing a fundraising campaign. It could create multiple AI agents to handle different parts of the process: one to analyze donor data, another to craft personalized outreach emails, and yet another to identify potential new donors—all happening at the same time. The result is a system that not only works faster, but also frees up human staff to focus on higher-level strategy and relationship-building. For nonprofits, this represents an opportunity to revolutionize operations by streamlining administrative tasks, optimizing donor engagement, and automating program delivery on an unprecedented scale.

The financial incentives for adopting agentive AI are compelling. By reducing costs, improving efficiency, and enabling scalability, it promises to stretch limited nonprofit resources further than ever before. However, this power comes with significant responsibility. As Sam Altman (2024), CEO of OpenAI, has shared with conviction, "Generative AI is not a replacement for human creativity, but rather a tool that can augment and enhance it."

Agentive AI has the potential to reshape the nonprofit sector, but this power must be wielded carefully. Over-automation—particularly in areas requiring human empathy and connection—could erode the very trust that fuels charitable giving. Human-to-human interaction is central to building relationships with donors, volunteers, and beneficiaries. Removing it risks turning philanthropy into a purely transactional experience, stripping away the emotional resonance that inspires generosity.

While the allure of automating routine human tasks is strong, nonprofits must remain steadfast in their commitment to preserving the human element. Decisions about automation should prioritize amplifying human impact, not replacing it. This requires a thoughtful and deliberate approach, with leaders asking tough questions about where automation enhances operations versus where it diminishes the authenticity of their mission.

Used responsibly, agentive AI's predictive decision-making could be transformative for nonprofits tackling complex, systemic issues. For instance, in disaster relief, AI could analyze historical data and current trends to predict where crises might emerge, allowing organizations to take proactive measures. A food bank, for example, could leverage AI to predict regions where food insecurity is likely to rise based on economic, environmental, and social data, ensuring resources are allocated before the need becomes critical.

The challenge, however, lies in defining boundaries. Nonprofits must resist the temptation to hand over full control to machines, especially in areas where personal interaction and ethical judgment are paramount. The future of agentive AI in the nonprofit sector will depend on how well organizations balance efficiency with empathy, automation with accountability, and innovation with humanity.

By leveraging agentive AI as a tool to augment—not replace—human intelligence, nonprofits can unlock new levels of productivity and impact while staying true to the values that make their missions meaningful. In doing so, they ensure that the rise of autonomous systems does not come at the expense of the trust and connection that form the foundation of philanthropy.

Immersive Storytelling Through AR and VR

As AI advances, its integration with augmented reality (AR) and virtual reality (VR) offers nonprofits transformative ways to connect with donors, volunteers, and beneficiaries. These immersive technologies enable organizations to create emotionally compelling experiences that bring their missions to life, fostering a deeper sense of empathy and connection.

What are AR and VR, and how are they different?

- Augmented reality (AR) adds digital elements—such as images, animations, or interactive features—to the real world, enhancing the environment as seen through devices like smartphones, tablets, or AR glasses. It's like a digital overlay on reality, allowing users to engage with their surroundings in new ways. For instance, AR could turn a brochure into an interactive experience where tapping on an image reveals video testimonials or live data about a cause.
- Virtual reality (VR), by contrast, immerses users in a completely digital environment, replacing the real world entirely. By wearing a VR headset, users can explore an entirely new setting, whether it's a bustling wildlife sanctuary, a disaster relief zone, or even a simulated classroom.

Imagine a nonprofit focused on wildlife conservation. Using VR, they could invite potential donors to step into the shoes of a field researcher in the Amazon rainforest, witnessing the challenges of deforestation firsthand. This immersive experience would help supporters feel the urgency of the problem in a deeply personal way, bridging the gap between abstract data and lived reality.

Similarly, an educational nonprofit might deploy AR in classrooms to create interactive lessons. A history teacher could use AR to bring historical events to life by overlaying digital recreations of ancient battles or civil rights marches onto the physical classroom environment, making the past feel tangible and immediate for students.

These technologies create powerful emotional connections that can inspire people to take action, whether through donations, volunteering, or spreading awareness. By immersing supporters in the mission, nonprofits can foster a sense of shared purpose and urgency.

While AR and VR hold immense potential, they also come with ethical responsibilities. The realism of immersive experiences could blur the line between reality and fabrication, raising concerns about misrepresentation. For example, an organization might inadvertently create an overly dramatic simulation that misleads participants about the severity of an issue. Nonprofits must ensure that the stories they tell through these technologies are accurate, transparent, and aligned with their mission of integrity.

Additionally, AR and VR often rely on data to deliver personalized or location-based experiences. This raises questions about privacy and data security. Nonprofits should be clear about how they collect, use, and protect data, ensuring their practices uphold the trust of their supporters.

When used thoughtfully, AR and VR can transform storytelling, turning passive supporters into active advocates. These tools allow nonprofits to connect with their audiences on a deeper level, bridging emotional and geographical divides. By blending cutting-edge technology with human-centered narratives, nonprofits can inspire meaningful engagement while staying true to their core values.

Quantum Computing: The Next Frontier

Quantum computing is set to revolutionize the future capabilities of AI, offering exponentially faster processing power and the ability to solve problems that were previously impossible. While still in its early stages, quantum computing holds enormous potential for nonprofits, particularly in data analytics and predictive modeling. Traditional computers process data in bits, which are either 1 or 0, but quantum computers use qubits, which can exist in multiple states simultaneously. This allows quantum computers to process vast amounts of data in parallel, making them incredibly powerful for tasks like simulating complex systems or optimizing resource allocation.

For nonprofits, quantum computing could lead to breakthroughs in program impact measurement and donor segmentation. AI systems powered by quantum computing could analyze massive datasets from multiple sources—demographics, economic indicators, social media trends—to create hyper-accurate predictions about donor behavior, program outcomes, and community needs. For example, a humanitarian organization could use quantum-powered AI to predict the spread of infectious diseases based on real-time data from across the globe, enabling faster, more targeted responses.

However, as quantum computing becomes more accessible, nonprofits will also need to grapple with the environmental impact of these technologies. Quantum computers, like all AI systems, require significant energy to operate, raising concerns about their carbon footprint. Nonprofits, many of which are focused on sustainability and environmental justice, will need to ensure that they are using AI in a way that aligns with their broader mission of protecting the planet.

Deepfakes and AI-Generated Content: Navigating Ethical Complexities

The rise of AI-generated content, including deepfakes—digitally created or altered videos and images that mimic reality—presents both opportunities and ethical challenges for nonprofits. Deepfakes have gained notoriety for their potential to deceive, but they also offer innovative tools for creative storytelling. Nonprofits could, for instance, use AI-generated videos to simulate potential futures, vividly illustrating both the positive impacts of their work and the dire consequences of inaction. These simulations have the potential to inspire donors by immersing them in the nonprofit's vision for change.

However, the growing use of AI-generated content, especially when deployed through automated "bots" or synthetic images portraying themselves as humans, creates ethical tensions that nonprofits must navigate with care. While there are strong financial and operational incentives to embrace such technologies for efficiency and scalability, the nonprofit sector operates under unique constraints that demand an uncompromising commitment to trust and transparency.

Efficiency versus Human-centric Mission: The Tension

The nonprofit sector is often resource-constrained, making efficiency gains from AI-generated content highly appealing. Automated storytelling bots can rapidly produce targeted messages, create personalized donor appeals, and even simulate real-world events at a fraction of the cost of traditional methods. This efficiency, coupled with the financial pressure to demonstrate impact while keeping overhead low, creates a compelling case for deploying these tools.

Yet nonprofits must tread carefully, as they bear a heightened responsibility to maintain trust—arguably their most valuable asset. Unlike for-profit organizations, nonprofits exist to serve communities, uphold societal values, and foster meaningful human connections. The authenticity of these connections is central to their mission, and any misstep in how AI-generated content is used could erode the very trust that sustains donor relationships and public support.

As Dr. Fei-Fei Li (2018), a leading voice in AI ethics and largely recognized as the "Godmother of AI," has emphasized: "There's nothing artificial about AI. It's inspired by people, it's created by people, and—most importantly—it impacts people. It is a powerful tool we are only just beginning to understand, and that is a profound responsibility." This responsibility is particularly acute in the nonprofit sector, where there is less room for compromise on transparency, honesty, and the human-centric approach that defines charitable work.

Nonprofits must recognize the fine line between leveraging AI for storytelling and creating content that misleads or manipulates. For instance, a deepfake video showing the potential impact of a climate initiative could inspire action, but it must be clearly labeled as a simulation to avoid misleading viewers. Transparency in how AI-generated content is created and used is critical to preserving credibility.

Moreover, the human element cannot be replaced. AI may efficiently generate content, but it lacks the empathy, intuition, and moral judgment required to build genuine relationships with donors, beneficiaries, and communities. While a bot might generate a heartfelt donor appeal, it is the follow-up conversation with a human representative that solidifies trust and commitment.

To navigate this complex landscape, nonprofits should consider the following principles when using AI-generated content:

1. **Transparency:** Clearly disclose when content is AI-generated and explain its purpose. Label deepfake simulations as visualizations rather than real events.
2. **Human Oversight:** Ensure that all AI-generated content is reviewed by humans before release, with an emphasis on maintaining alignment with the organization's values and mission.
3. **Ethical Storytelling:** Avoid creating content that overstates impact or manipulates emotions in a way that could be perceived as deceptive.
4. **Stakeholder Trust:** Engage donors and beneficiaries in discussions about how AI is used, reinforcing their role as partners in the mission rather than passive recipients of automated content.

The adoption of AI-generated content offers nonprofits a way to reach broader audiences, tell richer stories, and inspire action at scale. However, this must not come at the expense of the trust and authenticity that are the cornerstones of the sector. By committing to transparency, upholding ethical standards, and ensuring that humans remain at the center of their work, nonprofits can harness the power of AI-generated content responsibly—using it not just as a tool for efficiency but as a means of strengthening their mission to serve humanity.

Long-Term Vision: How AI Will Shape the Future of the Nonprofit Sector

As we look ahead to the next 3–5 years, it is clear that AI will fundamentally reshape how nonprofits operate, engage with stakeholders, and deliver services. The speed at which AI is evolving means that organizations must be future-focused and willing to adapt to new technologies as they emerge. The nonprofit sector, which has historically lagged behind the private sector in terms of technology adoption, must accelerate its AI integration to remain competitive and impactful.

Personalization at Scale: A New Era of Donor Engagement

AI's ability to process and analyze vast amounts of data will enable nonprofits to personalize donor engagement in ways that were previously unimaginable. Instead of sending mass communications, nonprofits will be able to tailor their outreach based on each donor's preferences, values, and giving history. AI systems will analyze data from multiple sources—donation records, social media activity, event participation—to create detailed donor profiles that allow for highly personalized messaging.

For instance, an AI-powered system could predict which donors are most likely to respond to a specific fundraising campaign, enabling nonprofits to optimize their resources and target their outreach more effectively. According to a 2023 report from McKinsey & Company, organizations that use AI to personalize donor engagement see an average increase of 30% in donor retention and a 20% increase in donations. As donor expectations continue to shift toward personalized, digital-first interactions, nonprofits that fail to adopt AI-driven personalization risk falling behind.

Predictive Analytics and Proactive Decision-Making

AI's predictive capabilities will also transform how nonprofits plan and execute their programs. By analyzing historical data and external factors, AI systems can predict future trends and challenges, allowing organizations to take proactive measures. For example, a nonprofit working in education could use AI to identify students at risk of dropping out based on a combination of academic, social, and economic factors. With this information, the organization could intervene early, providing the necessary support to keep students on track.

In the realm of humanitarian aid, AI could predict where natural disasters are likely to occur, enabling organizations to pre-position resources and personnel in high-risk areas. These predictive insights could save lives, improve program outcomes, and allow nonprofits to respond more efficiently to emerging crises.

AI's Role in Reducing or Exacerbating Inequality

While AI offers tremendous potential for nonprofits, it also has the potential to exacerbate inequality if not used responsibly. As discussed in previous chapters, AI systems often reflect the biases embedded in the data they are trained on. If nonprofits are not careful, they could inadvertently use AI in ways that reinforce existing power dynamics and systemic inequalities.

In their 2023 report on AI and inequality, the World Economic Forum warned that AI could increase income inequality by creating systems that benefit the wealthy while marginalizing lower-income groups. For nonprofits, whose missions often involve advocating for marginalized communities, the challenge will be ensuring that AI is used to promote equity, rather than exacerbating existing disparities.

One way nonprofits can address this challenge is by investing in data equity—ensuring that the data used to train AI systems is representative of the diverse populations they serve. This might involve collecting more data from underserved communities, collaborating with other organizations to share data, or working with data scientists to identify and mitigate biases in their algorithms.

Preparing for the Future: Steps Nonprofits Can Take to Stay Ahead

To ensure they are prepared for the future of AI, nonprofits must take proactive steps now. Here are some key strategies for staying ahead of the curve:

1. Invest in AI Education and Skills Development

AI fluency is no longer optional for nonprofit leaders and staff. Organizations must invest in training their teams to understand how AI works, how it can be applied to their mission, and how to ensure it is used ethically. Microsoft and Google have already launched AI training programs specifically tailored to the nonprofit sector, helping organizations build internal capacity for AI-driven innovation.

Nonprofit leaders should also stay informed about the latest developments in AI by attending conferences, listening to podcasts, participating in webinars, and engaging with industry experts. The Fundraising.AI initiative, for example, brings together thought leaders from across the global nonprofit and tech communities to explore how AI can be used responsibly and beneficially to advance social good.

2. Establish an AI Ethics Committee

As AI becomes more integral to nonprofit operations, it is essential to establish an AI ethics committee that can provide oversight and ensure that the organization's use of AI aligns with its mission and values. This committee should include diverse stakeholders, including board members, staff, beneficiaries, and external AI experts. By involving a wide range of perspectives, nonprofits can better anticipate and address potential ethical concerns related to AI.

The committee should also be tasked with developing an AI governance framework that outlines ethical guidelines for using AI, including principles of fairness, transparency, accountability, and sustainability. This framework will help ensure that AI is used in ways that are consistent with the organization's commitment to social good.

3. Prioritize Sustainability and Green AI

As AI systems become more powerful, they also require more energy to operate. Nonprofits, many of which are committed to sustainability and environmental justice, must ensure that their AI usage is environmentally responsible. This includes adopting green AI practices, such as optimizing algorithms to require less computational power and using renewable energy sources to power data centers.

According to a 2024 report from the Environmental Defense Fund, AI systems account for an increasing share of global energy consumption, with large language models like GPT-3 requiring the equivalent of hundreds of megawatt-hours of electricity to train. Nonprofits must advocate for sustainable AI practices, ensuring that the benefits of AI do not come at the cost of future generations.

4. Stay Flexible and Open to Change

The future of AI is uncertain, and nonprofits must remain adaptable and open to new developments. While it's impossible to predict exactly how AI will evolve, organizations can prepare by fostering a culture of continuous learning and experimentation. Nonprofits that embrace a mindset of flexibility will be better positioned to take advantage of new opportunities as they arise, while those that resist change risk being left behind.

The Future of AI for Nonprofits

As AI continues to evolve, the nonprofit sector stands on the brink of a transformative era. AI offers immense potential to improve efficiency, enhance donor engagement, and deliver more effective programs, but it also carries significant ethical and operational challenges. Nonprofit leaders must balance the drive for innovation with a commitment to humanity, ethics, and sustainability, ensuring that AI is used to amplify social good rather than exacerbate inequality or environmental degradation.

The choices made today will shape the sector's future for years to come. By investing in AI education, establishing strong ethical frameworks, and remaining flexible in the face of change, nonprofits can harness the power of AI to create a more just, equitable, and sustainable world.

18

Parting Thoughts

As we close this book, it's abundantly clear that the journey toward implementing artificial intelligence (AI) in the nonprofit sector has only just begun. The lessons shared throughout these pages are not merely academic exercises but a rallying cry for nonprofits to embrace the future with curiosity, optimism, and a deep sense of responsibility. AI is no longer a distant technological frontier; it is here, embedded in nearly every aspect of our lives, from the way we communicate to how we make decisions and solve problems.

Nonprofits stand at a critical juncture. As organizations historically dedicated to equity, social justice, and human connection, they have a moral imperative to adopt AI, not just for operational efficiency but to amplify mission and maximize the potential of their efforts.

A Future Shaped by AI: Humanity at the Core

AI has the power to unlock unimaginable possibilities for nonprofits. It can extend your reach, deepen your relationships with donors and beneficiaries, and provide insights that would have been unattainable without it. But even as we embrace these technologies, we must remind ourselves of the key takeaway from this journey: AI is a tool, and like any tool, its value is defined by how we choose to use it.

Throughout the book, we've emphasized the dual role of AI as both a solution and a challenge. On one hand, AI has shown promise in helping nonprofits personalize donor experiences, automate time-consuming administrative tasks, and make data-driven decisions that increase their impact. On the other hand, we have warned of the ethical challenges and risks of AI, from biases embedded in algorithms to the erosion of trust if AI is misused or misunderstood.

The key to navigating this new world of AI lies in maintaining a human-centered approach. While AI can process vast amounts of data, make complex predictions, and offer strategic insights, the compassion, empathy, and ethical decision-making that define the nonprofit sector must remain at the forefront of every AI deployment.

The Imperative for Urgent Action

The AI revolution is not waiting. Every day, governments, corporations, and organizations across the globe are investing in AI systems that will reshape the way we live and work. Nonprofits, too, must act swiftly. Time is of the essence. The longer you wait to integrate AI into your organization, the greater the gap will become between those who have adapted and those who remain stuck in outdated ways of operating.

Unlike corporate entities, whose primary motive is profit, nonprofits have a responsibility to act with a sense of urgency for the sake of humanity. The communities you serve count on you to ensure that technological advancements benefit them rather than leave them behind. The opportunity to leverage AI to tackle social challenges—from poverty to inequality, healthcare access, climate action, and education—is unparalleled.

However, there are clear warning signs that if nonprofits do not take the lead in ethical AI deployment, they risk being sidelined in the wider societal discourse. Governments and corporations will not be able to solve all the world's problems on their own. Nonprofits, as the guardians of social equity, have a unique role to play in filling the gaps that for-profit entities and state institutions cannot address. Your work often exists precisely because governments and businesses fall short in serving the most marginalized populations.

The question is: Will your organization be ready?

The Moral Imperative of AI Governance

As AI becomes a critical part of nonprofit operations, there is an even greater need to govern these technologies responsibly. AI can bring extraordinary benefits, but it also introduces risks that could undermine trust—the very currency that nonprofits rely on to function. The EU AI Act, the White House AI Bill of Rights, and the NIST AI Risk Management Framework are some of the global efforts aimed at creating a regulatory structure to govern AI use responsibly. Nonprofits must play a leading role in this movement.

You cannot wait for governments to regulate AI or for corporations to offer a roadmap. Nonprofits must take the lead by adopting AI governance frameworks that ensure fairness, accountability, transparency, and human oversight. By being proactive, you can demonstrate to your donors, volunteers, and communities that AI can be a force for good—when used responsibly.

Nonprofit organizations must also invest in training and educating their teams to become fluent in AI ethics. This is not just the responsibility of IT departments or data scientists—leaders, program directors, fundraisers, and everyone within the organization should understand how AI impacts the work they do and the lives of the people they serve.

The Practical Steps to an AI-Driven Future

As we look forward to the future, it's clear that nonprofits have an immense opportunity to shape the role AI will play in driving social good. But to do so effectively, organizations need to take practical steps to integrate AI into their operations in ways that are scalable, responsible, and aligned with their missions.

1. **Start by Conducting an AI Readiness Audit:**
   Assess where your organization currently stands in terms of data infrastructure, leadership buy-in, and AI fluency. Identify the gaps to be filled to successfully integrate AI into your operations. Determine what kinds of AI tools will have the most immediate impact and where you can begin to automate low-value tasks to free up staff for mission-critical work.

2. **Invest in AI Education Across Your Organization:**

    AI is not just a technology issue; it is a strategic issue. Nonprofits that fail to educate their leadership and staff about AI will struggle to implement it effectively. Leverage online courses, workshops, and AI certification programs to build your team's AI literacy. By creating a workforce that is knowledgeable and comfortable with AI, your organization will be better equipped to navigate the complexities of this new technological landscape.

3. **Adopt a Governance Framework:**

    Your AI initiatives must be grounded in ethical principles. Whether you choose to adopt the Fundraising.AI Framework, the NIST AI Risk Management Framework, or a custom governance structure, the key is to ensure that all AI-driven decisions are transparent, accountable, and in alignment with your organization's mission. The Singapore Model AI Governance Framework and the OECD AI Principles also provide globally recognized structures that nonprofits can adapt to their needs.

4. **Begin with Low-Risk AI Applications:**

    Don't feel the need to dive into complex AI implementations from the start. Focus first on automating routine administrative tasks, improving donor segmentation through predictive analytics, or utilizing AI-driven tools to enhance digital marketing efforts. Start small, but think strategically about how to scale your AI efforts as your organization becomes more confident in using these tools.

5. **Commit to Continuous Learning and Adaptation:**

    AI is not static. It is an evolving technology, and the most successful organizations will be those that stay curious and adaptable. Make sure your team has access to ongoing education, whether through AI conferences, webinars, or partnerships with tech companies. As the technology changes, so must your approach. The nonprofit sector cannot afford to fall behind in a world that is increasingly shaped by data and algorithms.

A Call to Action: Leading the Future of Social Good

Nonprofits have always been at the forefront of addressing society's most pressing challenges. From advocating for social justice to providing disaster relief, nonprofits are the heart of social change. AI is not a tool that will replace these efforts, but rather, it will empower nonprofits to scale them, reach more people, and solve more complex problems with precision and insight.

But this is not just a technological journey; it's a moral and ethical one. The decisions you make today about how to use AI will shape not only the future of your organization, but also the future of the communities you serve. The beneficial future of AI in the nonprofit sector is not inevitable—it is in your hands.

As the world continues to embrace AI, the nonprofit sector must be prepared to fill the gaps that corporations and governments cannot. The stakes are high, and the consequences of inaction are even higher. Nonprofits must lead by example, demonstrating how AI can be used responsibly and equitably to serve the greater good.

You are not alone in this journey. The tools, frameworks, and ideas presented in this book are the building blocks for a future where AI serves humanity, not the other way around. The time to act is now. The AI revolution is here, and it is up to you to ensure that your organization is ready to harness its power for good.

As you close this book, take with you a sense of urgency, responsibility, and optimism. The future of AI in the nonprofit sector is bright, but it is only bright because of the people—like you—who are willing to step up, take action, and lead the way.

The Future Is in Your Hands

For the love of this and future generations, it is our moral imperative to harness the power of AI in ways that amplify and elevate the missions of nonprofits, all of which are driven by the vision of a more just, equitable, and beautiful world. Nonprofits exist to bridge the gaps left by others, serving those who might otherwise be forgotten. With AI, we now have the tools to continue that service and scale it to levels once thought impossible. AI gives us the opportunity to deepen our connections with communities, optimize the resources we have, and create transformative impacts where they are needed most.

But this is not just a matter of convenience or efficiency—this is a profound responsibility. Philanthropy, grounded in the very meaning of "the love of humankind," compels us to use every tool at our disposal to uplift those in need. To stand still in the face of such potential would be to shirk our responsibility to those we are called to serve. AI offers us a chance to realize the missions we hold so dear, to envision and build a world where compassion, justice, and opportunity reach everyone, especially the most vulnerable.

As the guardians of humanity's conscience, nonprofits must take the lead in ensuring AI serves all people, not just the privileged few. We must guide the evolution of AI to ensure that it is used ethically, responsibly, and always in the service of love and justice. This is our moment to act, to embrace these tools not out of fear or obligation but out of the deep conviction that technology must be used to amplify the good we seek to create in the world.

The future depends on the actions we take today. For the love of humankind, let us boldly embrace AI as a tool for compassion, equity, and transformative change. Together, we can shape a future where AI helps create a world that is more efficient and more just, kind, and beautiful for all. This is our moral imperative. Let's step forward with courage and conviction, and let's ensure that the technology of tomorrow lifts humanity to new heights, fulfilling the missions that have always driven the nonprofit sector. The future is in our hands. Let's shape it together.

Appendix: Resources for AI Governance Templates and Frameworks

As AI becomes more embedded in nonprofit operations, establishing strong governance frameworks is critical to ensure responsible and ethical AI use. The following global frameworks and resources offer practical guidance for nonprofits implementing AI systems aligned with their missions.

Fundraising.AI Framework

Designed specifically for nonprofits, Fundraising.AI is a free global community representing 10,000 nonprofit professionals from 140+ countries which provides guidelines for the responsible and beneficial use of AI in fundraising. It emphasizes transparency, fairness, and human oversight to build trust with donors and ensure that AI systems are aligned with the mission of advancing social good.

- **Link:** Fundraising.AI

EU AI Act

The EU AI Act is the most comprehensive legislative framework for global AI governance. It imposes strict rules on high-risk AI systems, particularly those used in healthcare, law enforcement, and education. Nonprofits operating in Europe or working with European partners must ensure compliance with this act to protect fundamental rights.

- **Key Elements:** Risk categorization, transparency, fairness, and human oversight.
- **Link:** EU AI Act Overview

Singapore Model AI Governance Framework

This framework offers guidelines for building trustworthy AI systems that prioritize accountability and transparency. Nonprofits can use this framework to develop governance structures that mitigate AI risks while promoting innovation and inclusion.

- **Key Elements:** Transparency, human accountability, managing AI risks.
- **Link:** Singapore Model AI Governance Framework

NIST AI Risk Management Framework

The National Institute of Standards and Technology (NIST) developed this framework to help organizations manage AI risks, including bias, fairness, and accountability. It provides a comprehensive roadmap for identifying and mitigating risks associated with AI deployment.

- **Key Elements:** Risk management, fairness, transparency, accountability.
- **Link:** NIST AI Risk Management Framework

AI Ethics Guidelines by the European High-Level Expert Group on AI

This framework offers guidelines for designing AI systems that are trustworthy and aligned with ethical values. Nonprofits can use this resource to ensure their AI systems are designed with fairness, accountability, and transparency.

- **Key Elements:** Trustworthiness, fairness, transparency, accountability.
- **Link:** AI Ethics Guidelines

Glossary

THIS GLOSSARY IS designed to provide clear and concise definitions of key terms related to artificial intelligence (AI). Some of these terms appear in the book; others do not, but you are likely to come across them as you learn more about using AI. This glossary is to ensure you have a solid understanding of the language and terminology used throughout the book. Please note that the field of AI is rapidly evolving, and new terms and advancements are continually emerging. The definitions provided here are current as of the publication date of this edition, and we encourage readers to stay informed about the latest developments in this dynamic and fast-paced area.

A

AGI (Artificial General Intelligence) Artificial general intelligence (AGI) is a field of theoretical AI research that attempts to create software with human-like intelligence and the ability to self-teach. The aim is for the software to perform tasks it is not necessarily trained or developed for.

Agentive AI Agentive AI refers to systems that can undertake actions with a certain degree of autonomy, aiming to fulfill tasks as an agent for its user. These systems leverage advanced algorithms and machine learning techniques to understand and predict user needs, make decisions, and take actions that typically require human intervention.

AI (Artificial Intelligence) AI stands for artificial intelligence, which is the simulation of human intelligence processes by machines or computer systems. AI can mimic human capabilities such as communication, learning, and decision-making.

AI Ethics AI ethics refers to the issues that AI stakeholders, such as engineers and government officials, must consider to ensure the technology is developed and used responsibly. This means adopting and implementing systems that support a safe, secure, unbiased, and environmentally friendly approach to artificial intelligence.

Algorithm An algorithm is a sequence of rules given to an AI machine to perform a task or solve a problem. Common algorithms include classification, regression, and clustering.

Algorithmic Transparency Algorithmic transparency refers to the clarity and openness about how AI algorithms operate, make decisions, and process data, enabling stakeholders to understand and trust the system.

Application Programming Interface (API) An API, or application programming interface, is a set of protocols that determine how two software applications will interact with each other. APIs tend to be written in programming languages such as C++ or JavaScript.

Augmented Reality (AR) Augmented reality (AR) is an enhanced, interactive version of a real-world environment achieved through digital visual elements, sounds, and other sensory stimuli via holographic technology.

Automated Decision-Making Automated decision-making involves AI systems making decisions based on data inputs without human intervention. These systems are often used to improve efficiency and consistency in processes.

B

Beneficial AI Beneficial AI (BAI) goes beyond meeting ethical standards and short-term outcomes; it proactively ensures that AI technologies actively and consistently contribute to long-term human welfare, societal well-being, and environmental sustainability. BAI entails a proactive approach to minimizing adverse impacts and mitigating long-term negative implications. This means preventing harm and fostering positive outcomes across various domains, including economic equity, social justice, and ecological health. By prioritizing these objectives in the design and evaluation of AI systems, beneficial AI aims to create a future where technology enhances the quality of life for all individuals and communities, driving progress in a way that is inclusive, responsible, and sustainable.

Bias in AI   Bias in AI refers to the presence of systematic and unfair discrimination in AI systems' predictions or decisions, often resulting from biased training data or algorithms.

Bias Mitigation   Bias mitigation involves techniques and strategies used to reduce or eliminate bias in AI systems to ensure fair and equitable outcomes.

Big Data   Big data refers to the large data sets that can be studied to reveal patterns and trends to support business decisions. It's called *big* data because organizations can now gather massive amounts of complex data using data collection tools and systems. Big data can be collected very quickly and stored in a variety of formats.

Blockchain   A blockchain is a distributed database or ledger shared among a computer network's nodes. They are best known for their crucial role in cryptocurrency systems for maintaining a secure and decentralized record of transactions, but they are not limited to cryptocurrency uses.

C

Chatbot   A chatbot is a software application that is designed to imitate human conversation through text or voice commands.

Cognitive Computing   Cognitive computing is essentially the same as AI. It's a computerized model that focuses on mimicking human thought processes such as pattern recognition and learning. Marketing teams sometimes use this term to eliminate the sci-fi mystique of AI.

Computer Vision   Computer vision is an interdisciplinary field of science and technology that focuses on how computers can gain understanding from images and videos. For AI engineers, computer vision allows them to automate activities that the human visual system typically performs.

Cryptocurrency Cryptocurrency is a digital currency, otherwise known as digital tokens in which transactions are verified and records maintained by a decentralized system using cryptography, rather than by a centralized authority. Cryptocurrency allows people to make payments directly to each other through an online system. Cryptocurrencies have no legislated or intrinsic value; they are simply worth what people are willing to pay for them in the market.

D

Data Mining Data mining is the process of sorting through large data sets to identify patterns that can improve models or solve problems.

Data Science Data science is an interdisciplinary field of technology that uses algorithms and processes to gather and analyze large amounts of data to uncover patterns and insights that inform business decisions.

Deepfake A deepfake is a synthetic media created using AI and deep learning techniques to produce realistic but fake videos, images, or audio that mimic real people and events.

Deep Learning Deep learning is a function of AI that imitates the human brain by learning from how it structures and processes information to make decisions. Instead of relying on an algorithm that can only perform one specific task, this subset of machine learning can learn from unstructured data without supervision.

Digital Twin A digital twin is a virtual model of a process, product, or service that allows analysis of data and monitoring of systems to prevent problems before they occur, develop new opportunities, and plan for the future.

E

Emergent Behavior Emergent behavior, also called emergence, is when an AI system shows unpredictable or unintended capabilities.

Ethical AI Ethical AI involves designing, developing, and deploying AI systems in ways that uphold moral principles, including fairness, justice, and respect for human rights and dignity. Ethical AI serves as the underpinning framework of Responsible AI (RAI).

Explainable AI (XAI)   Explainable AI refers to AI systems designed to provide clear, understandable explanations of their decision-making processes. This is crucial for transparency and trust, particularly in high-stakes applications.

F

Fairness in AI   Fairness in AI is the principle that AI systems should operate without favoritism or prejudice toward any individual or group, ensuring equal treatment and opportunity.

Federated Learning   Federated learning is a machine learning technique that allows algorithms to be trained across multiple decentralized devices or servers holding local data samples, without exchanging them.

G

Generative AI   Generative AI is a technology that uses AI to create content, including text, video, code, and images. A generative AI system is trained using large amounts of data, so that it can find patterns for generating new content.

Guardrails   Guardrails refer to restrictions and rules placed on AI systems to make sure that they handle data appropriately and don't generate unethical content.

H

Hallucination   Hallucination refers to an incorrect response from an AI system, or false information in an output that is presented as factual information.

Hyperparameter   A hyperparameter is a parameter, or value, that affects the way an AI model learns. It is usually set manually outside of the model.

I

Image Recognition   Image recognition is the process of identifying an object, person, place, or text in an image or video.

Internet of Things (IoT)   The Internet of Things refers to the interconnection of everyday objects via the internet, enabling them to send and receive data. This network of connected devices can be used to collect and analyze data for various applications.

L

Large Language Model (LLM) A large language model (LLM) is an AI model that has been trained on large amounts of text so that it can understand language and generate human-like text.

Limited Memory Limited memory is a type of AI system that receives knowledge from real-time events and stores it in the database to make better predictions.

M

Machine Learning Machine learning is a subset of AI that incorporates aspects of computer science, mathematics, and coding. Machine learning focuses on developing algorithms and models that help machines learn from data and predict trends and behaviors, without human assistance.

Multimodal AI Multimodal artificial intelligence (AI) is a machine learning (ML) model that can process and analyze multiple data inputs, such as images, text, audio, video, and code, to produce more accurate outputs.

N

Natural Language Processing (NLP) Natural language processing (NLP) is a type of AI that enables computers to understand spoken and written human language. NLP enables features like text and speech recognition on devices.

Natural Language Understanding (NLU) Natural language understanding (NLU) is a subfield of AI that focuses on enabling machines to comprehend and interpret human language in a meaningful way.

Neural Network A neural network is a deep learning technique designed to resemble the human brain's structure. Neural networks require large data sets to perform calculations and create outputs, which enables features like speech and vision recognition.

Non-Fungible Token (NFT) A non-fungible token (NFT) is a unique digital identifier that certifies ownership and authenticity of a specific asset. NFTs are recorded on a blockchain, a public ledger that records transactions, and are often encoded with the same software as cryptocurrencies.

O

Overfitting Overfitting occurs in machine learning training when the algorithm can only work on specific examples within the training data. A typical functioning AI model should be able to generalize patterns in the data to tackle new tasks.

P

Pattern Recognition Pattern recognition is the method of using computer algorithms to analyze, detect, and label regularities in data. This informs how the data gets classified into different categories.

Predictive Analytics Predictive analytics is a type of analytics that uses technology to predict what will happen in a specific time frame based on historical data and patterns.

Prescriptive Analytics Prescriptive analytics is a type of analytics that uses technology to analyze data for factors such as possible situations and scenarios, past and present performance, and other resources to help organizations make better strategic decisions.

Prompt A prompt is an input that a user feeds to an AI system in order to get a desired result or output.

Q

Quantum Computing Quantum computing is the process of using quantum-mechanical phenomena such as entanglement and superposition to perform calculations. Quantum machine learning uses these algorithms on quantum computers to expedite work because it performs much faster than a classic machine learning program and computer.

R

Retrieval-Augmented Generation (RAG) Retrieval-augmented generation (RAG) is an AI technique that combines information retrieval with text generation, enhancing the generation process by incorporating relevant external data.

Reinforcement Learning Reinforcement learning is a type of machine learning in which an algorithm learns by interacting with its environment and then is either rewarded or penalized based on its actions.

Responsible AI Responsible AI (RAI) refers to the development and use of artificial intelligence technologies in a manner that is ethical, transparent, accountable, and respects privacy and human rights.

Robotic Process Automation (RPA) Robotic process automation is the use of software robots to automate highly repetitive, routine tasks typically performed by a human interacting with digital systems.

S

Sentiment Analysis Also known as opinion mining, sentiment analysis is the process of using AI to analyze the tone and opinion of a given text.

Singularity Singularity in AI refers to a future point in time when artificial intelligence (AI) becomes more intelligent than humans, surpassing human capabilities and reaching a new level of intelligence.

Structured Data Structured data is data that is defined and searchable. This includes data like phone numbers, dates, and product SKUs.

Supervised Learning Supervised learning is a type of machine learning in which classified output data is used to train the machine and produce the correct algorithms. It is much more common than unsupervised learning.

Synthetic Data Synthetic data is artificially generated information that mimics real-world data. It is often used to train AI models when real data is scarce, or privacy concerns prevent the use of actual data.

Synthetic Media Synthetic media refers to digital content that is artificially generated or altered using AI techniques, such as deepfakes or AI-generated art.

T

Token A token is a basic unit of text that an LLM uses to understand and generate language. A token may be an entire word or parts of a word.

Training Data Training data is the information or examples given to an AI system to enable it to learn, find patterns, and create new content.

Transfer Learning Transfer learning is a machine learning system that takes existing, previously learned data and applies it to new tasks and activities.

Turing Test The Turing test was created by computer scientist Alan Turing to evaluate a machine's ability to exhibit intelligence equal to humans, especially in language and behavior. When facilitating the test, a human evaluator judges conversations between a human and a machine. If the evaluator cannot distinguish between responses, then the machine passes the Turing test.

U

Unstructured Data Unstructured data is data that is undefined and difficult to search. This includes audio, photo, and video content. Most of the data in the world is unstructured.

Unsupervised Learning Unsupervised learning is a type of machine learning in which an algorithm is trained with unclassified and unlabeled data to act without supervision.

V

Virtual Reality (VR) Virtual reality (VR) is a computer-generated environment with scenes and objects that appear to be real, making the user feel they are immersed in their surroundings.

Voice Recognition Voice recognition, also called speech recognition, is a method of human-computer interaction in which computers listen and interpret human dictation (speech) and produce written or spoken outputs. Examples include Apple's Siri and Amazon's Alexa, devices that enable hands-free requests and tasks.

References

Altman, S. (2024) 10 Generative AI Quotes by OpenAI CEO Sam Altman. Skim AI. Available at: https://skimai.com/10-generative-ai-quotes-by-openai-ceo-sam-altman/ (Accessed: 17 December 2024).

Amazon Web Services (AWS) (2023). *Accelerating AI Skills in the United States*. Available at: https://assets.aboutamazon.com/e1/a0/17842ee148e8af9d55d10d75a213/aws-accelerating-ai-skills-us-en.pdf (Accessed: 22 Jan. 2025).

American Civil Liberties Union (n.d.) At Liberty Podcast. Available at: https://www.aclu.org/podcast (Accessed: 17 December 2024).

AmeriCorps (2023) Volunteering and Civic Life in America. Available at: https://americorps.gov (Accessed: 17 June 2024).

Bank for International Settlements (2023) *Artificial Intelligence, Income Inequality, and Global Economic Impact*. Available at: https://www.bis.org/publ/work1135.htm (Accessed: 17 December 2024).

Bernholz, L. (2021) How We Give Now: A Philanthropic Guide for the Rest of Us. The MIT Press.

Bruce, A. & Ward, A.S. (2022) The Tech That Comes Next: How Changemakers, Philanthropists, and Technologists Can Build an Equitable World. Wiley.

Carvana (2023, May 9) Carvana creates 1.3M+ unique AI-generated videos for customers. Available at: https://blog.carvana.com/2023/05/carvana-creates-1-3m-unique-ai-generated-videos-for-customers/ (Accessed: 17 December 2024).

Center for Effective Philanthropy (2024) *State of nonprofits 2024: What funders need to know*. https://cep.org/report-backpacks/state-of-nonprofits-2024-what-funders-need-to-know/

Chappell, N. (2023) Beyond AI Ethics: The Nonprofit Sector's Imperative for Responsible AI. LinkedIn. Available at: https://www.linkedin.com/pulse/beyond-ai-ethics-nonprofit-sectors-imperative-nathan-chappell/ (Accessed: 17 December 2024).

Chappell, N. (2024a) The Curiosity Code: Unlocking Your Superpower in the AI Age. LinkedIn. Available at: https://www.linkedin.com/pulse/curiosity-code-unlocking-your-superpower-ai-age-nathan-ozgkc/ (Accessed: 17 December 2024).

Chappell, N. (2024b) Humanity or Utility, or Humanity Over Utility? It's Your Choice. LinkedIn. Available at: https://www.linkedin.com/pulse/humanity-utility-over-its-your-choice-nathan-chappell-mba-mna-cfre-qsdpc/ (Accessed: 17 December 2024).

Chappell, N., Crimmins, B. & Ashley, M. (2022) *The Generosity Crisis: The Case for Radical Connection to Solve Humanity's Greatest Challenges*. Wiley.

Cooper, G. & Bailey, M. (2020a) *Responsive Fundraising: The Donor-Centric Framework Helping Today's Leading Nonprofits Grow Giving*. Liberalis.

Cooper, G. & Bailey, M. (2020b) *Responsive Fundraising: The Donor-Centric Framework Helping Today's Leading Nonprofits Grow Giving*. Wiley Publishing.

Das, M. and Vryn, M.F. (2024) *AI Equity Project Report 2024: Advancing Justice, Inspiring Action*. Available at: https://charityvillage.com/ai-equity-project-a-research-initiative-focused-on-ai-and-data-equity-in-the-nonprofit-sector/ (Accessed: 17 December 2024).

Dietz, N. and Grimm, R. T., Jr. (2023) The state of volunteer engagement: Insights from nonprofit leaders and funders. Do Good Institute, University of Maryland School of Public Policy. Available at: https://spp.umd.edu/research-impact/publications/state-volunteer-engagement-insights-nonprofit-leaders-and-funders (Accessed: 17 December 2024).

DonorSearch (2024) Children's Healthcare of Atlanta: Major gift fundraising success story. Available at: https://www.donorsearch.net/resources/childrens-healthcare-of-atlanta/ (Accessed: 17 December 2024).

DrivenData (n.d.) *Box-plots for education*. https://www.drivendata.org/competitions/4/box-plots-for-education/

Drucker, P.F. (1985) *Innovation and Entrepreneurship*. New York: Harper & Row.

Environmental Defense Fund (2024) Green AI: The Environmental Impact of Artificial Intelligence. Retrieved from https://edf.org/ai-environment-report

Erickson, M. (2022) Fundraising Strategy: A Guide to Increase Donations and Fundraising Effectiveness. Wiley Publishing.

Feeding America (2022) Annual Report. Available at: https://www.feedingamerica.org/about-us/financials/annual-report (Accessed: 17 June 2024).

Fundraising.AI (2025) Embracing AI and Mindfulness for Impactful Change with Randima Fernando. Available at: https://www.youtube.com/watch?v=eVFAaCt5w7U (Accessed: 21 January 2025).

Furniture Bank (2022) Furniture Bank's AI-driven holiday campaign. Available at: https://www.furniturebank.org/postcard/ (Accessed: 17 December 2024).

Furniture Bank (2023) Imagining furniture poverty: How AI helps tell our story. Available at: https://www.furniturebank.org/imagining-furniture-poverty/ (Accessed: 17 December 2024).

Gartner (2021) Gartner Hype Cycle. Gartner. Available at: https://www.gartner.com/en/research/methodologies/gartner-hype-cycle (Accessed: 17 December 2024).

GivingTuesday (2021) Millions of people come together to celebrate generosity, share kindness, and drive record-breaking giving on GivingTuesday 2021. Available at: https://www.givingtuesday.org/blog/millions-of-people-come-together-to-celebrate-generosity-share-kindness-and-drive-record-breaking-giving-on-givingtuesday-2021/ (Accessed: 17 December 2024).

Google (2021, March 24) How AI helps volunteers support LGBTQ youth in crisis. The Keyword. Available at: https://blog.google/outreach-initiatives/google-org/trevor-project-crisis-contact-simulator/ (Accessed: 17 December 2024).

Google for Nonprofits (2024, March 28) 3 insights from nonprofits about generative AI. Google. Available at: https://blog.google/outreach-initiatives/google-org/google-for-nonprofits-generative-ai-report/ (Accessed: 17 December 2024).

Hemple, J. (2018) Fei-Fei Li's quest to make AI better for humanity. Wired. Available at: https://www.wired.com/story/fei-fei-li-artificial-intelligence-humanity/ (Accessed: 17 June 2024).

HubSpot (2023, April 18) The state of generative AI & how it will revolutionize marketing. Available at: https://blog.hubspot.com/marketing/state-of-generative-ai (Accessed: 17 December 2024).

International Monetary Fund (2023) World Economic Outlook: Uneven Growth, Fragile Recovery. IMF.

Johnson, S. (1998a) *Who Moved My Cheese?: An Amazing Way to Deal with Change in Your Work and in Your Life*. G.P. Putnam's Sons.

Johnson, S. (1998b) *Who Moved My Cheese? An Amazing Way to Deal with Change in Your Work and in Your Life.* Putnam Adult.

JPMorgan Chase & Co. (2017) JPMorgan software does in seconds what took lawyers 360,000 hours. The Independent. Available at: https://www.independent.co.uk/news/business/news/jp-morgan-software-lawyers-coin-contract-intelligence-parsing-financial-deals-seconds-legal-working-hours-360000-a7603256.html (Accessed: 17 December 2024).

Kanter, B. & Fine, A. (2022) The Smart Nonprofit: Staying Human-Centered in an Automated World. Wiley.

Kozyrkov, C. (2024) *Cassie Kozyrkov LinkedIn profile.* [LinkedIn]. Accessed 19 November 2024. Available from: https://www.linkedin.com/in/kozyrkov

Lipstein, G. (2017) *A brief introduction to machine learning and 3 ways to make it useful.* DrivenData. https://drivendata.co/blog/intro-to-machine-learning-social-impact/

McCarthy, J., Minsky, M.L., Rochester, N., & Shannon, C.E. (1955) A proposal for the Dartmouth Summer Research Project on Artificial Intelligence. Available at: https://archive.computerhistory.org/resources/access/text/2023/06/102720392-05-01-acc.pdf (Accessed: 22 January 2025).

McKinsey & Company (2023) The Impact of AI on Nonprofit Fundraising. Retrieved from https://mckinsey.com/nonprofit-ai-impact-report.

Microsoft (2024) *2024 Work Trend Index Annual Report.* Available at: https://news.microsoft.com/annual-wti-2024/ (Accessed 21 January 2025).

Ng, A. (2017). AI is the New Electricity. Stanford Graduate School of Business. Available at: https://www.gsb.stanford.edu/insights/andrew-ng-why-ai-new-electricity (Accessed: 17 December 2024).

Nonprofit Finance Fund (2021) State of the Nonprofit Sector Survey. Available at: https://nff.org/survey (Accessed: 17 June 2024).

NTEN (2018) Nonprofit Technology Staffing and Investments Report. NTEN.

Obermeyer, Z., Powers, B., Vogeli, C., & Mullainathan, S. (2019). Dissecting racial bias in an algorithm used to manage the health of populations. Nature. Available at: https://www.nature.com/articles/d41586-019-03228-6 (Accessed: 22 January 2025).

Pichai, S. (2017) Google Is Now an AI-First Company. Google Blog. Available at: https://blog.google/technology/ai/google-ai-first/ (Accessed: 17 December 2024).

Pluralsight (2024) AI Skills Report 2024: The State of AI and What It Means for the Workforce. Available at: https://www.pluralsight.com/resource-center/ai-skills-report-2024 (Accessed 17 December 2024).

Princeton University, Georgia Tech, Allen Institute for AI, and IIT Delhi (2023) Generative engine optimization: Revolutionizing content creation for AI search engines. Available at: https://www.searchenginejournal.com/researchers-show-how-to-rank-in-ai-search/504260/ (Accessed: 17 December 2024).

Salesforce (2023) Nonprofit Trends Report. Available at: https://salesforce.org (Accessed: 17 December 2024).

Suleyman, M. (2023) The Coming Wave: Technology, Power, and the Twenty-First Century's Greatest Dilemma. New York: Crown Publishing Group.

The Giving Block (2022) Annual Report 2021: The State of Crypto Philanthropy. Available at: https://thegivingblock.com/annual-report/ar21/ (Accessed: 22 October 2024).

The Nonprofiteers (2024) Social Impact Staff Retention 2024. Available at: https://www.thenonprofiteers.com/sisr (Accessed: 17 June 2024).

Tufekci, Z. (2017) We're building a dystopia just to make people click on ads. TED. Available at: https://www.ted.com/talks/zeynep_tufekci_we_re_building_a_dystopia_just_to_make_people_click_on_ads (Accessed: 17 December 2024).

U.S. Bureau of Labor Statistics (2023) *For-profit, nonprofit, and government sector jobs in 2022.* https://www.bls.gov/spotlight/2023/for-profit-nonprofit-and-government-sector-jobs-in-2022/

Virtuous (2024) Future trends in AI fundraising: What nonprofits need to know. Available at: https://virtuous.org/blog/ai-fundraising/ (Accessed: 17 December 2024).

World Economic Forum (2020) The Future of Jobs Report 2020. Geneva: World Economic Forum. Available at: https://www.weforum.org/reports/the-future-of-jobs-report-2020 (Accessed: 17 December 2024).

World Economic Forum (2023) AI and Inequality: The Growing Divide. WEF Global Risks Report.

World Economic Forum (2025). *Future of Jobs Report 2025: Jobs of the Future and the Skills You Need to Get Them.* Available at: https://www.weforum.org/stories/2025/01/future-of-jobs-report-2025-jobs-of-the-future-and-the-skills-you-need-to-get-them/ (Accessed: 22 Jan. 2025).

About the Authors

Nathan Chappell, MBA, MNA, CFRE, is a thought leader, public speaker, author, and artificial intelligence (AI) inventor, recognized globally as an expert at the intersection of AI and generosity. He has led AI initiatives for many of the largest nonprofits in the U.S. and co-founded Fundraising. AI, an advocacy organization promoting responsible and beneficial AI in the nonprofit sector. His award-winning 2022 book, *The Generosity Crisis*, was hailed as "required reading" by NonProfit Pro. With over 20 years of nonprofit leadership experience, Nathan is a sought-after keynote speaker, advisor, and contributor featured in *The Chronicle of Philanthropy*, NPR, Forbes, and more. His podcast, *Fundraising. AI*, ranks among the top nonprofit technology podcasts worldwide.

Scott Rosenkrans, MS, is a leading voice on the use of artificial intelligence for nonprofits. As an experienced data science leader, he has built and implemented custom machine learning models that drive fundraising success for nonprofits of all sizes. A founding member of Fundraising. AI and cohost of the *Fundraising. AI* podcast, Scott advocates for responsible and beneficial AI, helping organizations navigate the opportunities and challenges of AI adoption. With over 15 years of nonprofit experience, he is known for bridging complex AI solutions with the human-centered missions of nonprofits. His work has earned recognition from Fast Company's World Changing Ideas Awards, highlighting his commitment to innovation and impact.

Index

A/B testing, 93, 97, 152
Accelerator, 194
Accountability. *See also* Fairness;
        Transparency
    in agentive AI, 199
    in beneficial AI, 137
    and bias, 140
    education for, 154
    establishment of, 130
    ethical focus on, 18, 186, 207
    in Fundraising.AI initiative, 133, 143
    global standards for, 142, 216–217
    governance over, 186, 211
    in responsible AI, 127
    trust through, 128, 136, 147
    via XAI, 21
ACLU (American Civil
        Liberties Union), 6
ADA (Americans with
        Disabilities Act), 141
Adaptation:
    and continuous learning,
        138, 143, 212
    in growth mindset, 42
    and innovation, 8
    need for, 135
    perpetual, 122
    to trends, 23
Advocacy, 10, 64, 89, 90, 92–93, 98
Agentive AI, 23, 198–200, 219–220
AGI (Artificial General Intelligence), 219
AI adoption, 167–178
    analysis of, 49–50
    in beneficial AI framework, 136–138
    caution in, 30
    change management in,
        112, 113–114
    collaboration in, 40
    cultural challenges of, 168–169
    cultural resistance to, 170–171
    ethical concerns of, 37, 42–43, 128
    experimentation in, 116
    expertise for, 45
    external factors of, 174–175
    failing fast concept in, 121
    in fundraising, 76–77
    Fundraising.AI initiative for, 133
    goals for, 114
    governance for, 186
    implications of, 126
    innovation in, 54

AI adoption (*Continued*)
  leadership roles in, 119
  limitations of, xii–xiv
  in marketing, 97–98
  multidisciplinary teams in, 115, 116, 120
  in nonprofit operations, 100, 143
  philanthropic R&D for, 121
  planning for, 181–183
  and privacy, 131
  proactive, 48
  in program development, 64–66, 176–178
  risks of, 164
  scaling of, 114–115
  stakeholder input for, 134, 138
  technical challenges to, 171–174
  transparency in, ix
  and trust, 127, 175–176
  and volunteer management, 87–88
  volunteers' roles in, 120
AI Bill of Rights, 216
AI Equity Project Report, 127, 130
AI-first organizations, 47–55
  AI-last organizations vs., 170
  becoming, xiii, 54–55
  front-of-house and back-of-house functions in, 53–54
  future of, 123
  impact of, 47–48
  importance of, 50–51
  innovation in, 54
  meaning of, 51
  private sector vs., 49–50
  proactive strategies in, 48–49
  as problem solvers, 51–52
  scalability of, 52
  Trevor Noah's views on, 53
AI fluency, 33–46. *See also* AI literacy
  in AI-first organizations, 47
  in AI readiness audits, 211
  current state of, 36–38
  definition of, 35
  future of, 43–45
  importance of, 35–36, 46, 206

  increasing, 192–193
  key components of, 38–41
  and nonprofit workforce changes, 41–43
AI-generated content, 22, 42, 96, 202–204, 226
AI hype cycle, 29–30
AI implementation:
  assessment of, 156
  budgeting for, 184
  case studies of, 30
  expert help with, 65
  goals for, 181
  human oversight for, 132
  low-risk, 212
  managing expectations of, 174
  objectives for, 26
  in open cultures, 88, 171
  partnerships for, 156
  strategies for, 114–116
  sustainable, 170, 182
AI insights, 81, 105–106. *See also* Data-driven insights
AI-last organizations, 170. *See also* AI-first organizations
AI literacy, 33, 36, 48, 192–193, 196, 212. *See also* AI fluency
AI mindset, 191, 195
AI readiness audits, 211. *See also* Audits
AI selection, 145
AI teams, 115, 117, 118, 120, 185. *See also* Multidisciplinary teams
AIDA (Artificial Intelligence and Data Act), 142
Algorithms:
  for AI training, 25
  bias in, 5, 11, 129, 165, 206, 210, 221
  black box, 72
  for budgeting, 109
  in data science, 222
  in deep learning, 38, 222
  definition of, 220
  evolution of, 155
  in federated learning, 223

in generative AI, 19
in generosity crisis, 8
in green AI, 207
in machine learning, 10, 16, 19, 52, 86, 220, 224
overfitting of, 225
overoptimization of, 165
for pattern recognition, 225
in quantum computing, 225
in reinforcement learning, 226
for social media, 6
for stakeholder engagement, 9
in supervised learning, 226
in unsupervised learning, 227
Algorithmic transparency, 220
Altman, Sam, 199
Amazon Web Services (AWS), 35, 194, 196
American Civil Liberties Union (ACLU), 6
Americans with Disabilities Act (ADA), 141
AmeriCorps, 7
Application Programming Interface (API), 220
AR (Augmented reality), 200–201, 220
Artificial General Intelligence (AGI), 219
Artificial Intelligence and Data Act (AIDA), 142
Ashley, M., 7
Asia, 142
Audience engagement, 92
Audits:
  for AI readiness, 211
  for bias, 146, 149
  continuous, 129, 131, 132
  for evaluation, 132
  for failure assessment, xiii
  as governance, 186
  need for, 166
  for privacy, 140, 146
  for quality control, 173
Augmented intelligence, 27–29
Augmented reality (AR), 200–201, 220

Autonomous systems, 20, 23, 26, 161, 166, 198, 200
AWS (Amazon Web Services), 35, 194, 196
AWS Nonprofit Credit Program, 194–195

Back-of-house functions, 52–54
Bailey, Mckenna, 5, 29, 37
Bank for International Settlements, 50
Beneficial AI (BAI), ix, 18, 136–138, 143, 149, 220–221
Bernholz, Lucy, 43
Beyond AI Ethics: The Nonprofit Sector's Imperative for Responsible AI (Chappell), 127
Bias:
  algorithmic, 11, 129, 155–156, 165, 206, 210, 221
  assessment of, 100
  auditing for, 129, 131, 132
  in data, 25, 198, 206
  and data enrichment, 69
  definition of, 221
  diverse teams against, 185
  and ethics, 37, 40, 140, 142, 191, 220
  evaluation of, 149
  and fairness, 140
  and fluency, 44
  governance of, 43, 186
  in healthcare, 164, 166
  mitigation of, 149, 173
  NIST framework for, 216
  questioning, 163
  recognizing, 36
  reducing, 137
  reinforcement of, 165
  and transparency, 72
  trust vs., 127–128, 154
Bias mitigation, 221
Big data, 5, 8, 16, 221
Bing Chat, 96
Black-box algorithms, 72
Blockchain, 5, 221, 225

Bots, 202, 203. *See also* Chatbots
Bruce, Afua, 126, 128–130

California Consumer Privacy Act (CCPA), 129, 141
Carvana, 90
Center for Humane Technology, 2
Change management, 43, 113–114
Chappell, Nathan, 7, 33, 53, 67, 96, 114, 127, 159
Charity Navigator, 51
Chatbots, 20, 49, 92, 97, 141, 194, 221. *See also* Bots
ChatGPT, 89, 96
Children's Healthcare of Atlanta, 76
Children's Online Privacy Protection Act (COPPA), 141
Client involvement, 152–153
Cognitive computing, 221
COIN (contract Intelligence) software, 49
The Coming Wave (Suleyman), 197
Communication. *See also* Marketing
 automation of, 20, 25–26, 28
 with donors, 48, 71, 97, 115, 194
 as front-of-house operation, 53
 future of, 98
 in HR, 106
 impact reporting for, 62
 improving, 61
 internal, 103
 mass, 205
 personalized, 80, 102, 117, 148, 180, 195
 with prospects, 71
 as soft skill, 107
 with stakeholders, 104
 streamlining, 160, 194
 transparent, 116, 186
 with vendors, 175
 with volunteers, 82–85, 88
Compassion. *See also* Equity
 AI as tool for, 27, 31
 and decision making, 29
 efficiency vs., 165
 fatigue from, 7
 human oversight for, 26, 32, 37, 129, 162, 210
 in nonprofits, 2, 159
 and philanthropy, 214
 and technology, 12
Computer vision, 20, 221–222
Content creation, 20, 90–91, 96, 98, 102, 106, 171
Content optimization, 90
Contextual understanding, 29
Continuous learning:
 and adaptation, 135–136, 138, 143, 212
 in AI fluency, 40
 for AI literacy, 193
 commitment to, 66
 embracing, 38
 for fundraising, 69–70
 in immersion, 182–183
 importance of, 31, 42, 188
 investing in, 143
 mindset of, 112, 115
 opportunities for, 185
Contract intelligence (COIN) software, 49
Convenience, 33–34, 160–161, 163–164, 214
Cooper, Gabe, 5, 29, 37
COPPA (Children's Online Privacy Protection Act), 141
Coursera, 39, 190, 195
COVID-19 pandemic, 3–4
Crimmins, B., 7
CRM systems, 8, 126, 150, 195
Cross-functional learning, 196
Cross-functional teams, 41, 43, 117, 120, 174, 183
Cryptocurrency, 4, 221, 222, 225
Cultural resistance, 37, 170–171
Currency of trust, 38, 41, 127–130
Customization:
 for advocacy, 92
 in collaborative partnerships, 176, 177

Index 241

for data retention policies, 146
for donor engagement, 76, 148
generic models vs., 152
of government frameworks, 212
for HR, 103, 106
of invitations, 95
of learning materials, 60
for media production, 96–97
need for, 155
off-the-shelf products vs., 172
of personalized emails, 22
of reports, 62
and scalability, 151
of support, 60
for video creation, 90
for volunteer outreach, 83

Dartmouth College, 14, 15
Das, Meena, 128–130
Data analytics, 5, 39, 190, 201
Data-driven insights, 182. *See also*
    AI Insights
  application of, 26
  and collaboration, 58
  in crisis situations, 51
  decision making through, 10, 29, 45
  for fundraising, 117
  value of, 105
Data enrichment, 68–69, 77
Data literacy, 192, 195
Data mining, 222
Data privacy. *See also* Security
  addressing, 110
  and AI fluency, 44
  and bias, 11, 136
  convenience vs., 160–161
  of donors, 134
  ethical concerns about, 5, 37, 130–131, 155, 191
  and federated learning, 22
  governance over, 43, 173, 186
  importance of, 128, 197
  insufficient, 155
  leadership for, 119

regulations for, 141, 156
  in responsible AI, 226
  security for, 137, 139–140, 146, 201
  standards for, 118
  and synthetic data, 226
  and trust, 131
Data quality, 25, 65–66, 149, 172–173
Data retention, 146
Data science, 25, 42, 109, 190, 191, 222
Decision-making:
  accountability in, 130
  adaptability in, 136
  AI-enhanced, 43, 45, 51, 179, 188
  automated, 220
  bias in, 149
  communication about, 133, 136
  data-analysis for, 80, 119
  data-driven, 15, 31, 196
  ethical, 27, 29, 210
  in explainable AI, 223
  in HR, 100, 105
  human, 27, 132, 134, 137, 163–164
  immersion for, 182
  improving, 1
  ineffective, 151
  maximization for, 182
  predictive, 199
  under pressure, 86
  proactive, 205
  real-time, 21, 150
  transparent, 153–154
Deep learning, 16, 19, 38, 59, 222, 224. *See also* Machine learning
Deepfakes, 220–222
Deliberation, 163–164
Digital divide, xii, 5, 11
Digital literacy, 42
Digital Technology and Democratic Theory (Bernholz), 43
Digital twins, 222
Donation cycles, 73
Donation reminders, 75
Donor-centricity, 5, 148, 156

Donor engagement:
  agentive AI for, 199
  AI for, 18, 23
  consequences of, 166
  customized, 148, 152
  enhancing, 24, 34, 130
  example of, 75
  as front-of-house operation, 53
  fundraisers' role in, 117
  future of, 98, 208
  generative AI for, 74
  human element in, 138–139, 160
  impact reporting for, 10
  long-term, 148
  and mission impact, 116
  NLP for, 20
  personalized, 55, 120, 169, 205
  in precision philanthropy, 67
  predicting, 19
  traditional approaches to, 112
Donor welcome journeys, 75
DrivenData, 109
Drucker, Peter, 8

Edge AI, 22
Education Resource Strategies (ERS), 109
EdX, 191
Efficiency:
  in AI adoption, 188, 189
  and AI fluency, 43, 47
  automation for, 103, 108
  compassion vs., 26, 165
  in corporations vs. nonprofits, 127
  early adoption of, 48–49
  empathy vs., 162
  expertise for, 45
  in fundraising, 67, 75
  human-centric vision vs., 203
  and human values, 159–160, 166–167
  impact reporting for, 62
  investments in, 37
  machine learning for, 71, 122
  marketing for, 97
  metrics for, 177
  operational (*see* Operational efficiency)
  opportunities for, 112
  problem solving for, 21, 192
  of programs, 17, 61
  savings through, 184
  streamlining for, 101
  and technological interaction, 14
  and volunteers, 79, 84, 85–86, 119
Einstein, 195
Emergent behavior, 222
Emotional intelligence, 28, 42
Empathy:
  -driven interactions, 24, 28
  in agentive AI, 199
  in AI-first organizations, 51, 55
  as AI goal, 27
  in augmented intelligence, 27–28
  efficiency vs., 162
  and emotional intelligence, 28
  and ethics, 129, 164
  example of, 86, 97
  human element in, 204, 210
  as soft skill, 42
  and storytelling, 200
  training for, 107
Environmental Defense Fund, 207
Equity. *See also* Compassion; Inclusivity; Inequality
  AI as tool for, 214
  in beneficial AI, 221
  data protection for, 127, 128, 206
  and ethics, 26, 128
  and fairness, 137
  nonprofits' responsibility for, 159, 163, 206, 209
  oversight for, 25
  power dynamics vs., 162
  protecting, 15
  trust through, 130, 143
  value of, 31
Erickson, Mallory, 5
ERS (Education Resource Strategies), 109

Ethics, 125–143
   and adaptability, 135–136
   beneficial framework for, 136–138
   and bias, 140
   currency of trust in, 127–130
   and data privacy, 139–140
   definition of, 220
   governance in, 133–135
   guidelines for, 217
   human oversight over, 138–139
   legal considerations vs., 139
   legislating, 141–142
   standards for, 126–127, 142–143
   from user's perspective, 130–132
Ethical AI:
   as core purpose, 128
   definition of, 222 (*See also* Responsible AI (RAI))
   global standards for, 142
   governance for, 186
   importance of, 44, 210
   myths about, 26
   standards for, 157
EU AI Act, 142, 211, 216
European High-Level Expert Group on AI, 217
European Union (EU), 141–142
Evaluation, 145–157
   in AI adoption plans, 181–182
   and AI fluency, 35, 38
   of AI tools, 87, 100, 114, 187
   audits for, 132
   of bias, 149
   of client involvement, 152–153
   criteria for, 145–146
   of customized and generic models, 152
   of data, 165
   and data security, 146
   donor-centric, 148
   and forecasting, 101
   of harmful solutions, 154–155
   for HR, 108
   by humans, 139
   for impact reporting, 62
   importance of, 182–183
   metrics for, 76–77, 136, 177
   for multidisciplinary teams, 116
   of partnerships, 175–176
   for program development, 58
   real-time, 51
   reassessing, 155–157
   rescoring in, 150
   scalability in, 151
   and transparency, 147
   and trust, 153–154
   of value alignment, 160
   and verification, 41
Event promotion, 94–95
Explainability, 129, 132, 147. *See also* Transparency
Explainable AI (XAI), 21, 147, 223

Failing fast concept, 121
Fairness. *See also* Accountability; Transparency
   auditing for, 129
   in beneficial AI, 125
   and bias, 140, 149, 191
   ethical focus on, 18, 207, 222
   ethical standards for, 126–127
   in Fundraising.AI framework, 133, 215
   global standards for, 142, 216–217
   governance over, 211
   importance of, 130
   in NIST framework, 216
   trust through, 132, 135, 137
Fairness in AI, 223
Farmlink Project, 3
Federated learning, 22, 223
Feedback:
   from employees, 108, 170, 187
   from end users, 131, 154
   gathering, 65
   personalized, 60, 108
   post-event, 95
   for product development, 175
   public, 20
   sentiment analysis of, 62

Feedback (*Continued*)
  from stakeholders, 156, 170
  use of, 100
  from volunteers, 81, 82, 84, 88, 120
Feedback loops, 65, 88, 132, 186–187
Feeding America, 3, 54
Fernando, Randima, 2
Fine, Allison, 35
Front-of-house functions, 52–54
Fundraising.AI framework:
  accountability in, 133, 143
  for AI adoption, 133
  fairness in, 133, 215
  human oversight in, 215
  transparency in, 143, 146, 156, 212, 215
Furniture Bank, 96–97

Gartner, 29
General Data Protection Regulation (GDPR), 129, 141, 146
Generative AI (GenAI), 19, 223
Generative engine optimization (GEO), 90, 95–96, 98
Generative pre-trained transformer (GPT), 16
The Generosity Crisis (Chappell et. al.), 7, 67
The Giving Block, 4
Giving days, 5
GivingTuesday, 5
Global standards for regulation, 141
Google.org, 86, 194
Governance:
  for AI adoption, 186
  of AI roadmaps, 211
  of bias, 43
  committees for, 207
  ethical, 139, 186
  moral imperative of, 211
  in regulatory landscape, 141
  responsible, 136–138
  role of nonprofit sector in, 133–135
GPT-3, 207
GPT-4o, 194

Graphics processing units (GPUs), 16–17
Green AI, 207
Guardrails, 223

Habitat for Humanity, 3
Hallucination, 223
Harvard University, 191
HIPAA, 146
HubSpot, 90
Human-in-the-loop approach, 134, 137
Human oversight:
  and accountability, 137
  in beneficial AI, 137
  in decision making, 26, 138–139
  in Fundraising.AI Framework, 215
  global standards for, 142
  governance for, 134, 211
  guidelines for, 129
  importance of, 25, 132, 204
  need for, 166
Human resources (HR), 99–110
  AI empowerment of, 105
  AI insights in, 105–106
  automation in, 103–104, 107–108
  content creation for, 102–103
  ERS example of, 109
  future forecasting in, 101–102
  importance of AI in, 99–100
  overview of, 109–110
  recommendations for, 100
  streamlining, 101
  tailored content in, 106–107
Humanity:
  AI in service of, 31, 44, 55, 143, 204, 213
  AI's impact on, xii, 197
  challenges for, 113
  conscience of, 214
  future of, 209–210
  as guiding principle, 163
  innovation with, 8, 199, 208
  prioritizing, 29, 159, 163–164
  tranformational shifts in, 13–15
  utility vs., 160, 166

Hurricane Katrina, 2–3
Hype cycle, 29–30
Hyperparameters, 223

IBM, 195–196
Image recognition, 223
Immersion, 181, 182–183
Impact-driven goals, 114
Impact measurement, 57–66
    AI for, 61
    automation for, 63–64
    data-driven, 62–63
    enhancing, 10
    goal of, 114
    quantum computing for, 202
Impact reporting, 5, 62, 75
Inclusivity, 107, 129, 134, 138, 154, 162–163, 182, 221. *See also* Equity; Inequality
Income inequality, 50
Inequality, 50, 55, 133–134, 137, 206, 208, 210. *See also* Equity; Inclusivity
Innovation, 1–12
    in agentive AI, 199
    and AI fluency, 36, 41, 44, 46
    catalysts for, 3–6
    collaboration for, 156
    and creativity, 39
    culture of, 54, 114, 174, 185, 187–188
    in data processing, 17
    education for, 177, 206
    embracing of, 11–12
    enablement of, 50
    as force for good, 135, 138
    funding for, 184, 194–196
    for generosity crisis, 7–8
    in HR, 99
    imperative for, 8
    lack of, 68
    laws concerning, 139
    leadership for, 119, 208
    in multimedia creation, 22
    need for, 1–2, 47, 67, 112
    in nonprofit sector, 2–3, 14, 110
    in open-source communities, 17
    in philanthropic research, 121–122
    pitfalls of, 197–198
    planning for, 179, 182
    prioritizing, 175
    in problem solving, 28
    purposeful, 130
    sparking, 40
    in storytelling, 202
    synergy in, 28, 128
    trends in, 9–11
    for volunteer engagement, 68
    wealth vs., 53
International Medical Corps, 52
Internet of Things (IoT), 21, 223–224

Johnson, Spencer, 34, 111
JP Morgan, 49

Kanter, Beth, 35
Key performance indicators (KPIs), 186–187
Kozyrkov, Cassie, 170

Large language models (LLMs), 16, 19, 26, 38, 224, 226
Li, Fei-Fei, 203
Limited memory, 224
LinkedIn Learning, 39, 190, 195

McCarthy, John, 14
Machine learning. *See also* Deep learning
    in agentive AI, 220
    in AI hype cycle, 30
    algorithms for, 10, 16, 19, 52, 86, 220, 224
    AWS for, 194
    for connection measurement, 72
    for content creation, 90
    data for, 68, 69
    and deep learning, 222
    definition of, 19, 224
    EdX for, 191

Machine learning (*Continued*)
  efficient nature of, 71, 122
  and federated learning, 223
  in multimodal AI, 224
  overfitting in, 225
  for personalization, 22
  for predictive AI, 10, 19, 59, 70, 93
  in quantum computing, 225
  regression models vs., 70
  and reinforcement learning, 226
  rise of, 16
  for social initiatives, 22
  and supervised learning, 226
  and transfer learning, 227
  and unsupervised learning, 227
  for volunteer training, 86
McKinsey & Company, 205
Marketing, 89–98. *See also* Communication
  advocacy in, 92–93
  AI fluency in, 40
  and AI teams, 185
  content creation in, 90
  for events, 94–95
  failures of, 187
  by FurnitureBank, 96–97
  future of, 98
  generative AI for, 20
  low-risk, 212
  recommendations for, 97–98
  SEO vs. GEO in, 95–96
  social media in, 91–92
  visual campaigns for, 74
Massachusetts Institute of Technology (MIT), 191
Maximinization:
  in AI adoption plans, 181–182
  of AI benefits, 64, 76–77
  by cross-functional teams, 174, 196
  of donor engagement, 94, 150
  of efficiency, 79
  of impact, 8, 47, 48, 81, 97, 100, 117, 159
  of limited resources, 179
  via machine learning, 122
  of mission-driven initiatives, 112
  by multidisciplinary teams, 120, 185
  of productivity, 35
  of resource allocation, 188
  of ROI, 195
  via social media, 91–92
  for sustainability, xiii
  of utility, 160, 165
  of volunteers, 80, 84, 88
MealConnect program, 54
Mentorship, 94, 193, 194
Microsoft, 53, 196, 206
Microsoft AI for Good Program, 194
Microsoft Global Nonprofit Leaders Summit, 53
Minsk, Marvin, 14
Mission delivery, 18–19, 21, 47, 51–53, 55, 115–116
Mission impact, 8, 34, 43, 116, 177
Model Building, 152–153
Monitoring:
  of AI performance, 87
  of campaign performance, 95
  continuous, 25, 60, 98, 100, 129
  of occupancy and turnover rates, 62
  of progress, 61, 76
  for reporting, 62
Morgan Stanley, 49
Multidisciplinary teams, 116–117, 120, 123, 185, 188. *See also* AI teams
Multimedia creation, 21
Multimodal AI, 224

National Institute of Standards and Technology (NIST), 216
Natural language processing (NLP), 20, 22, 30, 86, 90, 96, 224
Natural Language Understanding (NLU), 224
Netflix, 60
Neural networks, 16, 19, 224
Ng, Andrew, 13, 190
NGOs, xi, 2

NIST AI Risk Management Framework, 211, 212, 216
Noah, Trevor, 53
Non-Fungible Tokens (NFTs), 224–225. *See also* Tokens
Nonprofit Finance Fund, 4
NTEN, 36

Occupancy rates, 62
OECD AI Principles, 212
OpenAI, 194, 196, 199
Operational efficiency:
   in AI-first organizations, 51
   back-of-house functions for, 53
   and ethical standards, 145
   human elements of, 110, 164
   and purpose alignment, 137
   and social impact, 134
   streamlining for, 61
   for sustained impact, 179
   and transparency, 5
   trends towards, 21
   and trust, 153
   for volunteers, 84
Opinion mining, 226. *See also* Sentiment analysis
Opt-out mechanisms, 132
Over-optimization, 164–165
Overfitting, 225

Pain points, 87, 114
Pattern recognition, 28, 221, 225
PerplexityAI, 96
Personalized engagement, xiv, 198. *See also* Donor engagement
Personalized outreach, 20, 21, 73, 77, 198
Philanthropy:
   and agentive AI, 199–200
   changing patterns in, 4
   and creation of AI, 14–15, 31
   diversity of, ix, 11
   ethics of, 130
   funding from, 184
   generational attitudes towards, 7

   obligation of, 214
   precision, 67–69
   predicting, 81
   research for, 121–122
   strategies for, xiii
   transparency in, 72
   trust in, 38
Pichai, Sundar, 48
Poverty porn, 97
Precision philanthropy, 67–69
Predictive analytics. *See also* Sentiment analysis
   benefits of, 10
   cloud-based, 25
   definition of, 225
   for donations, 68, 162, 212
   example of, 122
   goals for, 180
   laws concerning, 141
   in machine learning, 19
   and mission delivery, 52
   mission-driven work through, 198
   for personalized outreach, 77, 148
   and proactive decision-making, 205
   for program design, 58–59
   for program management, 117, 194
   tools for, 195
Prescriptive analytics, 225
Princeton University, 96
Privacy, *see* Data privacy
Proactive decision-making, 205
Problem solving, 10, 15, 28, 41–42, 51–52, 192, 195
Program delivery:
   analysis for, 9
   and bias, 149
   future of, 45
   human oversight of, 134, 137
   and immersion, 183
   innovation for, 39
   machine learning for, 122
   personalized, 59–61
   and social impact, 130
   streamlining, 57, 179, 198
   teams for, 185

Program design, 58
Program development, 57–65
Program management, 60–61, 190, 194
Project management, xiv, 43
Prompts, 102, 225
Prospects, 68, 70–72, 76
Purpose alignment, 137

Quantum computing, 201–202, 225

RAG (Retrieval-augmented generation), 225
RAI, *see* Responsible AI (RAI)
Real-time insights, 60, 150
Recruitment, 8, 79, 80, 82, 85, 94, 105
Red Cross, 3
Regulatory frameworks, 18, 101, 141–142, 211
Reinforcement learning, 20, 226
Relationship focus, 148
Rescoring, 150
Research and development (R&D), 121–123
Reskilling, 42
Resource allocation:
    analytics for, 150
    data for, 26
    ERS for, 109
    forecasting for, 101
    goals for, 180
    human oversight for, 138, 166
    maximizing, 183
    optimizing, xiv, 9, 36, 117, 188
    predictive AI for, 94
    reinforcement learning for, 20
    rules for, 23
Resource-constrained nonprofits, 22, 59, 91, 160, 180, 203
Responsible AI (RAI):
    accountability in, 127
    and data privacy, 140
    data privacy in, 226
    defining and implementing, 127
    definition of, 226 (*See also* Ethical AI)
    discussions about, 44
    environmentally, 23
    expert opinion on, 65
    frameworks for, 133, 142
    transparency in, 226
    trust through, 143
Responsive Fundraising (Cooper and Bailey), 5, 29, 37
Retrieval-augmented generation (RAG), 225
Roadmaps:
    for AI fluency, 39, 41, 46
    creating, 183–184
    governance of, 211
    need for, 168, 176
    in NIST framework, 216
    in strategies, 179
    tenets for, 133, 136
Robotics, 18, 20
Robotic process automation (RPA), 226
Rochester, Nathaniel, 14
Rockefeller Foundation, 14
Royal Bank of Canada (RBC), 49

St. Jude Children's Research Hospital, 54
Salesforce, 49, 195–196
Scalability:
    in agentive AI, 199
    in AI-first organizations, 52
    of AI tools, 172
    and customization, 151
    and ethics, 203
    in evaluation, 151
    from IT professionals, 118
    and mission delivery, 52
    steps towards, 211
    in training scenarios, 86–87
Search engine optimization (SEO), 90, 95–96, 98
Security. *See also* Data privacy
    analysis for vendors, 183
    and data privacy, 137, 139–140, 146, 201
    evaluation for, 146

IT's responsibility for, 118
of personal information, 134, 140
standards for, 141
trust in, 175
Sentiment analysis, 20, 25, 62, 148, 226.
    See also Predictive analytics
Shaff, Brittany, 96
Shaff Fundraising Group, 96
Shannon, Claude, 14
Singapore Model AI Governance
    Framework, 212, 216
Singularity, 226
Skill Development, 88, 189,
    191–192, 206–207
The Smart Nonprofit (Kanter
    and Fine), 35
SMART (specific, measurable,
    achievable, relevant,
    time-bound) goals, 180, 188
Social good initiatives, 22
Social media:
    analysis of, 10
    campaigns, 22, 74
    changes in, 6
    data from, 17, 64, 161
    integration with, 150
    management of, 91–95
    marketing of, 98
    personalization of, 205
    and quantum computing, 202
Soft skills, 42, 107
Spotify, 60
Stakeholder engagement, 9, 21, 125,
    126–127, 130, 132, 135
Stanford University, 13, 190
State of the Nonprofit Sector Survey, 4
Stop Soldier Suicide, 64
Storytelling, 74, 83, 197, 200–204
Strategies, 179–188
    for AI adoption, 181–183
    AI's role in, 179–180
    budgeting for, 184–185
    continuous improvement
        in, 186–188
    goals for, 180–181

governance for, 186
multidisciplinary teams in, 185
roadmap for, 183–184
Structured data, 226. *See also*
    Unstructured data
Success Metrics, 26, 177
Suleyman, Mustafa, 197
Supervised learning, 226. *See also*
    Unsupervised learning
Sustainability:
    budgets for, 185
    collaboration for, 120
    in communities, 53, 66
    environmental, 47, 202
    feedback for, 170
    governance of, 134
    and green AI, 207
    investment in, 23
    leadership for, 119
    long-terms, 138
    in marketplace, 176
    maximization for, xiii, 182
    for missions, 77
    partnerships for, 177
    planning for, 175
    prioritizing, xiii
    and productivity, 30
Synergy, 27–29
Synthetic data, 226
Synthetic media, 222, 226

Targeted advertising, 93–94
Task scheduling, 61
"Tech With Tim" YouTube channel,
    190
"3Blue-1Brown" YouTube channel,
    190
Tokens, 222, 226. *See also* Non-Fungible
    Tokens (NFTs)
Training, 189–196
    AI literacy in, 192–193
    building capacity for, 189, 195–196
    financial resources for, 193–195
    resources for, 190–191
    skill development in, 191–192

Training data, 149, 221, 225, 227
Transfer learning, 227
Transparency. *See also* Accountability; Explainability; Fairness in AI
  algorithmic, 220
  auditing for, 129
  in beneficial AI framework, 125, 136
  committees for, 207
  in communication, 116
  in customization, 152
  in data collection, 129, 173
  in decision making, 153
  demand for, 4
  for donors, 5
  education for, 154, 170
  ethical, 11, 18, 77, 135, 226
  and explainability, 147
  in Fundraising.AI framework, 143, 146, 156, 212, 215
  global standards for, 142, 216–217
  governance over, 186, 211
  impact, 5–6
  importance of, 125–127
  lack of, 155
  oversight for, 166
  principles for, 204
  in responsible AI, 226
  for stakeholders, 130–133, 140
  in storytelling, 201
  trust through, 132, 135, 161, 203, 223
Trevor Project, 86–87
Tufekci, Zeynep, 164
Turing test, 227
Turnover, 62, 82, 105–106

Udemy, 190
UNESCO, 142
Unstructured data, 19, 222, 227. *See also* Structured data
Unsupervised learning, 226, 227. *See also* Supervised learning
Upskilling, 42, 97, 115, 185, 190, 195
Utility, 160, 166

Virtual reality (VR), 200–201, 227
Voice recognition, 227
Volunteer engagement, *see* Volunteer management
Volunteer management, 79–88
  AI for, 85–86
  coordinating, 84
  example of, 83, 84–85
  maximizing, 84
  needs for, 80–81
  recommendations for, 87–88
  role of, 79–80
  And Trevor Project, 86–87
Volunteerism, 7, 73

Ward, Amy Sample, 126
Wealth data, 68, 72
Who Moved My Cheese? (Johnson), 34, 111, 112, 116
World Economic Forum, 41, 50, 206

XAI (Explainable AI), 21, 147, 223

YouTube, 190–191, 195

Zipline, 53